FLEETWOOD

FLEETWOOD

MY LIFE AND ADVENTURES WITH FLEETWOOD MAC

MICK FLEETWOOD

WITH

STEPHEN DAVIS

SIDGWICK & JACKSON

LONDON

First published in Great Britain in 1990 by
Sidgwick & Jackson Limited

Copyright © 1990 by Mick Fleetwood and Stephen Davis

Reprinted October 1990
Reprinted December 1990

ISBN 0 283 99679 X

Phototypeset by Rowland Phototypesetting Limited,
Bury St Edmunds, Suffolk
Printed and bound in Great Britain by
Mackays of Chatham PLC, Chatham, Kent
for Sidgwick & Jackson Limited,
1 Tavistock Chambers, Bloomsbury Way
London WC1A 2SG

For Peter Green

Contents

Part One

Chapter 1:   Two sticks and a drum   3
Chapter 2:   Crusade   15
Chapter 3:   The Green God   36
Chapter 4:   Trees so bare and beautiful   62
Chapter 5:   Hypnotized   86

Part Two

Chapter 6:   Like a charmed hour and a haunted song   109
Chapter 7:   Piggy in the middle   132
Chapter 8:   Not that funny   157
Chapter 9:   Transcension   189
Chapter 10:   Comeback   210
Acknowledgements   227
Index   228

Part One

———————————

Write a book, they ask
A book about what?
Well, let's see how all this started
Sitting here at the beginning
Looking back
It will, I think, do me good
To do just that!

M. F.

CHAPTER ONE

Two Sticks and a Drum

'All right, Mr Fleetwood, you're all through. Sign here please.'

Wearily, I took the clipboard and autographed the invoice. With that, my furniture and instruments, already loaded in the van, were taken off to storage until I could find a new place to live.

It was June 1984, and I had just been forced to file for bankruptcy. The newspapers were saying that I had lost eight million dollars and much of it had gone up my nose. At least that's what they said. My band, Fleetwood Mac, one of the biggest groups in the world, hadn't played together in two years. My relationships were in a shambles, and I felt isolated and humiliated by press accounts of my economic plight. And I was drinking a bit more than my fair share as well.

It looked like the long party was over. I was thirty-seven years old.

I watched the van carrying my possessions rumble down the canyon road towards the Pacific Coast Highway, and then walked back into the empty Blue Whale, the big Malibu ranch house that I'd just had to sell – cheap. I walked through the echoing rooms that had once been filled with music and constant parties. Then I locked up the house and garages, sat down by the pool and wiped my eyes and listened to the ocean wind through the acacia trees.

'Oh my God,' I thought. 'Eight million dollars!'

For more than fifteen years I had been an utterly driven man, obsessed with the Fleetwood Mac family and all its works and adventures. My life had hinged – and un-hinged – on the band, and when the band retired, my life fell apart. Without my central obsession, Fleetwood Mac, to occupy me, I felt bored, listless, without the vision so essential to an artistic life. I had no one to blame but myself.

I put my head in my hands, and heard my late father's voice in the middle of my head. 'Come on, Mick, cheer up! It's only money, and you can make it back.'

'Dad,' I thought, 'I wish you were here to tell me what to do.'

'I'm telling you what to do,' he said. 'You can make it back, old boy. Don't forget who you are. Keep a stiff upper lip and don't be too proud. Ask your friends for help. Ask Stevie. And McVie. And Christine and Lindsey. Go ahead. Don't be shy. They'll help you!'

I came out of this reverie and felt something different, as if my old obsession were still glowing weakly in my heart like an ember at the bottom of a cold fireplace. Fleetwood Mac only barely existed at that point, but I knew that if I could rekindle the flame and revive the band, I could turn things around. I also knew it wouldn't be easy and would take years; but somehow I now felt optimistic. I mean, what else could happen to me now that I had hit bottom? I had to be optimistic.

But first I wanted to take stock, a personal inventory of experience and memory. I had to figure out who I was and what had happened to me. Along the way, I've discovered that Memory Lane is often a painful address, but one where the elusive answers to many questions can be found.

My journey begins in Cornwall, England, right after the war . . .

If I sometimes think of myself as a rock soldier, a drummer who does his duty, it is because the Fleetwoods are a service family who have served English kings and queens on land and sea beyond the stretch of the family's memory. My grandfather, John Fleetwood, was killed at Gallipoli in the Great War. My father, Mike Fleetwood, was born in Liverpool in 1915 and never knew his father. His mother, the beautiful Alice Kells, brought him up in Ireland. Eventually Mike followed his father into the army and for a time was one of the plumed and caparisoned guardsmen of the Household Cavalry. But Dad was a poet – he wrote good verse all his life – and the cavalry was stuffy and snobbish, so he bought himself out of the army. For a time he thought about joining the British police force in Palestine, but instead joined the Royal Air Force in 1936. His wing of RAF aviation cadets was trained to fly at Salisbury Plain and of course were destined to become among the Heroic Few, who saved England from the numerically superior Luftwaffe during the Battle of Britain. Actually, my father distinguished himself even before the great air battles of the war. In February 1940, he led a flight of three Lockheed Hudsons from an RAF Coastal Command base at Thornaby-on-Tees. Their mission was to find the *Altmark*, the tanker and prison ship of the Graf Spee, the

German 'pocket battleship' that terrorized trans-Atlantic shipping in the early days of the war. The *Altmark* was heading to Germany with 300 British seamen, captured after the Graf Spee had sent their ships to the bottom. Eventually Mike Fleetwood sighted the *Altmark* lurking in a Norwegian fjord, where the Royal Navy trapped it and freed the prisoners. He got the DSO for finding the ship.

By that time Mum and Dad had already found each other and married. Mum is Bridgid Brereton, born in Somerset and called Biddy by all of us who adore her. After the war had started in earnest and my sister Sally had arrived, Mike was posted to South Africa. Biddy and Sally were to join him, and dutifully shipped out to Capetown aboard the freighter *City of Nagpur*, which was almost immediately torpedoed by a German U-boat and sunk. Mercifully, my mother and sister were rescued by the destroyer *HMS Hurricane* (which happened to be captained by an old Fleetwood family friend) and taken to Scotland. Dad survived the war too, emerging as Wing Commander Fleetwood. My sister Susan was born around then, and I came along in 1947, entering this life on 24 June in Redruth in northern Cornwall, not far from St Devel aerodrome where Mike was stationed. My very first memories are of the family house in Hayling Island, Hampshire. The child's eye recalls the dappled light on the Solent, the blue water off the southern coast of England in May.

In 1950 my father was posted to Egypt, and of course we went with him. I have incredible memories from there, some bright, some dim. I almost drowned twice. The worst time was when an iron ladder fell off the raft I was trying to climb onto, pinning me underwater. I saw fish and tried in vain to breathe. My father saved my life. I recall the servants in their long blue *gallabayas*. I remember the tension and barbed wire of the 1956 Suez War era. Dad wore a pistol with his uniform. We spent holidays in Cyprus, nestled in the cool mountains, relieved to be away from the dusty heat of the Nile.

One of my most painful memories from this time involves the strange warps and twists that began to wrack my body in childhood. The frame that would eventually elongate into six feet six inches started out decidedly knock-kneed, and in Egypt I began to experience excruciating growing pains. 'He *can't* grow up knock-kneed,' my mother cried. 'He won't be able to wear shorts!' So they slapped steel and leather braces on my legs when I slept at night. Utter agony!

A bit later Dad was assigned to a NATO base in Norway, and so we moved to northern climes. I went to the English school there for three years, and learned to speak pretty fluent Norwegian. My body continued its relentless extension in Norway, where I quickly shot up in height. As a ten year old, I could just about look my six foot one inch father in the eye, and I must say the view up there was fine; my dad was a splendid man – handsome, high-spirited, sarcastic and poetic. He was a man who put his family before the air force at almost every turn, and his military career probably suffered a little in the process. He would take us on wonderful family holidays during our Norwegian days, camping in the summer, skiing in the short winter days.

Like most sons of English families serving abroad, I was sent home to boarding school. My academic career began at an old manor called Wyndlesham House, tucked amid the Sussex Downs.

It was actually a prep school, designed to get its young charges through their first important exams and into a proper public school. Here's my first night: lights out, in bed in my pyjamas, twenty-five boys in the dorm, not feeling great, a little sheepish. Suddenly a torch is shining on me. A voice shouted: *'Fleetwood!'* I wanted to cry. I'd always been called Mick. I didn't know what was going on so I froze. The voice again: *'Fleetwood! Stand up!'* So I stood up. Several voices hissed, 'Take your trousers down!' This is the first night of boarding school, right? So there was Fleetwood standing on his bed, and a voice asked: 'What are you, Roundhead or Cavalier?' I didn't know what the hell he was talking about. Something to do with the English civil war? Later I learned that they wanted to know whether I was circumcised. The whole school was divided into Roundheads and Cavaliers for informal athletics. This was the first ritual of boarding school, and I just stood there with my dick hanging out of my pyjamas, not knowing what to say. (The rest of my school days went much the same way.) Eventually, they established I was a Roundhead and that was the end of it.

I was unhappy at being away from my family, and an undiagnosed learning disability made my attempts to pass my exams seem rather pathetic. My teachers couldn't understand why I didn't learn, and I developed a revulsion for being taught anything. At the same time, I got along well with everybody and was good at sports. Even today, my problems with learning can affect my playing. It's very difficult for me to repeat anything the same way twice, such as a certain rhythmic pattern. This can be extremely soul-destroying in the recording studio, believe me. I think I never really learned to concentrate, for some reason, as if my mind equated concentration with anxiety. Sometimes people will tell me I've played a certain way, and I really don't know what they're talking about. This gets me annoyed and reminds me of how awkward I sometimes felt at school.

I did learn to cope, after a fashion. First, there was the traditional school fagging system to survive. When a new boy comes to school he is classified as a 'fag' and is subject to the whims of sadistic older fellows called prefects. Torture was definitely the order of the day. We underwent various ordeals in the school boiler room. You had to hang by your hands from hot metal pipes, and there was one fucker, a prefect with a split razor hidden in his crocodile belt. He was a monster at flicking that thing, the vindictive creature. The pipes are hot, you're scrambling hand over hand and he's flicking at your calves to keep you up there. If you fell, up you'd go again. Later the blisters would break and I would cry myself to sleep. There were also book tortures, where they'd make us hold books at arm's length until we fainted.

One of the most vivid memories of those days is of the year that the government introduced the hideous disease myxomatosis to control a plague of rabbits on the Sussex Downs. The poor rabbits, dazed on the cricket pitch with oozing blinded eyes, didn't have a chance against the army of schoolboys that went hunting them with improbable homemade spears.

It was a difficult experience, that school, and I ran away from it as often as I could. The first time was when I was taking part in a Sea Scout exercise in the school grounds. We were camping out, and I was lying in my tent thinking about my sister Sally, then at art college in London. I was upset because it looked like I was going to be kept back to repeat the year over again while all my friends moved up normally. Suddenly I decided to go to London and connect with my sister. So off I went. It was late afternoon. I walked down the school's long driveway and hopped on board a double-decker bus bound for the station. But somone must have seen me go because I was soon dismayed to discover Mr Charles, the headmaster, driving behind the bus in his car. At the next stop he pulled over and I realized I'd had it. Back at school the kindly headmaster and his wife made me a cup of tea, listened to my problems, and then decided to move me up so I could be with my friends.

But my parents decided to try another school, and the following term I was sent to a special school, a 'crammer' run by a Mr Ratchett at Broomham, near Hastings. Less than an hour after my parents left me at the school, I ran away. This time I decided to go overland, but while I was crossing an enormous pasture full of thistles a bull spied me and began to charge. I ran so fast that I lost my precious penny-loafers during my flight. Despite the bull, I went back into the field to retrieve them. I had no idea where I was, but I started to follow a row of giant electric pylons, figuring they would lead me to civilization. I remember dodging adders as I walked cross-country. Eventually I came to the road and a teddy boy on a motor bike gave me a lift to the station. I made my way to Havant, Kent, where Mike and Biddy were living on board a cozy barge moored in an old canal. My dad had by now retired from the air force. I crept into a little cedar hut my dad was using to write in, where I was soon discovered and taken back to Broomham.

The school was really just what I needed – small classes, extra attention – but I still failed the exams. I did learn to fence, however, and this gave me great confidence. Here my long arms helped me. I enjoyed the awesome reach with the foil, and conquered all my opponents. Our team was so good that we fought public school teams, bigger chaps than us, and won. Other memories are nastier. For instance, the underground life of the school revolved around a black market in tuck – English school slang for snacks. You had your own tuck box. I built this false bottom into mine at home and brought it to school with me at the start of term. There I kept extra tuck and used it to buy off the school bullies; it was tuck for protection or else watch your step! There were tuck-for-homework cartels, extortion, wicked stuff. Once I stole some tuck at Broomham, one of my few crimes. I saw a chocolate bar in a locker. I took it and ate it. It got reported and the whole school was placed in detention because I had taken the wretched thing and just could not own up to it.

The school couldn't help me, and I left after a year.

It was the drums and the love of music that gave me my self-respect and led me to believe that more lay on my far horizon than my miserable luck at school presaged.

I think it started with my father. Mike was a good drummer, one of those people with a constant rhythm about them. I remember in Norway my dad jingling the coins in his pockets while I beat on a leather *toofta* cushion we had brought from Egypt. I loved to hear dad play drums and water glasses at the officers' parties, and I've been beating on things as long as I can recall. By the time I was thirteen, in 1960, I was beginning to be obssessed by the drums. I collected catalogues and dreamt about owning a huge kit. Dad bought me my first set of drums that year. It was called a Gigster, almost a toy kit, but it did have a calfskin snare, a little four-inch cymbal, a high hat, a bass drum and one tom-tom the size of a tambourine. I taught myself to play the Gigster by thumping along to the radio. No lessons, just me and the Everly Brothers, plus Cliff Richard and the Shadows (Tony Meehan on drums). They were my real teachers.

I didn't pass the common entrance exam for public school, so instead I went to the equivalent for under-achievers like myself, King's School in Sherbourne. Here I got really obsessed with drumming, to the exclusion of almost everything else except the school's theatre group. It was at King's School that I discovered that I had a thing for dressing up in ladies' clothes. Not that I'm really much of a drag queen, but this goes way back with me. As a baby I used to be dressed in a Victorian christening gown by my older sisters and paraded around to the amusement of the neighbours. At Sherbourne, I was cast and costumed as a willowy Ophelia in the school production of *Hamlet*, and there are those alive who saw the play who still tell me how beautiful I looked.

King's School was housed in a stately manor with gilded ceilings. They tried their best with me, but I cared only for the drums. It was there that I swore, during a long solitary walk with tears streaming down my face, after some academic debacle, that it would only be a couple more years before I'd be a professional drummer playing the clubs of London's West End.

My situation was getting pretty desperate, and Mike and Biddy were beginning to wonder if I might be uneducable. (I couldn't say I blamed them.) At the time the family was living in a Georgian house called Little Court, in Gloucestershire. My dad was working with farmers on agricultural projects, not earning a hell of a lot, and up to that point my education had been an expensive failure. But they decided I needed another chance in a less-structured atmosphere, so I was enrolled as a day student in a nearby Rudolph Steiner school, which offered a rigidly artistic curriculum instead of the normal memorization of facts at which I proved so useless. The Steiner school was eccentric, but tolerant of my foibles, and I was very happy to be living with my family. At first I lived in the attic. I ran a wire from the family radio up to my room, rigged up a speaker, and drummed and dreamed along with Don and Phil Everly. Then the Beatles exploded out of Liverpool. Later I moved out to the old stable behind the house and started a nightclub for my schoolmates. I called it the Club Keller. It was my first venture into show business, other than the little school band we'd had at Sherbourne. I used to invite the boarders to the house at the weekends; they were the Club Keller's customers. I had my drums, a gramophone, Coca Cola and some fish netting on the wall. The lights were low and we'd listen to music and have a giggle. Word of the club eventually got back to the school, and a teacher came out and asked my parents if we kids were taking drugs. Dad and Mum knew this was a farce, but it didn't much help my standing at school.

By the time I was fifteen years old, it was clear to all that my schooldays were nearing an end. I was an outsider at school, unable to fit in, useless at the eurythmic dance patterns required by Steiner education. I was especially tired of disappointing my parents. Dad wanted me to have the education that he hadn't had. When I first ran away from Broomham, I remember just sitting with my father, and him crying.

After the Steiner thing petered out, he asked me what I wanted to do. I was fifteen-and-a-half. I said, 'Dad, I'm not going to achieve anything more at school. I can't pass exams with flying colours and don't think I can go to university.' He was sad, but resigned.

The Fleetwoods are a service family, but one that really encourages the arts. Sally had been at art college, and Susan was at acting school. Sally was now married to a young London art dealer, John Jesse; they lived in Notting Hill Gate and had a spare room in the attic. Since I wanted to be a West End drummer, it was decided that I would go to London, live with my sister, and pursue my dream. That was it.

Leaving home was not easy. A lot of tears were shed over this decision. I was jobless, without a proper education, and had never even played with a real band. My father, bless his heart, bought me a proper drum kit – my first full, brand-new set. It was a Rogers kit: two rack toms, bass drum, floor tom, a couple of cymbals, high hat, black and glittery, *very* gaudy. It was my only qualification for migrating to London and calling myself a drummer. Yet I knew there was a revolution brewing down there. The Beatles now had their own weekly radio show on the BBC and were transforming British youth culture in the process. The Rolling Stones were breaking out of London clubs and becoming a national sensation, their naughty ways endlessly hyped in the press. I had (almost) complete faith that I could find or make a place for myself in this widening gyre of new music and style.

Mike and Biddy drove me to Gloucester station one damp morning in early 1963. My leaving home meant that their nest was now empty, so it was a profound moment for the three of us as the London train pulled into the station with a roar. Many years later, my father, a true soldier-poet, wrote these lines about that melancholy day.

ROCK STAR

Gloucester, station, wet and dreary.
  A Mum, a Dad, and a teenage boy
Stand together, yet apart,
  Dreading the last goodbye.

The London train pulls in and waits.
  The boy climbs in, it's the acid test.
Their last young fledgling
  is leaving the nest.

The train door slams,
  Everything tensioned,
as all three unburdened thoughts
  unmentioned.

Mum says,
  Don't forget to wrap up
and not get a chill.
  We don't want to hear
you are sick, or ill.

The boy smiles.
  Don't worry Mum.
I'm as fit as a flea,
  I'll be all right,
just you wait and see.

Dad, do you think the
  drum kit will make it?
It's in the guard's van,
  wrapped in a blanket.

The whistle blows,
  it's all too much.
Dad blows his nose, Mum sheds a tear.
  The embryo Rock Star
hides his fear.

The train jerks forward.
  The umbilical is broken.
It's raining. He's gone,
  They are alone.

He seeks his fortune,
    with eyes full of fun.
To conquer the world,
    with two sticks and a drum.

Through years of gigs,
    sordid clubs.
Dead-beat roadies
    and randy fans.
Endless journeys
    in broken-down vans.

Crooked managers
    exploiting talent.
Pusher, Junkie, Rocker and Mod.
    Dolly girls, poofs,
and Children of God.
    All played their part
to make or mar
    The dream of a boy
on his way to a star.

Then suddenly, he's there.
    He'd out-rocked the rest.
People stand and stare,
    from the Albert Hall in London,
to New York's Madison Square.

Rock star, Super Star.
    He is the lot.
Knowing in his inner heart,
    it's all just tommy rot.

Still a boy with a dream,
    and eyes full of fun,
who had been through the mill
    and made it,
with just two sticks,
    and a drum.

The London that welcomed me that rainy day in 1963 was a city coming alive again after the re-building post-war years. Mini-skirts and Mini cars filled the streets. All the bus conducters were Jamaican, and their Bluebeat music filled the clubs that year with exotic rhythms and rude dancing. The Beatles still lived in Liverpool; the Rolling

Stones filled a dancehall on Eel Pie Island every weekend. Meanwhile the whole nation was rocked by the so-called Profumo scandal, in which a defence minister was forced to resign after admitting an affair with a girl whose other lovers included a Russian naval attaché. In my sister Sally's Notting Hill Gate neighbourhood, this scandal was much savoured since it also involved peripherally one of the area's biggest landlords as well.

My sister Sally says that I arrived at her house in a pleasant cul-de-sac called Hawbury Mews wearing my school blazer, a porkpie hat, and carrying a girlie magazine under my arm. Sounds about right. So I moved in with her and John and their little boy, Kells. I had a corner of the attic that I reached via a precarious wrought-iron ladder. I set up my drums in the huge double garage where the horses had originally been kept, and began to bash around on my own, waiting for something to happen.

I didn't know a soul apart from Sal and her family. So I followed the country boy routine: you're down in the bustle of London on your own, you gotta get a job. So I traipsed around and eventually was hired by Liberty's, the posh department store in the West End, in Regent Street. It was my first (and only) job of the kind where you had to clock in. I remember that I walked into this glass-walled cash office to talk to this rather swish old fellow about the job. He thought I was well-spoken, with the right accent, and took me on. He put his arm around my shoulders and told me that, if I stuck with it, I might be in an office like this someday. I looked around: it was like being in a cage.

I hated every minute. I worked on the sanction desk – clearing people for credit – and I could barely recite the alphabet. There were all these folders on my desk that I couldn't read. I went into terrible sweats, and ended up clearing everybody. John Jesse was working nearby in an art gallery in Bond Street, selling Henry Moore sculptures and beginning to collect the *Nouveau* and *Moderne* pieces for which he would become quite famous. I used to steal away to the gallery at lunch time to stare at the sculptures and share a sandwich with John. I still treasure those moments because I so loathed Liberty's. I did my best to make myself repugnant there. Instead of the *de rigueur* collar and tie, I would wear a mod roll-necked polo shirt. I chewed gum and grew my hair. Other workers didn't like it and complained. Eventually I got fired and that was the end. I've never had another job.

What was I going to do? I didn't know right then, but I somehow felt something would happen, and it did.

One day in Hawbury Mews I was playing drums in the garage by myself. As I doodled out a pattern, the garage door opened and a boy about my own age poked his head in and listened. I recognized him. His name was Peter Bardens and he lived three doors down from us in the mews.

Pete got me my first gig, and thus began my career as a professional musician, 'with two sticks and a drum'.

CHAPTER TWO

Crusade

It was like a crusade.
Eric Clapton, on the British blues
movement in the sixties.

Pete Bardens was an organist who had already been playing with his own trio at the Marquee and other West End clubs for about a year. He told me he was thinking of putting a pop group together to feed off the explosion of energy coming out of Liverpool and the London R&B scene, especially the Rolling Stones. In the meantime he got me my first London gig with a group called the Senders. We played in a church youth club, mostly Shadows instrumentals. It was a tiny gig but it was my baptism by fire, the first time I'd ever played with a real band. That's how I got started.

By July 1963 Pete was ready and formed his band, The Cheynes, named after fashionable Cheyne Walk in Chelsea. Pete sang and was on organ, I was on drums, the bass was Peter Hollis and Eddie Lynch played guitar and sang. We worked out of the Rik Gunnell Agency in Gerrard Street and did clubs and college gigs along with our contemporaries the Yardbirds, the Animals, Manfred Mann, and the Spencer Davis Group. We played Bo Diddley, Little Richard, Buddy Holly and a few originals; we were billed as 'Britain's Most Exciting Rhythm & Blues Sound' and I must admit that the Cheynes were a hot band. We played at seedy clubs like the Mandrake, off Wardour Street, that operated all night. At the age of fifteen I was too young to be working at three in the morning; but I was so tall that no one ever suspected I was under age.

So I began to learn my trade. We played with the Yardbirds a lot and had experiences both great and loathsome. We played for love of the music and only second for money. We were extremely green, and were ripped off by crooks and club owners, and allowed the same terrible things to happen over and over again. We signed papers that made us the owners of a transit van and an expensive PA system that put us in crushing debt. From the gitgo, we found ourselves working for the company store. We played our brains out and never could quite get over the hump. At the end of a gruelling week we were grateful to get a few shillings each for beer. We felt totally ripped off, all the time. We played horrendous dives for as little as £15 a night, then drove all night in freezing little vans to make it to the next gig on time.

The Cheynes played the Cavern Club in Liverpool at the height of Beatlemania. Our manager stuffed our equipment in a Daimler limousine and drove around Liverpool promoting the gig with our PA. We went on at the Cavern wearing fruity little suede jerkins and white shirts; the guitars weren't tuned and the show was a disaster, but we had come from London and were identified with the Rolling Stones, so the Cheynes got some screamers in the provinces.

I loved being in the Cheynes after the initial hardships of starting a band. Gradually I saved a little money and moved out of my sister's house and into a bed-sitting room in Bayswater with Roger Peacock. We boiled tea on a gas ring and I ironed my one pair of brown mohair trousers until they rotted. I also acquired my first form of transport, an old London taxi I bought from a driver who lived in Hawbury Mews. During 1964, the Cheynes worked relentlessly and even began to record. We travelled with the Stones' famous 1964 tour of British cinemas as backup band for the Ronettes, and I would sit transfixed as Ronnie Spector talked about Phil Spector as a drummer; how, during recording, he would suspend drummers from platforms perched literally halfway up the wall – the legendary Wall of Sound. I was too cowed to suggest anything like this when the Cheynes began to record singles that year. Eventually we cut three, including covers of 'Respectable' and 'It's Gonna Happen To You', but they weren't hits, and by early 1965 the Cheynes were starting to fade.

Since the Cheynes worked out of the Gunnell brothers' agency, we played the same circuit as the other Gunnell bands – Georgie Fame and the Blue Flames, Chris Farlowe and the Thunderbirds, Ronnie Jones and the Nighttimers (with John Paul Jones on bass and Johnny McLaughlin on guitar) and John Mayall's Bluesbreakers. The Bluesbreakers' bass player gradually became a good friend of mine.

John McVie.

He had been with Mayall since 1963, the year Mayall had come to London from Manchester to pursue his dream of the ultimate British blues band. John Mayall was one of those blues fans who had been converted by Muddy Waters' famous 1958 tour of England with an electric band that featured Otis Spann and the best of the Chicago blues stars. Muddy's hard-edged Chicago blues inspired British blues fans like Alexis Korner and Cyril Davies to take up instruments and convert the young. By the time the Cheynes folded during 1965, Davies was dead, Korner was scuffling and Mayall was running a jumping, harp-driven blues band. The other bands that had started as R&B groups like the Stones and Yardbirds had gone to America and left 'purist' blues behind. Mayall stayed, and by 1964 was the backup-band-of-choice for touring blues stars who came through England, like John Lee Hooker and Sonny Boy Williamson. Such was the musical education of McVie, arguably the best bass player in England at the time.

He was born in Ealing, West London, in 1945. His father Reg was a sheet metal worker, later a Weetabix rep. His mother, Dorothy, is a love. When he was about fourteen he and a group of friends got guitars. McVie continues:

I started out as a bass player on guitar, playing Shadows songs, because everyone else was strumming or playing lead. Everyone wanted to be Hank Marvin, the Shadows' lead guitar player. Nobody wanted to play bass. Who wants to be a bass player? So I took the top two strings off my guitar, the C and B strings, and I had a bass. The family loved music and was very supportive, although I don't think my mum was convinced until she saw my picture in the local paper one day. Eventually, Dad bought my first bass – a pink Fender – on credit. He brought it home one day as a present and I went mad. I stood in front of the mirror in my room and dreamed I was Jet Harris, the Shadows' bassist, because he played a pink Fender too.

John went to Walpole Grammar until he was sixteen, then started a nine-month civil service training in a tax office. The first day of training coincided with his first gig with John Mayall.

John lived across the street from Cliff Barden, who played bass for the Cyril Davies All Stars. One day in the spring of 1963, Mayall phoned up Barden and asked him to join the Bluesbreakers, but Cliff was happy in his gig and gave Mayall McVie's number. John:

John Mayall phoned up and said, 'Be at the White Hart, Acton, at six o'clock'. My dad drove me to the White Hart, and there's John Mayall, Davie Graham and some other musicians. John said, 'OK, we'll do a 12-bar in C.' I said, 'Wot?' I'd only been in a little band before that, doing 'Blue Moon' and 'Bonanza' and Shadows stuff. So John Mayall taught me the blues and somehow I got the job. During the week I kept working in the tax office, while Mayall was a commercial artist. On weekends we'd leave our jobs and play a Friday all-nighter in London, then drive way up north and do Saturday and Sunday shows, arriving home by five on Monday mornings. I'd have to be at the tax office at nine to talk to enraged Irishmen about their screwed-up tax returns. At the end of nine months I said, 'This is enough', and turned professional.

I remember meeting Mick Fleetwood vividly, like it was yesterday, at the Flamingo Club on Wardour Street. At the time we were playing on the same circuit with other bands – Zoot Money Big Roll Band, Georgie Fame, Long John Baldry, Graham Bond. Mick was in a band called the Cheynes, with Peter Bardens.

The Bluesbreakers had played up north and then came down to London to play the all-nighter at the Flamingo until dawn. That night it was the Cheynes, John Mayall and Georgie Fame, in a basement club with cinema seats, a small stage and two dressing rooms. I was near the stage and looked down the aisle and in comes Mick and his sister Sally. I couldn't tell the difference, because both had thin faces and very long straight hair. I asked who it was and someone said, 'That's the drummer from the Cheynes.' Later we had a couple of pints and became friends. I was living at home in Ealing and Mick had a flat, and I used to hang out there a lot, smoking and talking about music and pulling girls.

The Cheynes collapsed in the spring of 1965, just as the music of the Swinging London era neared its peak. Pete Bardens left to join Them, the Belfast band led by Van Morrison, which had moved to London, the planet's epicentre of hipness in those days. Pete and I stayed good friends; we shared a flat that was really more of a crash-pad in Frognall, Hampstead, north London. We had one amp with reverb and Van Morrison sitting around, singing and playing guitar. Van liked to listen to old Bobby 'Blue' Bland records, pausing occasionally to vent his

Virgo temper by chasing around the kitchen table with a butcher knife.

Needing work, I put an advert in the *Melody Maker* and was quickly hired as a drummer for the Bo Street Runners, a late version of a pop group, named for Bo Diddley, that had won the *Ready Steady Go* TV talent show in 1964. When I joined them, they were already on their way out, picking up gigs on the strength of their TV success. It wasn't exactly a musical adventure for me, but it paid my part of the rent, and vocalist John Dominic has stayed a good friend over the years. My initiation into this band, incidentally, speaks volumes about the wars between the Mods and the Rockers that were part of growing up in England in the sixties. The gig was at an unlicensed venue in Nottingham, and we went around to the pub between sets. On our way back, we were set upon by a dozen rockers who saw us, dressed in our stage gear, and assumed we were part of the local Mod gang with whom they had been feuding, no doubt over someone's stolen motorbike. I hated this sort of thing. John Dominic and others wound up in the gutter with bottles broken over their heads. Eventually it was determined that the Bo Street Runners were not the local Mods, and we were escorted back to the club by the Rockers. I assumed this was normal for the band, and wanted to quit right there, but was persuaded to stay at least through early 1966.

It was an incredible time to be alive and working as an artist in London. Swinging London now seems like *fin-de-siècle* Paris, or Hollywood in the twenties; one of those lost eras when Art reigned supreme and a new generation was hatching out. If you were young, you could only make money by being a designer, a model, a fashion photographer or a pop star. Period. All these people met and mingled at clubs and cross-pollinated each others' ideas. It was an adventurous and inspiring and very creative time, and I was proud to exist on the very fringe of it, mostly because of my prolonged courtship of the beautiful Jenny Boyd, who knew quite well the undisputed kings of Swinging London, the Beatles.

I met Jenny when I was still in the Cheynes. I used to get up very late and have breakfast at the Coffee Mill in Notting Hill Gate. I'd see Jenny coming home from school, a stunning fifteen-year-old in white socks. I lost my heart to her immediately. I had a *massive* crush on her, but was so shy I couldn't even say anything to her. I knew then, at sixteen, that this was the girl I was destined to marry. I mean, I actually stood outside her house at night and watched her light go out. That's how much I loved Jenny.

Helen Mary Boyd was born in Surrey the same year as me. Her sister Patti, three years older, had a favourite doll called Jenny, and this was the name that stuck on the family's younger daughter. Like the Fleetwoods, the Boyds went abroad after the war, and Jenny and her sister were brought up in Kenya around the time of the Mau Mau uprisings. Jenny's father, like mine, was an RAF pilot; but one who had returned from the war badly wounded. After her parents' divorce, the family returned to England, where Jenny and Patti were enrolled first at St Martin's Convent in Barnet, then as day girls at a school at Holland Park, near where I lived by Notting Hill Gate. They were two of the most beautiful girls in London.

As Jenny recalls:

While we were at school, Patti met George Harrison. The mod girls at school who loved the Beatles *hated* Patti for being his girlfriend. They'd pull her hair and push her into the road. George would pull up to our house in his E-type Jaguar and our schoolmates would die of envy. I would go around sometimes with Patti and George, so some of this envy sort of rubbed off on me too.

I must have met Mick around this time, perhaps 1964. My best friend Dale made a figurine out of a wire hanger. It was of a boy with long, long legs, which she would sit on her desk at school. 'It's this wonderful boy I've met in Notting Hill Gate,' she told me. 'His name is Mick and he's the drummer in a band called the Cheynes.' Dale wanted to introduce me to Mick, so we went to a restaurant around the corner where he hung out, called the Mercury. And there he was, very shy, hiding behind the long hair that fell over his eyes, eating his omelette. I think we were both sixteen years old.

So we met, and Mick asked us to go to a Cheynes gig in Brentwood, North London. While they were setting up, Mick put his foot next to mine, and I felt a strong emotion coming from him. But he didn't say anything, so I paid attention to the singer, Roger Peacock, and then went out with him for a year.

The thing was, I *couldn't* say anything to Jenny. That's the way I am about these things, to this day. Even though the singer in the Cheynes was the first to grab her, still I knew there was this underlying feeling between Jenny and me. So I just waited for the right time. Meanwhile, this *was* Swinging London, and I was a pretty boy with very long hair. The first time I jumped in bed with anyone was with a Chelsea sophisticate named Suzanne. She was the Vamp of Savannah, and pointed to me after a Cheynes gig at the London School of Economics and said, 'I want *you.*' Everything in London was Chelsea Chelsea Chelsea, and she was a real Chelsea-ite, with lots of queer boyfriends and other things I had no idea about at all. That went on for a bit, my first excursion into the world of the pillow and sheet.

But like any romantic, I was longing for something that combined love and destiny, and this I knew meant Jenny Boyd. So I pursued her in my half-arsed way, and gradually won her. By the time I was in the Bo Street Runners, she had followed Patti into modelling; she was working at a Carnaby Street shop, Foale and Tuffin, where I used to visit her. When she told Roger Peacock goodbye, he was furious and threatened to knife me at the Marquee club.

Jenny and I started going out. At first we were so shy that we went to the movies a lot so we didn't have to talk. But as her picture started to appear in *Vogue* fashion spreads, we gradually infiltrated the edges of the mid-sixties London avant-garde. Mostly we rode happily on the coat tails of the Beatles. When the Beatles toured America, Patti and Jenny would stay at George and Ringo's flat in Knightsbridge. When they were in town, we'd go with George and Patti to the clubs – the Ad Lib, the Scotch of St James's, the Cromwellian – and literally stay all night. I got to know Brian Jones of the Rolling Stones through Jenny, an acquaintance I'll always treasure. We'd see the Beatles, always sitting together for protection, with their manager Brian Epstein hovering nearby. The clubs were full of pop stars, aristocrats and artists laughing and getting loaded. Ah, Swinging London – if one could only recreate that lost, heady air of freedom and opportunity that was sweeping over sleepy, stuffy London town during the mid-sixties.

All this was idyllic for me; less so for Jenny, who broke up with me during the summer of 1966.

Jenny:

I had left home and rented a flat with Judy Wong, our friend from San Francisco, and went to work as a freelance model, mostly for *Bride's.* Patti and I did a spread in *Vogue* that was shot by David Bailey, and a lot of offers came my way. So I went to a job in Rome, and Mick didn't come to say goodbye. Well, I met someone in Rome and became involved. I told Mick when I got home and he got *really* upset. It was a very big break-up. I was shocked at how terribly he took it, because he'd always been so cool and understated about everything. And it was hard for me also, because I'd got to know the Fleetwoods, and they'd become like my own family. Mick's father Mike was wonderful, always laughing, and he'd never let me sit there and be shy. Mealtimes were incredible compared to my own family. We were encouraged by Mike and Biddy to laugh and talk about sex and everything else that was taboo. So it was a very big break-up for us both. Later his sister Sally said to me: 'Look, Mick's always had life easy. He's such a trusting soul, and this is the first whammo that's ever happened to him. He thought you were the perfect couple, like brother and sister.'

Truer words were never spoken.

I was a Bo Street Runner just long enough to do a session with them that resulted in a single, 'Baby Never Say Goodbye'. But in February 1966 I was recruited by Peter Bardens to play drums in his new band, Peter B's Looners (later shortened to the Peter Bs). It was an instrumental band, the brainchild of someone at the Gunnell agency, designed to cover the Stax soul sound of Booker T and the MGs – organ-based contempo R&B that the agency billed as 'Cool Blue Pop'. Pete was the organist, I was on drums, Dave Ambrose played bass; the original guitarist, Mick Parker, left the lineup the following month and was replaced by an eighteen-year-old English bluesman from Putney who was playing his first professional gigs with us.

Enter the Green God.

Peter Greenbaum was born in the East End of London in 1946. His family later moved to Putney in southwest London, where Peter was given a Spanish-style guitar when he was ten years old. He has said that his earliest musical influences were Muddy Waters, Sister Rosetta Tharp, and 'some old Jewish songs' that were around the house.

By the time he was fifteen, he was calling himself Peter Green and playing bass with Bobby Dennis and the Dominoes, the Muskrats, and a west London dance band called the Tridents, through which had passed another young guitarist named Jeff Beck. By day he laboured as a butcher and a furniture polisher. Eric Clapton soon inspired Peter Green to foresake the bass for the lead guitar. (Peter even got a Les Paul guitar because that's what Eric played.) In 1965, Clapton had left the red hot Yardbirds because he was turning into a blues fanatic and the other Yardbirds wanted a hit single. Eric left the band the day after the session that produced 'For Your Love'. He was replaced in the Yardbirds by Jeff Beck (after Jimmy Page turned down the job). Eric almost immediately joined John McVie and John Mayall in the more purist Bluesbreakers. Left alone to play the blues and R&B with Mayall, Eric began to soar, and by the summer of 1965 'John Mayall and the Bluesbreakers Featuring Eric Clapton' were the best live band in Britain. And wherever the Bluesbreakers played in London in those days, there was Peter Green, watching Eric and listening carefully. But Peter Green was a blues scholar as well; he went to the same sources that Clapton had tapped: B. B. King, Freddie King, Albert King, the living masters of the modern blues guitar. Peter Green learned this music cold, as Eric had, and by the autumn of 1965 was even able to step into Eric's shoes! This happened when restless Eric impulsively decided to take a break from the Mayall group and travel to Greece to play with a romantically itinerant group of gypsy musicians. One night Mayall was buttonholed at the Zodiac club in Putney by a handsome youth with longish hair and mutton-chop sideburns who was demanding a chance to play guitar in Clapton's absence. Pete played a few gigs with Mayall, who was impressed. But when Eric came back from Greece, Peter Green was out in the cold. A few months later, he came to us.

I was hanging around the Gunnell agency when Peter Green came in to audition for the Looners, but I don't remember much about it. Fortunately Judy Wong was also there, and she has a better memory than mine. Judy was from Sacramento. She came to London in 1965 after college and started hanging around with the musicians who played at Klook's Kleek, near where she lived in Hampstead.

Judy:

One night I went to see Bo Diddley at the Flamingo on Wardour Street. The Peter Bs were the support act, and I thought Mick Fleetwood was so tall that he looked comical when he stood up from the drums. I then got involved with Peter Bardens and started hanging out at Rik Gunnell's. There I met Eric Clapton, who made me give him one of my silver rings for good luck.

I met Peter Green when he came in to the audition for the Peter Bs. He was this young fellow in a chair with mutton-chop sideburns and a mod Liberty print shirt. Peter Bardens said, 'You're the new guitarist? Those sideburns will have to go right away.'

Eventually Judy and Peter became good friends, and Judy got to see how much Peter idolized Eric Clapton. One afternoon, they were walking in Notting Hill Gate and saw Eric standing with his guitar case, waiting for a bus outside the Mercury Restaurant. They asked where he was going and Eric replied he was going to the studio to cut his first-ever vocal. So Judy and Peter jumped on a bus with Eric and ended up at Decca studios, where John Mayall's Bluesbreakers were recording their breakthrough British blues masterpiece, the *Blues-breakers* album. There Eric cut a soulful vocal track for his version of Robert Johnson's 'Ramblin' On My Mind'. On the way home in the bus, a dejected Peter Green slumped against Judy, put his head in his hands, and said: 'Oh shit. He can *sing* too.'

So Peter Green idolized Eric Clapton, and at first I thought that was all he was, a supercharged fan who was in water over his head. At the audition he told us he had mostly played bass, but that he realized there were a lot of guitarists out there, making a mint of money without being all that hot. Pete thought he could do better. But I remember that Dave Ambrose and I weren't that keen on having him in the band. He had a couple of licks he played very well, and that was it. But Bardens stuck to his guns and hired Peter Green, who *blossomed* right away. I still haven't heard anything like it, to this day. Greenie had got into the blues with a friend of his, a young singer on the London scene named Rod Stewart, and before our eyes Peter developed an incredible tone, a lingering blues wail that floored people who first heard it in the smoky, pre-dawn West End clubs. The first time I recall hearing Peter's magic was at one of the all-night jams at the Flamingo. Zoot Money called Peter Green up to play and he took out his guitar and let loose some blues that made my hair stand up.

Gradually I became very good friends with him. Peter Green was a talented, ambitious musician from a poor family who knew what he wanted, in a healthy sense. He was incredibly strong and noble, once he gained confidence as a working musician; he was a great judge of character, a guy with no bullshit about him. If anyone could teach the unteachable Mick anything, it was him; and what he taught me was to play the blues along with him. There was nothing bogus about Peter Green. As Judy Wong says, quite rightly: 'Peter was a Scorpio, with piercing eyes and instant sus. He was *very* direct with people, even to the point of hurting them, but he was someone who had the ring of truth about him. He was very influential on our circle of friends, and we all got to be a little in awe of him.'

What I remember most about Peter Green from those times are his hands. They were beautiful, delicate musician's hands, with fingers elongated from constant practise. They were hands that even at rest had some strange kind of eloquence and majesty of their own.

The Peter Bs were well-liked by the Swinging London set and we managed to land some prestige gigs. Along with the Lovin' Spoonful, we were selected to play at Tara Brown's twenty-first birthday party in Ireland. Young Tara was one of the heirs to the Guinness brewing fortune and knew many of the musicians on the London scene. His party, at a great Irish country house, was a spectacular event attended by royalty and members of the Beatles and the Rolling Stones. People wore splendid costumes, and great blocks of Moroccan hash were everywhere. (When Tara was killed in a car crash in 1966, his passing was immortalized in the Beatles' 'A Day in the Life'.)

The Peter Bs existed long enough to cut one single, 'Do You Wanna Be Happy', in early 1966. By May we had added two singers and turned ourselves into a soul showband called Shotgun Express. The singers were Beryl Marsden, who was sharing a flat with Jenny, and Rod Stewart, who had worked with Long John Baldry and another group, Steampacket. This lineup was quite successful for a few months; we had a lot of work, playing mostly Northern clubs, and we went down well because Rod, who liked to sing Sam Cooke songs, and Beryl put on a good show, and Peter Green was getting *very* hot. Eventually the band lost momentum, cutting a couple of singles without being able to break out nationally. Plus Beryl was always at the hairdressers, Rod was always in bed, and after Peter Green left to join John Mayall, his successor didn't always make it to the gigs. The Shotgun Express lasted until early 1967, but the piss really went out of the band when Peter left in July 1966, after an unhappy affair with Beryl.

By then, Eric Clapton had been with Mayall for a little over a year. CLAPTON IS GOD declared graffiti writers in the London underground. The *Bluesbreakers* album was a worldwide smash that made Eric a star in his own right. On several dates in 1966, John McVie had been replaced by bassist Jack Bruce, and drummer Ginger Baker was starting to hang out at Mayall gigs as well. Eventually, Mayall and McVie realized that Eric was about to leave. McVie remembers being a little annoyed one night when Clapton came to the gig and displayed a poster announcing his new band with Baker and Bruce, which they were calling Cream.

How do you replace Eric Clapton? John Mayall had the good sense to reach into Shotgun Express and pull out Peter Green, who proceeded to blow everyone away. When he first appeared on the Mayall bandstand in his muttonchops, blue jeans, Canadian lumber jacket and sneakers, there were shouts from the fans: Where's Clapton? Where is God? Peter responded by grandstanding to top Clapton, playing the *Bluesbreakers* songs with his typical fire and haunting, sustained single notes. It was a drag for Peter to have to step into Eric's shoes and compete for his audience, but Peter had supreme confidence in himself and his abilities. Plus he had the bluesman's faith in the music, that the power and magic of it would carry him through.

John Mayall was due to go into Decca's West Hampstead Studios in October 1966 to record the successor to *Bluesbreakers*. Imagine the shock of Decca executives and engineers when Mayall walked in with an almost completely different band and announced he was ready to record. Gone was Eric Clapton, replaced by an unknown. Aynsley Dunbar had taken over from Hughie Flint on drums. McVie was still in the band, but only by the skin of his teeth, having been let go several times because of his taste for a drink. The puritanical Mayall was quite candid about this; in the liner notes to *A Hard Road*, the album produced at these sessions, he wrote: 'Although John McVie has been through good and bad times with us, I know from experience that a better blues bass guitarist would be difficult to find in this country.' The producer of Mayall's sessions, a young Decca staffer named Mike Vernon, was at first dismayed to find Mayall in the studio without Eric, because Peter Green was completely unknown to him; but at the moment of truth, when it came time to play, everyone was amazed. The energy was there, as well as the power of a world-class blues player. It was, one and all agreed, as if Eric had never left. A new star was in the making.

For Greenie was indeed hot during the *Hard Road* sessions. He played blistering licks on Freddie King's 'The Stumble', sang on a couple of tracks, and wrote the first of his mystic, evocative instrumentals, 'The Supernatural', which used elongated notes (played on a vintage Les Paul guitar with the top pickup removed and the amp set on reverb) combined with blues grandeur to produce a kind of desert nomad saga, as if someone had just told you a scary story.

Soon there was new graffiti on the wall.

PETER GREEN IS BETTER THAN GOD.

During a cold February, 1967, we folded the Shotgun Express. Rod Stewart joined the Jeff Beck Group to sing the blues, and I was out of a job for the first time since arriving in London four years earlier. It was a low point for me. Still, I had to eat, so I started a decorating and window cleaning business with an artist friend, Dave DaSilva, who occasionally used to sit in with the Peter Bs on congas. We borrowed money from my dad, bought some ladders, and proceeded not to get any gigs. As winter turned to spring, my sister Sally noticed we were starving and gave us a job painting her new digs across from her husband's gallery in Kensington Church Street. One day the phone rang while we were working, and I answered with paintbrush in hand. It was Peter Green. He said, 'Mick, how do you fancy joining John Mayall?'

I was stunned. I couldn't think of anything to say, except, 'What's happened to Aynsley?'

And he said, without being derogatory, that Aynsley was playing too much. I didn't get this, because I wasn't under any illusions that I was a better drummer than Aynsley, a super-powerful drummer who liked to solo for twenty-five minutes and had a lot of technique, which I've never had at all. In fact, I'd never played a drum solo in my life. I've never been a 'performing' drummer of the Keith Moon variety. I want the effect of my playing to be that people feel the emotion I'm trying to create with rhythms; but there's not a lot in what I do. I try to keep it to the simplest manner possible. For me, the point of the craft is to complement your fellow players and not get frustrated – the drummer's malady – wanting to show off, wanting to get noticed. Since Mayall already had one of the best in England, why did he want to hire me? But Peter said he'd talked to Mayall, and I should come down to the gig and have a look.

I didn't audition for the Bluesbreakers. I drove down to a Mayall gig, somewhere near London, in my little Deux Chevaux. It was awkward; Aynsley was still in the band, and I felt weird, but Mayall had said to come. I was horrified to see that Aynsley had his own vocal following among the fans and also played very well. Nevertheless, he was fired that night while I was there. As it happened, I didn't keep the gig long either. I joined the Bluesbreakers in April 1967. I took the gig, still muddled about Mayall's reasoning, and said to him, 'John, if this doesn't work out, don't feel bad about asking me to go.'

I was really thrilled to have, somehow, broken into one of the top bands in the country. What was I doing there? I wasn't a blues drummer and had never considered myself one. I never sat in a room and tried to copy records or practise a paradiddle. I wasn't even a drum fanatic; I just played what I played, simple stuff. Mayall was very professional – he managed the band, arranged travel, got many of the gigs – and very meticulous, and was in general a pleasure to work for. Plus the band made me feel very welcome. My first Bluesbreakers gig was at some out-of-town club. We walked in and I could hear the fans literally howling for Peter and John. I took a gulp. This was the big time, the Bluesbreakers! As I sat down at the drum kit, there were shouts from the audience. 'WHERE'S AYNSLEY?' My heart sank, and we started to play. Then another punter screamed out at me, 'YOU'RE NOT AS GOOD AS AYNSLEY!!' I wanted to die, but suddenly John McVie stopped playing bass, walked up to the mike, and yelled. 'WHY DON'T YOU FUCK OFF AND LISTEN?' I loved John McVie from that moment on.

McVie's comment gave me back my confidence and put the whole thing right. And off we went. Our friendship has been cemented ever since the day he stuck up for me. John and I got on great together instantly. From the moment I joined we did a lot of heavy drinking; in fact we were drunk most of the time, the two of us, and this had a lot to do with me receiving my marching orders from Mayall shortly thereafter. I didn't have a drinking problem when I joined John Mayall, but I may have had one by the time I was fired. I was *very* sad to leave the Bluesbreakers. I loved playing with McVie, whose style perfectly complemented my own. I play slightly behind the beat, while John plays slightly ahead of it. We meet somewhere in the middle and to us it sounds just right.

My departure, of course, was not unexpected. Indeed, it could have been predicted. I even maintained a graph of how I was doing, taped to the wall of the Bluesbreakers' van, and the graph kept going . . . down. McVie had already been fired and rehired four times for alcoholism and fucking up. I remember one night when John and I had had a few; Peter didn't show up for the gig, having come down with flu, so Mayall started to improvise and I got completely lost. At this point, John Mayall probably realized that one drunken musician in the band was enough.

My actual downfall came in Ireland. McVie and I had a few drinks before we played, and I was fired before we flew back to England the following day. I had been in the band less than six weeks. I regretted being sacked, mostly because Peter Green was *incredible*. He was playing 'The Stumble' and other torrid Freddie King stuff. His show-piece was 'The Supernatural', which was really Pete's jump out of the heavy blues influence. That song *was* Peter, in terms of how he excited and transported people when he played. It was a real blow to leave Peter Green and John McVie.

Yet the seeds of Fleetwood Mac had been sown, quite unbeknownst to me. I wasn't in the Bluesbreakers long enough to formally record any material with them except for an EP with Paul Butterfield; but John Mayall happened to give Peter Green some studio time for his birthday. So Peter, John and I went into Decca's studios and recorded two sides of a single, 'Double Trouble' and 'It Hurts Me Too'. We also recorded three instrumentals; two of them, 'Curly' and 'Rubber Duck', were later released as B-sides of the singles. The third instrumental was a three-minute twelve-bar R&B shuffle with a fast tempo tapped on the high hat cymbal, Peter picking nimble blues changes. It was a real Chicago-sounding track, especially when Peter overdubbed a growling harmonica part, in the style of the immortal Little Walter. This third track, Peter later told us, was named after his favourite rhythm section, Fleetwood and McVie. I remember Peter Green writing down the name on the tin can that held the finished tape: 'Fleetwood Mac'.

Fired from John Mayall's band in May 1967, I did nothing for a while. I lived in Sally and John's attic and dreamed of Jenny Boyd. She had given up her flat in Knightsbridge for six months and gone to San Francisco to visit our friend Judy Wong. I missed her and felt more strongly than ever that we should be together. But then in June, Peter Green left the Bluesbreakers and my life got so hectic that I could barely think of anything else for the rest of the year.

Fleetwood Mac didn't start out, as some have suggested, as a sinister plot to get Peter Green to leave Mayall and form a band. Indeed, the opposite was true. I had been replaced in the Bluesbreakers by Keith Hartley and I think Peter felt there was some loss of rapport. In any case, Peter decided he'd had enough. He simply didn't want to do it any more, especially since he hated the whole star-guitar-as-God kind of hype that was beginning to plague him. Peter just wanted to play the blues and write a few songs. I don't believe he had any intention of starting a band when he left Mayall, and at first I didn't have any direct communication from him at all. Yet there was no way Peter Green couldn't form a band of his own in the London music scene. Cream and the Jeff Beck Group were the big bands of the day, goaded by a madman genius from Seattle who had taken up residence in Chelsea, Jimi Hendrix. The Beatles had just released *Sergeant Pepper's Lonelyhearts Club Band*. Peter himself had been replaced in the Bluesbreakers by a fluid young blues prodigy named Mick Taylor, who in turn would replace Brian Jones in the Rolling Stones.

We all knew that Peter Green had to do something. He was being not-so-gently prodded by a pair of London music biz guys who were well known to us. Clifford Davies was a booker at the Gunnell agency who had long been after Peter to go solo so he could manage him. And Mike Vernon was a blues fan and staff producer at Decca who had supervised most of Mayall's records, as well as an album Pete had done with Chicago blues pianist Eddie Boyd. Vernon had started a private label for blues fans called Blue Horizon Records, which had some strong sales with limited edition pressings by Mayall and Clapton (produced by Jimmy Page!), as well as the earliest recordings by the Savoy Brown blues band. Now Vernon saw Pete as a way out of working for Decca if he could sign him to Blue Horizon. So Vernon and Davies worked on Pete, who really didn't have any plans at all. After Pete realized that he was most comfortable out in front of the music we had recorded as a trio, he allowed himself to be convinced.

In late June he phoned me up at Sally's again.

'How'd you fancy playing some drums?' he asked. I said, Yeah, sure. It was no big deal at the time. And that's the way we started. At first there were just the two of us, him being the boss. We went on from there.

It was Peter Green who named his new band Fleetwood Mac. Wanting to downplay his starring role, he decided it would be unusual to name the group after the rhythm section. He also liked the way it sounded. Even after McVie had initially proved reluctant to join, Pete was so confident of his ability to persuade him that he decided to name the band Fleetwood Mac anyway.

The first days of Fleetwood Mac in the summer of 1967 were taken up with mundane tasks. While Peter negotiated our record deal with Blue Horizon, I got our van together; we wanted to own our own transport so we wouldn't start out owing anything to anybody. The next thing was to find a bass player. The original idea was of course to have John McVie play bass, but he refused. He had earned a good living with Mayall for four years and wasn't keen to chuck it in and join an untried band, no matter how much he preferred the idea of playing with Peter and me. Plus McVie hated our manager, Clifford Davies. John told us he would hang on with Mayall, and we said all right and that was the end of that. It was ironic. We were naming the band in part after him, but McVie declined. So we went looking elsewhere. I remember a short stint with Rick Grech, and a few rehearsals with Dave Ambrose. Dave wanted the job but his wife said no. So Peter took out one of those little ads in *Melody Maker* that said 'Bass player wanted for Chicago-type blues band' with a phone number. As it happened, the number was misprinted by the paper, but one musician managed to track Peter down to a south London council flat in Putney. When young Bob Brunning showed up at his door and Peter introduced himself, Brunning stammered, 'Do you know about the Peter Green who plays with John Mayall?'

'You bloody idiot,' Peter said, 'I *am* Peter Green.' Bob stumbled through the audition and was promptly told by Peter that he was in the band. Brunning asked when the band's first gig was, expecting to be told the name of some little club. Peter instead told the astonished Brunning that the first gig was to be the prestigious Windsor Jazz and Blues Festival, in a month's time.

From the beginning, Peter Green was adamant that he share the spotlight with another guitarist. The loathing Pete felt for the concept of Guitar God or Axe Hero simply cannot be overstated. He was appalled by pretension and cant. In the era of Clapton as God and Beck as Prince of Flash, Peter Green just wanted to play the blues with as much integrity as the system would allow. He was ambitious, but he was also shy.

So Mike Vernon found another musician to share Fleetwood Mac's front line. He was a tiny demon of a slide guitarist, an Elmore James disciple named Jeremy Spencer. Vernon, scouting the provinces for Decca, had seen Jeremy playing in an awful band, the Levi Set, in a church in Lichfield, near Birmingham. The other guys couldn't play but it didn't matter because Jeremy, all five feet of him, played Elmore's awesome slide licks on a large F-hole semi-acoustic and sang as if he were Elmore's lost English son. Mike Vernon brought the band to London to audition, but the tapes they made were so bad that Vernon didn't bother to play them for Decca. But when Jeremy told Vernon he had talked to Peter Green at a Mayall gig, Vernon decided to play the tape for Peter. When he heard Jeremy's Elmore James thing, Peter Green went white and said simply, 'My God!'

There was a strong Elmore James cult among English rock musicians in the late sixties. Clapton, Beck and Page had recorded an album's worth of Elmore jams back in 1965. The Beatles, especially Paul McCartney, were big Elmore fans as well. Elmore, born in the Mississippi delta in 1918, was himself a disciple of the legendary Robert Johnson, especially the bugle-call slide riff Robert played on 'Dust My Broom'. By 1939, three years after Robert's death, Elmore was playing Robert's howling blues in the delta with a band that included sax and drums. After the war, Elmore plugged in and became one of the first electric bluesman in the delta, living and working in Chicago in 1951 as part of Sonny Boy Williamson's band. Elmore's own version of 'Dust My Broom' was a big hit on the R&B charts in 1952. That incredible clarion 'Dust My Broom' riff was not to be denied. It had originated in Kokomo Arnold's 1925 recording of 'Sagefield Woman'. Robert Johnson adapted and evolved

Kokomo's riff into a murderous full octave slide, which Elmore in turn played on the electric guitar with devastating flourish. The riff sustained Elmore James and his band, the Broomdusters (which included Ike Turner and J. T. Brown on sax), until Elmore died in 1963. The riff also inspired almost every major English blues and rock guitarist of the sixties and empowered the early Fleetwood Mac.

Two days after Peter Green heard Jeremy Spencer's tape, he drove up to Lichfield, grabbed Jeremy by the scruff of the neck and said, 'Right, you're in my band.' I wasn't involved with hiring Jeremy at all. Peter had made up his mind, but when I saw Jeremy play for the first time, I understood what Peter had been raving about. Jeremy was a *performer*; all he did was play Elmore James. That *was* Jeremy, just this little guy beating the shit out of his guitar with a bottleneck slide. But Jeremy was way past merely copying Elmore James. He was a chameleon in the best sense of the word. He acted the blues, lived the blues with the conviction that really matters in music. He was only eighteen years old and had a fifteen-year-old wife, Fiona, and an infant son named Dicken. Jeremy turned up in London one day in August 1967 with nothing but the clothes on his back and his guitar in a cloth bag. And he turned out to be a *fucking little monster*! He was shy for about the first half hour and then out came this line of patter and running commentary that was both non-stop and extremely vulgar. 'Oi, Mick!' he'd greet me. ''Ow's yer dick? Well if it's 'alf as big as yer nose then you're a lucky man indeed and so's yer old lady.' He was a wild man, this new discovery from the north. If he was staying at your house and didn't have a key, he'd break a window and crawl in rather than wait for you. 'Had to get in somehow' he'd say. He was so tiny and guileless and funny it was impossible to get mad at him. And when he finally took the guitar out of the bag it was incredible. Mike Vernon had said he was good, but I was amazed anyway. It was like Jeremy *was* Elmore James. I could hardly believe that this sound came out of this tousled-haired little man. But there it was. Peter Green made up his mind and off we went.

So the first lineup of Fleetwood Mac began to rehearse as a quartet in a pub in the Fulham Road called the Black Bull. We played Elmore James all the time, Peter letting Jeremy's powerful Elmore act become Fleetwood Mac's earliest repertoire. When we moved rehearsals to a beautiful house in Windsor owned by Peter's girlfriend, Sandra Ellsdon, Pete began to dabble with some of the songs he was writing. Mostly he was content – no, thrilled – to let Jeremy Spencer front the band.

Oh, for a time machine to revisit our first gig, the Seventh National Jazz, Pop, Ballads and Blues Festival, held on the Balloon Meadow at the Royal Windsor Racecourse from Friday, 11 to Sunday, 13 August 1967 – the Summer of Love. The Small Faces and the Move headlined on Friday night, supported by the Marmalade. On Saturday afternoon Yusef Lateef, Zoot Sims and Al Cohn played a jazz show with some of the regulars from Ronnie Scott's club. Paul Jones and Pink Floyd headlined Saturday night, with Ten Years After, The Crazy World of Arthur Brown, and the Aynsley Dunbar Retaliation opening (Aynsley was presumably retaliating against Jeff Beck, from whose hit-bound group he had just been fired.) On Sunday afternoon a folkie show was headlined by Donovan.

Our turn came on Sunday night. Billed as 'the debut of Peter Green's Fleetwood Mac Featuring Jeremy Spencer', we played way down on a bill that included The Pentangle, Denny Laine's Strings, Alan Bown and P. P. Arnold. Headlining the evening show were the three star bands of the day: Cream, the Jeff Beck Group, and John Mayall. I remember the concert quite vividly. We stepped on stage in front of an immense crowd which had come to be dazzled by Clapton and Beck. Pete motioned Bob Brunning up to the mike to announce the first song. Brunning cleared his throat and said, 'We'd like to play . . .' and stopped, having forgotten the name of the song! Yet within seconds the audience was on its feet and dancing, Jeremy's 'Dust My Broom' riff having passed through them at top volume like a thunderbolt from the gods. Then it was Peter's turn – emotional, liquid blues runs and rich, straight-from-the-soul singing. After the first ten minutes of our short twenty-minute set, I felt Fleetwood Mac was destined to be a big success. I could feel it in my deepest bones.

We also played a second set at Windsor, a more relaxed hour-long show at a fringe blues mini-festival in a tent later that night. Again we went over great with the audience, many of whom appeared to want their blues pure and simple, free of the psychedelic excursions being undertaken by the other big bands. It was at this fringe affair that we met John McVie, who, instead of joining Fleetwood Mac, had spent the summer touring Spain and Morocco with Mick Taylor. The two of them had spent several weeks in a hotel room in Tetuan, smoking hash and dreaming. I remember Peter trying to make John join us. 'Come on, John, you've got to come in!' But McVie had his security with Mayall and kept refusing to come with us.

I also remember a big commotion over a hot new blues band from

Birmingham called Chicken Shack, word having got around that the singer and keyboard player was a beautiful blonde named Christine Perfect. We all went to see Chicken Shack's set at this blues event, and everyone in Fleetwood Mac immediately fell in love with Christine.

So Fleetwood Mac more than survived its baptism by fire; in fact we instantly started doing quite well. We had great press from the festival proclaiming Peter Green one of the deities of the electric guitar. Fleetwood Mac was heralded as the new champion of 'pure' Chicago blues in England. Peter Green, a great bass player himself, worked hard with Bob Brunning to teach him the blues. Brunning wasn't bad, but with all due respect we wanted John McVie to be there. Desperately. (I remember Peter saying all Bob did was look at girls anyway.)

We spent the autumn of 1967 doing our venues – the 100 Club and the Marquee in London, Sheffield University, Bradford College, the Nottingham Boat Club, Enfield Technical College, and clubs all over: Wolverhampton, North Wales, Manchester, Brighton, Grimsby, Leicester. We played Cook's Ferry Inn and The Chelsea Cat. We honed our raw and vulgar blues music almost every night for three months until we were as tight as a drumhead.

Then John McVie decided to join Fleetwood Mac, at last. It was December 1967, and we were playing the Ram Jam Club in Brixton when we got the call.

McVie:

I didn't want to join Peter's band because I had a good living and some security. I was making £40 a week and felt I was doing well. But Peter kept tugging at me all that fall, telling me I *had* to join Fleetwood Mac. At the same time, John Mayall was getting into brass. He put a couple of horns in the band and I didn't like it. I thought it was too jazzy, and I just wanted to play Chicago. One night we were in Norwich, and Mayall told the horn section to play free-form. I was appalled. I said to myself, OK, that's it. We played one set and I marched to the phone box across the street with all the indignation a blues purist could muster. I called up Pete and said, Do you still want me in the band? He said he did, so I gave my notice to Mayall and that was it.

John McVie joined Fleetwood Mac in December 1967. Bob Brunning knew he was only temporary, and went right from us to the Savoy Brown Blues Band and a long career in the British blues.

As soon as John McVie joined, Fleetwood Mac changed from being a good band to a fire-breathing blues dragon. John really knows how to rock a band; he kicked us so hard my bum still smarts today, twenty odd years down the road.

CHAPTER THREE

The Green God

*Peter Green, he's the only one that ever
gave me cold sweats. He had the sweetest tone I ever heard.*

B. B. King

Fleetwood Mac's earliest recording sessions were illicit late-night raids
on the supposedly closed Decca West Hampstead studio after gigs at
the Railway Hotel, about a hundred yards away. Decca had been
extremely interested in signing Peter Green when Greenie left Mayall,
but they wouldn't offer their staff producer, Mike Vernon, a label deal
for his Blue Horizon Records, for which Peter had agreed to record.
So Vernon used his key to the studio to record us after hours; these
were the tapes (some with Bob Brunning on bass) used to sell us (and
his label) to CBS Records.

Our first session in CBS's Bond Street studio wasn't a big production.
We went in, set up our PA, and played our live set. Our first two
albums were basically Fleetwood Mac's live show. But it was a show
that was the hottest in Britain at the time, the last half of 1967. Our
early grassroots success in the clubs and colleges happened because we
were playing hard blues loud when everyone else was going psychedelic. But if our performances struck a chord in our British fans, it took
our recordings a while to catch up. Fleetwood Mac's first single was
released in November 1967, and it didn't sell. This was Jeremy's
version of Elmore James's 'I Believe My Time Ain't Long', backed with
'Rambling Pony', a Peter Green blues.

Fleetwood Mac didn't really take off until our first album was
released in February 1968, establishing us nationally as the new

crusaders of the English blues movement. Recorded in only three days, credited to 'Peter Green's Fleetwood Mac', *Fleetwood Mac* was a showcase for both Jeremy's torrid slide guitar and Peter's soulful blues re-creations and original songs, including two pieces that Peter would develop into that mystic, timelessly *triste* Fleetwood Mac trademark. 'I Loved Another Woman', with its icy reverb and faintly Cuban beat, was a perfect example of the majestic sonic airway along which Peter was beginning to fly. This song remains a part of our concert set to this day, along with Peter's 'The World Keeps on Turning', now compacted and changed around a bit and known as 'World Turning'.

The album was an instant smash, to our surprise. It spent seventeen weeks in the British Top Ten (and almost a year on the charts), climbing to number four. *Melody Maker*'s review was succinct: 'This is the best English blues LP ever released here.' There was an incredible flurry of Macmania – people actually fighting to get into our still small gigs – and blues revivalism as other bands like Savoy Brown and Ten Years After cashed in on our success. Suddenly we found ourselves covered in the press like the Beatles and the Stones. Clifford Davies, who was managing us, booked us on the BBC where we were heard by the whole country. All this without a hit single. We tried to correct this in March '68 when we released Peter's new song, 'Black Magic Woman'. Three minutes of sustain/reverb guitar with two exquisite solos from Peter, 'Black Magic Woman' was descended from 'I Loved Another Woman' with one of our trademark fast 12-bar shuffles as a coda. It wasn't a big chart success either when it came out, but it was played on the radio all the time and helped establish us in Britain and Europe even more.

'*Put a spell on me, baby . . .*'

That's how we felt at the time. It was a magic era for us, the first extremely heady days of Fleetwood Mac in 1968.

After a while we got tired of being blues purists. Our shows started to get extremely vulgar as Jeremy's personality began to flower. For the first three months of Fleetwood Mac, Jeremy was comparatively unassuming and quiet. He lived in Lichfield with his parents, wife and son. He read a lot and was very religious. He travelled with a tiny bible sewn in the lining of his duffel coat and was very sensitive, as if to compensate for the ferocious energy he displayed onstage. After he got to know us and began to relax, the real Jeremy came out. First he was revealed as a compulsive parodist, a gifted mimic, a kind of ultimate imitator. If you had an idiosyncracy, he'd home in on it and throw it back in your face. This really got to Peter, who had a strong personality of his own. Then Jeremy began to get vulgar onstage. He'd rave and curse filthy suggestions at the audience. He'd fill condoms with milk or beer and hang them from the pegs of his guitar and swing them out over the appalled audience of blues purists. The rest of us loved it; such a refreshing antidote to the seriousness of the Mayall approach to music and being in the band. Night after night, Jeremy would convulse us all in drunken laughter as he thought up and carried off some new outrage. The worst of these was Harold, the pink sixteen-inch rubber dildo that eventually became part of our show.

Our roadie, Hugh Price, would bring out Harold on a big platter, as if he were the butler delivering tea. Harold would be attached to my bass drum by way of a suction cup at his base, and would spend the evening quivering and vibrating in an erect position at the ladies in our audience. I got into the spirit of things by nicking a pair of big wooden balls from the end of pub lavatory chains and letting them hang from my belt whenever I played. My long-awaited drum-solo consisted of my stepping out in front of the drum kit and dancing while clacking these balls together: playing my balls. I still have these wooden balls, and I never play without them. In fact, they've become somewhat totemic; if I didn't have them or something happened to them, I'd be very loathe to play at all.

But there was more to Jeremy than vulgarity. He was a great rock & roll connoisseur who had seriously studied the early greats: Elvis, Buddy Holly, Little Richard, Cliff Richard. His abilities as a talented mimic and parodist meant that he could replicate their styles as well as he could Elmore James', and eventually our stage show would divide into half blues jams and half Jeremy's fifties pop parodies.

Then there was Jeremy the dreamer, the inherently lazy musician who refused to write anything of his own. We were always snarling at him to pull his weight in Fleetwood Mac. Despite his rapier wit, he was sensitive to criticism. He could dish it out but couldn't take it. He was so lazy. We'd come round to pick him up to go north and work, and he'd have his carpet slippers on. Got yer guitar, Jeremy? 'Oh, yeah, all right, just a minute . . .' He'd say goodbye to Fiona and Dicken, they would pray together, and it would be very touching. Then, that night, he would be transformed into this filthy-mouthed clown of rock. The contrasts were incredible.

I don't mean any of this as criticism of Jeremy, because it would be hypocritical. Amongst us lads, he was considered extremely funny.

We roomed together on the road and I became his complete stooge and straight man.

And then it got even worse. As the band got wildly popular, Jeremy started getting away with more, even insulting the audience a bit, and the whole vulgar thing snowballed. That was our early act. I'm not sure I'd want my daughters to see it today.

Harold the dildo stayed at home when we first toured Europe in the late winter of 1968. On the continent we were more serious blues scholars, and as such we were taken seriously, especially in Germany where Mac fans who knew us through our records caused mini-riots at the clubs and other venues we played. Back home we continued to record. There were at least three albums' worth of songs done under the name Fleetwood Mac, as well as countless hours spent in the studio as house band for Blue Horizon. In this capacity we backed Otis Spann, Muddy Waters' legendary piano player, bluesman Eddie Boyd, English blues harpist Duster Bennett as well as John Lee Hooker, with whom Pete jammed endlessly.

Fleetwood Mac arrived in America during the first week of May 1968, after several months of frothing anticipation on our part. We came straight to Los Angeles and played the Shrine Auditorium with The Who, Pacific Gas and Electric, and Arthur Brown. From there we went to San Francisco, where we were met at the airport by Judy Wong and two local musician friends of hers, Jerry Garcia and Phil Lesh of the Grateful Dead. Our first album hadn't yet been released in the States (it would be in June), but the Dead had heard about Peter's playing via the transatlantic rock grapevine, and they wanted to meet The Green God in the flesh.

San Francisco was everything we'd heard – hippie capital of the Aquarian Age – and more. We were cruising with Judy through Golden Gate Park one afternoon when our car was pulled over by a wolf pack of Hell's Angels. I swear I almost shat myself, but all they wanted was a joint from Judy. We played the Carousel and the Fillmore, our first intro to the American ballroom circuit on which we would make our living for the next few years. And it was wonderful: we met the big acid-rock bands of the day, and our music even sounded better, since the ballroom PA systems were much more sophisticated than those in the pubs where we had cut our teeth. We loved San Francisco in those days! Jeremy and I were staying with Judy Wong, while Peter and John lived with a pair of beautiful twins named Lynn and Laura Sanchez. Jeremy's cutting attitude still got in the way; his snide remarks upset Judy and occasionally had her in tears, since she was basically supporting him. He'd be out in the street, screaming obscenities at four in the morning and the neighbours would complain.

We got quite friendly with the Grateful Dead, playing with them on triple bills that Bill Graham promoted, and even letting their rambling, jamming acidic style rub off on us. The Dead took good care of Fleetwood Mac, keeping us high, occasionally putting us up in their Haight-Ashbury house, and getting us gigs. We were good friends with their sound man, the legendary Owsley, Augustus Stanley Owsley III, who was always urging us to try some of the superior lysergic acid diethylamide he was alchemizing. Being nice little English boys at the time, we politely thanked him and said no. We were scared of LSD. In fact, we were scared enough just being in America without tripping into the hippie fantastique of that era. Anyway, our first little 'tour' of the West Coast was just a short trip. We had played well and had got noticed. (*Rolling Stone* called Fleetwood Mac 'honest and professional'.) So we told Owsley that when we came back later in the year for a longer stay, we'd try some of his visionary product.

We returned to England full of our new experiences, feeling like grizzled veterans of the San Francisco scene. I mean, we had watched a raw young guitarist named Carlos Santana successfully audition for a job with Bill Graham. We felt part of the community, vicariously through Judy Wong, and we all wanted to get back as fast as we could.

Fleetwood Mac's second album, *Mr Wonderful*, was released during the summer of 1968. It was recorded in four days, and it sounds like it – ragged, low-down blues by the seat of the pants. Mike Vernon brought horns and a piano player into the session to augment our basic sound. 'Just blow,' Jeremy told the visitors, and away we sailed into the album with no rehearsal whatsoever. Like our live show, Peter and Jeremy alternated tracks. Pete started with a wild vocal and searing solo on 'Stop Messin' Round'. Jeremy counters with a revision of 'I've Lost My Baby', and so on. Pete's 'Love That Burns' was a slow blues, one of his typically bittersweet lyrics, that featured a piano solo by the pianist Mike Vernon had brought to the session.

Enter Christine Perfect, briefly.

I remember her sitting at the piano in the hot studio. She was gorgeous, and preoccupied with her part. We said hi to each other, and that was it. We knew her from Chicken Shack, the group she had with Stan Webb and Andy Sylvester. It was like she was Andy's sister, when I first met her. I knew her only as a fellow player who was very attractive. She was a band person, a team player; that was obvious because she could have been a star on her own. I could also see she was very strong without asserting herself, except when necessary. You wouldn't dream of pushing her around, and you couldn't if you tried. She was fun to have a drink with – no glitz, no pretension. We all *loved* Christine. Pete fancied her and she fancied him in this period, which was quite complicated because John McVie was also taking a shine to her and she to him. Anyway, Christine made her debut with Fleetwood Mac at that session.

Peter filled out the album with some thrilling guitar on a superb blues dirge, 'Trying Hard To Forget'. This touching song about poverty and deprivation in childhood was Peter Greenbaum baring his soul about growing up in Whitechapel, London's Jewish ghetto. The late Duster Bennett played a mournful harmonica, and for almost the first time I could feel the pain, hurt and sense of loss that Peter was expressing through the solace of the blues.

Peter decided to record Fleetwood Mac's third single, Little Willie John's 'Need Your Love So Bad', after John Mayall played him B. B. King's lush rendition of the song. True to his infatuation with the King style, Pete ordered up a string section for our version. The record was released on 5 July 1968 and was a hit, enjoying a brief sojourn on the British singles charts. In contrast to Fleetwood Mac's growing reputation as foul-mouthed stage pornographers, 'Need Your Love So Bad' was a tasteful, low-key, meditative blues that spotlit Pete's more reflective side.

Our stage presentation, however, continued on its ribald and obscene course, culminating in Fleetwood Mac being banned from London's most prestigious rock venue of the day, the Marquee in Wardour Street. It wasn't the first time we had got into trouble. Club owners all over the United Kingdom had complained to our booking agency about our unkempt appearance and bad language. And it was true. We played in our street clothes, jeans and shirts, and swore terrible oaths and displayed emblems of phallic narcissism onstage. 'A lot of people don't want to know us because we're so ragged and use bad language on stage,' Pete told one of the music papers. 'But if I want to say fuck then I will, because if I say it normally in my speech then I'm going to say it onstage too, at least until I get arrested.'

We didn't get arrested, but we did get banned. The final straw for the Marquee came during our second set one night. By this time we had got bored with Jeremy's Elmore act, and had prevailed on him to do a fifties parody set at our gigs by buying him a gold lamé suit. The suit somehow liberated Jeremy's ability to perfectly mimic every old rocker from Jerry Lewis to Gene Vincent to Little Richard. Jeremy launched into his Elvis show, having left the stage and returned clad in gold lamé. Tiny Jeremy, five foot nothing, came onstage carrying his huge guitar, which he then lifted to reveal yard-long Harold the dildo sticking out of his fly, and off we went with the immense pink phallus swinging in the faces of our customers. We thought this terribly funny, but the audience was aghast. The guy who ran the place came back afterwards and fired us, and we didn't play there for a long time.

Fleetwood Mac was really into this phallic trip, especially me and Jeremy. We tried to put an obvious phallic symbol on the cover of *Mr Wonderful*, whose original title, *A Good Length*, was rejected. Then we wanted *Udder Sucker* as the title, and I even went down to my Godmother's farm in Kent to pose for a cover photo under a cow. This burst of inspiration was also turned down by the label. Instead I posed naked for the cover, clad only in a loincloth and a depraved stare. Then I had a little engraved silver dildo made for the gearshift of my Alvis automobile, complete with a soft leather pouch to cover it up when parked. On my keychain were a little pair of silver balls, miniatures of my gig pub-chain balls, that my sister Sally had given me for my twenty-first birthday, a month before. This was Fleetwood Mac. We were a rude, wild, fun-loving bunch of people who simply didn't give a fuck. Fleetwood Mac never wanted to be pure blues like Mayall or rock like Hendrix or Cream. We were a funny, vulgar, drunken vaudeville blues band in that time, playing music as much to amuse ourselves as please an audience and make money.

So, banned from the Marquee and other clubs, we played quite a few outdoor festivals that summer. Typical of these was the Woburn Abbey Music Festival held that July in the grounds of Woburn Abbey in Bedfordshire. The lineup was heavy: Pentangle, Alexis Korner, Roy Harper and Al Stewart on Friday. The Jimi Hendrix Experience, T. Rex and the Family on Saturday. 'An Afternoon of Donovan' on Sunday. We headlined the last show on Sunday night, supported by, ironically, John Mayall, Champion Jack Dupree, Duster Bennett, the Taste, and American singer Tim Rose, with John Bonham on drums.

All during this time, John McVie had been courting Christine Perfect, Chicken Shack's singer. They had met at the Windsor Jazz Festival and kept bumping into one another on the English blues circuit we all used to play. As John remembers, 'One night we were at the Thames

Hotel, Windsor, and I was sitting with Chris, and I asked if she would care to go out to dinner one evening. She said she would, and it was quite romantic.'

They went out for a while, and then John disappeared to America with Fleetwood Mac. Chris went to Germany with Chicken Shack for a ten-day stint at the Blow-Up Club in Munich. A crazy German DJ asked her to marry him (men were *always* asking her to marry them). She turned him down and, as she says, wrote a long letter to John McVie. When we came back to England, John proposed. Chris was quite mad about John and said yes. They were married ten days later, in August 1968, amid mighty celebration, to the general delight and envy of Fleetwood Mac. They probably would have waited a bit longer, but Chris's mother was dying, and the wedding was really for her. True to the lifestyles we were all living back then, both musicians immediately went on the road with their separate bands. It would be almost another year before John and Chris had a real opportunity to live together.

In those days, Peter Green became restless and began to grumble about what we were doing. Peter felt that Fleetwood Mac needed to go beyond pure blues and old rock & roll parodies, into more free-form and improvisational jamming, the heady atmospherics of the West Coast bands who were taking the music to more experimental levels. And he was very aware that Jeremy Spencer was beginning to hold him back. Jeremy was like a band within a band, which was fine; he was a mainstay of Fleetwood Mac's all-important stage performance. But Peter Green was frustrated. Jeremy wouldn't try any new stuff and couldn't seem to change. More and more, Pete began to feel oppressed by the weight of carrying Fleetwood Mac on his shoulders. He was in that frame of mind where he didn't want to be lord and master – which he naturally was, without even trying. But he wanted very much for us to be a *band*, with every musician pulling equal weight. This was very important to him, and in terms of music he eventually realized that Jeremy simply wasn't going to go anywhere.

So Pete hired a third guitar player for Fleetwood Mac, a nineteen-year-old lad named Danny Kirwan.

We met Danny at a little club we used to play in Brixton, The Nag's Head. It held about eighty people and was one of our mainstays. Our first publicity photo had been taken outside the club almost a year before. One night we played with a local band from Brixton called Boilerhouse. The band wasn't very good, but Pete noticed the guitar player straight off. Danny played beautifully, getting a subtle tremolo effect from his fingering. He sounded a little like bluesman Lowell Fulson. Peter raved about Danny to Mike Vernon, who booked Boiler-house into his own club, the Blue Horizon, in Battersea. Gradually Danny became Peter's protégé and fan, following us around to London clubs and sitting at Peter's feet while Pete made his guitar cry and wail the bitter canon of the blues. Pete loved to play with Danny. They could play long melody lines together; in many ways it was a near-perfect match of sensibilities. At first Peter tried to find Danny a competent band of his own, since Boilerhouse was shit. They took out an advert in *Melody Maker* and auditioned a bunch of players. In the end Peter asked what I thought of having Danny join Fleetwood Mac. I agreed, and John said he felt all right about it. We'd all been encouraging a reluctant Danny to dump Boilerhouse anyway, so in the end we just took him in ourselves.

Danny worked out great, from the gitgo. Playing live he was a madman, Peter's harmonic foil, full of ideas that helped move Fleet-wood Mac out of the blues and into the rock music mainstream. He was an exceptional guitar player who in turn inspired Peter Green into writing the most moving and powerful songs of his life. Pete was at the top of his form during that autumn. His stature and authority as one of Britain's great guitarists was at its peak. Peter was so respected, even by the usually churlish music press, for his simplicity and integrity that the monthly newspaper *Record Mirror* ran a regular feature titled 'The Peter Green Column', which was dictated in part by Pete. 'Hello again, my flowers,' began one such essay. 'Hope you're all making out all right on nuts and cheese [Pete had been espousing vegetarianism in previous columns]. Have you heard our new single "Albatross" yet? I think it's the best thing I've ever composed . . .' Peter goes on to tell Fleetwood Mac fans that we were recording new music, including an EP of Jeremy's music that was supposed to come out with the next Mac album. He also notes that Danny had got himself an original Les Paul guitar, and that the whole band had been fitted out with new Orange amplifiers. 'They do a great reverb as well, which has become my pride and joy.' In passing, he also says that the band will soon undertake a change in material, which in retrospect seems a clear signal that Fleetwood Mac's days as a blues band were numbered.

I remember that we went to Paris around that time, and played a few other Euro gigs as well. Fleetwood Mac was big all over the continent. Even a meat-and-poatoes blues track like 'Shake Your Moneymaker' had gone to the top of the charts in Scandinavia earlier in the year, and every place we played was sold out and raving. In France we did a TV show with the Troggs, who slayed us with their live version of 'Wild Thing'.

Fleetwood Mac continued to record during the autumn of that year. As soon as he was hired, Danny was told, right – you have half the next album. Pete took him into the studio and Danny proved he could cut it with a Django Rheinhardt instrumental called 'Jigsaw Puzzle Blues' that moved through all kinds of key changes, and a rock song, 'One Sunny Day', as well as several other tracks. But our first big hit was written by Pete and recorded at Decca's studio in London.

'Albatross' was intended as a single, never as part of an album. It was an example of Pete's moody Santo and Johnnie thing. I remember a lot of overdubbing, conversations between the two guitars, lots of echoey, thematic playing – Pete's great one-note style. I played muffled tom-toms with mallets. The effect of all this Peter Green called 'Caribbean music' and titled 'Albatross'. There was never any question of lyrics. The song as an instrumental conjured up a floating sensation, a feeling of repose and release from anxiety. I loved it as soon as I heard the final playback. It's been a top ten hit in Europe three times in the past two decades.

'Albatross' was released in Britain in November, while we were in the States. I recall a bit of concern over the single because it was our first official step away from the blues format that had been successful for us in the past. We needn't have worried. As soon as it was out it was played as background music on a BBC pop radio programme. The producer of *Top of the Pops* heard it and put 'Albatross' on television. Within three weeks it was the number one record in Britain, and Fleetwood Mac was officially launched on its long career as a pop group. Such is fate.

Fleetwood Mac's second tour of America began the first week of December 1968. We were scheduled to do thirty dates (including playing before 100,000 at the Miami Pop Festival), and most had sold out in advance. The first gig was opening for our friends, the Grateful Dead, at the Fillmore East. It was there, after the show, that we reconnected with Owsley, who was still after us to try some of his acid. It was all in fun to him; he was like a mischievous goblin. 'C'mon, take it!' he would rasp. So we all had a go. We figured he made the best, most pure LSD available. We all wanted to try it, and if not his, whose? We didn't want to play on acid, so we took it back to our usual

New York digs, the Gorham Hotel on West 55th Street, and . . . did it.

Oh God.

I don't really remember much. We sat around and looked at each other. Are you tripping yet? We had no idea. After an hour or so, Fleetwood Mac had a massive anxiety attack. Our brains were broiling and we had no idea what was going on. We huddled together and held hands in a circle, trembling, terrified that we were undergoing a . . . bad trip! A bummer! With every new lysergic rush, we moved closer to the dreaded freakout. We'd heard about bad trips and damaged chromosomes and permanent LSD psychosis and all this stuff, but we hadn't the foggiest notion of what to do. I looked at Peter and saw him dead, a skeleton without flesh. I couldn't even look at the others. It was a horrible, helpless feeling. Just then the phone rang, and we all jumped out of our skins. It was Owsley, calling out of the blue to see if we were enjoying ourselves. We began to weep and blubber for help, and so Owsley most expertly talked us down: soothing words, firm directions, and soon we were calm again and merely . . . flying. Owsley. Our mentor.

Many strange adventures befell Fleetwood Mac at the Gorham. On off nights we'd hang out at the hip club of the day, Steve Paul's Scene. Jimi Hendrix would come in to jam, turn Pete's guitar upside down so he could play it left-handed, and off he'd go. It was unbelievable. Strange women and various nut cases would follow us back to the Gorham from the Scene and terrible events would ensue. Almost as soon as we had arrived in New York, Pete had pulled a girl from the Scene and was entertaining her in his room. But Pete didn't know they had been followed by her psychopath boyfriend. Soon I could hear Jeremy screaming down the hall in a panic, 'Help! Call the front desk, there's a maniac in our room!' Sure enough, I run into the hall of our suite and some guy is sticking a gun through the chained door and yelling, 'I'm gonna fucking kill you all.' I mean, we're Fleetwood Mac straight out of Ealing Broadway, and here we are with street-level New York violence in our room. Total terror.

Harold came along with us to America as well. He had been retired for a time after we were banned from the Marquee, but in America he again became a vital part of our show. Once again he was brought on stage by roadie Hugh Price, who looked like the classic English butler. He'd come on with a towel over his arm and a tray bearing Harold and his tacky attachments – French ticklers and various bizarre toys – surrounded by four large brandies. Harold would be attached to the bass drum so he could quiver and undulate with every downbeat. This of course had alienated some of our British fans, but in America our audiences understood it as a joke and loved it. The dirtier we got, the more positive the response we got from the fans. It was quite outrageous in a naïve and juvenile way, and our blues-based audience was a raucous group anyway, so we all had a good laugh over it. I remember opening for Big Brother and the Holding Company at the Fillmore West, and Janis Joplin laughing backstage as she watched Jeremy gird himself with Harold and go out to do his oldies act during our second set.

We got really crazy a little later at the Whisky A Go Go in LA. One night, blind drunk, the whole band draped around the microphone, we sang the most revolting song that Jeremy ever wrote: 'I'm going to fuck all the piss/That's swimming around your vagina,' and other 'lyrics' to that effect. Looking back, I can scarcely believe it. At the end of the set, if I were drunk enough, I'd destroy my kit. It wasn't really part of the act, but every now and then the leg would go out and over went the drums. Or I'd come out and take my big drum solo – playing my balls – while Jeremy threw milk-filled rubbers into the audience. As I said before, I was Jeremy's stooge on the road. He'd make me tune his guitar for him because he just didn't care enough to do it himself. Halfway through this second tour he had played so many gigs with milk-filled condoms hanging from his guitar that I used to have to tune the instrument with pliers because the tuning pegs were so rusted and clotted with milk.

The Fleetwood Mac that plied the ballroom and college circuit had a reputation for playing *loud*. Dinky Dawson, our sound man, liked to crank it up loud as bombs. So we blew the walls off the Electric Factory in Philadelphia and the Boston Tea Party, which we played so often in 1969 that it felt like a residency. Our intrepid sound department today takes credit for several innovations and techniques, such as a separate overhead vocal PA and the 'snake cable' that joins stage equipment to a mixing console in the middle of the audience. (This system was in part devised because Peter Green had taken to throwing things at Dinky Dawson when he didn't like the sound Dinky was getting, mixing from the wings.)

In January 1969, we were in Chicago, opening for our idol Muddy Waters at the famous Regal Theater. While we were there, Mike Vernon found out Chess Records was going to close down its fabled studio and decided that Fleetwood Mac had to record in the home of the Chicago blues before it shut down. He asked us if we wanted to cut tracks with some of the local legends, and of course we jumped at it. Working with Marshall Chess, the son of Chess's founder, Vernon prevailed upon Willie Dixon, the bass player who wrote 'Hoochie Coochie Man' and most of Muddy's other early fifties hits, to organize the sessions. So for two days Fleetwood Mac sat at the feet of our most revered masters: Otis Spann, Muddy's piano player and creative partner; Walter 'Shakey' Horton, originally a teenage harp wizard from Mississippi who became the premier Chicago soloist after the war; Honeyboy Edwards, a guitarist and contemporary of Robert Johnson; J. T. Brown, who for years had played his 'nanny goat' sax in Elmore James's Broomdusters; as well as Guitar Buddy, S. P. Leary (Dixon's house drummer at Chess) and Willie Dixon himself.

At first our heroes seemed condescending to us. But Peter Green dazzled the Chicagoans with the sheer feel of his playing and somehow pulled us through. Pete surprised them, I think. They learned that without the stacks of Marshall amps and that dread label – 'English Blues Band' – we were still a good little band, a cut above what they usually saw. As soon as Pete's respect for their music became apparent, they stopped treating us like tourists. The music was fine too, as long as the Scotch whisky kept flowing during our two days at Chess. Jeremy about wet his pants over J. T. Brown, who had played with Jeremy's god, Elmore. Afterwards we were taken to dark little South-Side clubs where, we were informed, white kids usually weren't welcome. Pete sat in with local musicians, and got the sense that he was being appreciated. Willie Dixon took him to one low-life joint where some hoodlum pulled Pete into the back room and Dixon had to step in to prevent Pete getting cut up.

The recording went well, we all thought. J. T. Brown blared out great tenor solos as Jeremy fantasized about being the reincarnation of Elmore James. Shakey Horton and Otis Spann supercharged Fleetwood Mac into some of the best blues playing we ever achieved. But it was ironic, for these Chess sessions produced the last blues that Fleetwood Mac would record. We were about to mutate into another kind of band altogether.

When we landed at Heathrow Airport a week or so later, we were thrilled to find 'Albatross' the number one record in Britain. Where our first two singles had failed commercially, 'Albatross' put us into the pop mainstream at home. Something in Peter's moody, soothing song had clicked, and it was on its way to selling a million copies in Britain. Our manager had been complaining that it was getting hard to find jobs in the UK because of our ragamuffin attitude; when 'Albatross' went on the charts we suddenly found ourselves on TV and in demand to play much larger venues than before. This was a new era for us.

Happy to be home, I was living in Ealing with my three cars: the Alvis, an Austin 7, and a Bristol. And I was still carrying a torch for Miss Jenny Boyd.

In the early days of the band, John and Peter would pull girls. Jeremy did not, because he missed his wife and son and actually preferred spending evenings reading the New Testament or watching TV. I was terrible at pulling girls, never having been a roadhog in the great rock & roll tradition. Since John and Chris had got married, John was out of that race too. But Peter loved having girls attracted to him. I would moralize, saying that I was still in love with Jenny, and that what he needed was a true romantic love to get him over his deep down episodes.

I had told Judy Wong that I was determined to marry Jenny when we stayed with her on our first trip to San Francisco. During our second tour, encouraged by Wong, I wrote to Jenny to tell her I thought we should get married. But a lot had happened to Jenny in the eighteen months we had been apart. She had spent six months in San Francisco in 1967, living with Judy Wong during the prime of the Haight-Ashbury scene, trying acid, attending the Monterey Pop Festival protected by Hell's Angels, and getting quite mellow. She wrote to her sister Patti, who soon arrived in San Francisco with George Harrison. Jenny took them down to the Haight and it was pandemonium. Huge crowds of hippies formed as the Beatle made his progress. People were laying joints on George and then harassing him, and soon it all got too much and they had to run for the shelter of the limo. On her return to England, Jenny moved in with Patti and George in Surrey. Then Jenny opened the Apple boutique in Chelsea and gave a lot of interviews, once again caught in the thick of the London pop scene.

Donovan was after her too, writing 'Jennifer Juniper' for her. The song was a hit for Donovan, a huge star in England in those times, but Jenny was unswayed. 'I liked him,' she remembers, 'but I didn't want a boyfriend.'

Thank God.

Jenny continues:

It was sometime during 1967 that my sister Patti decided she wanted to learn to meditate. She went to hear Maharishi Mahesh Yogi with a girlfriend, and told George about it. He thought it sounded good, and eventually we met the Maharishi, who was obviously *very* pleased; there was much talk of the Beatles opening a big Maharishi Centre in London. Later on in the fall, I went down to Wales with the Beatles on a retreat with Maharishi. We all went by train: Paul McCartney and Jane Asher, Ringo and Maureen, Mick Jagger and Marianne Faithfull, George and Patti, and John Lennon (his wife Cynthia missed the train). While we were in Wales we learned that Brian Epstein had died in London. It was an incredible experience, first the experience of the meditation, then the incredible sadness of Brian's death by overdose. Brian had been the bridge between Lennon and McCartney. It really felt like the Beatles ended that weekend, and *everyone* felt it.

A few months later George asked me if I wanted to go to India along with him and Patti, and of course I was thrilled. I had been undergoing a spiritual awakening, no longer looking at things in terms of heaven and hell but instead in terms of karma and re-birth. George had been to see Ravi Shankar, and now wanted to go back to the Maharishi's ashram in the foothills of the Himalayas.

So I spent two months in 1968 at the Maharishi's with a group that included George and Patti, John and Cynthia Lennon, Mia Farrow and a few other seekers. At first it was quite glorious – bathing in the Ganges, monkeys roaming around at breakfast – although I wasn't quite sure about the Maharishi, as if something were not quite right. I was meditating almost all the time, and getting quite hot, like I had a fever. It turned out to be dysentery, but the local doctor diagnosed tonsillitis. I sat with John Lennon a lot, since he didn't feel well either from terrible jet lag and insomnia. He would stay up late, unable to sleep, and write the songs that appeared later on the Beatles' *White Album*. When I was at my lowest, he made a drawing of a turbanned Sikh genie holding a big snake and intoning, 'By the power within, and the power without, I cast your tonsil lighthouse out!'

Sometimes, late at night, I can still hear John singing those sad songs he wrote during those evenings, like 'I'm So Tired'.

Eventually our group was joined by several others. Donovan came over to be with me, but I had other ideas. Then Magic Alex arrived. He was the Beatles' technical wizard and inventor, and he came because he didn't approve of the Beatles' meditating, and he wanted John back. He made friends with another girl in our party, and I could see them walking the grounds of the ashram together, obviously cooking something up.

And so we left, prematurely. First Patti dreamed that the Maharishi wasn't what he seemed. Then Mia Farrow said that Maharishi had come on to her, and another girl said the same thing. There was a mass decamping after that. But by this time I was getting into it and didn't want to leave. George said that I was under their protection and had to go with them. Poor Maharishi. I remember him standing at the gate of the ashram, under an aide's umbrella, as the Beatles filed by, out of his life. 'Wait,' he cried. 'Talk to me.' But no one listened. We went back to the hotel in Delhi and George and John tried to decide what to do. 'Should we tell the world that the Beatles made a mistake?' John asked. 'He isn't what's happening at all.' Everyone was so disappointed. So George, John and Paul hooked up with Ravi Shankar and went to the south of India where Ravi was touring with his troupe. There George got dysentery, and thought the Maharishi had put a spell on him. Ravi got him some amulets and things and George was immediately better.

Back in England, Patti and I opened an antique store in Chelsea that we called Juniper. We sold art nouveau and deco things and had lots of fun. That's when I got a letter from Mick, who was on tour in America, saying we should get married. I was staying with Alice Ormsby-Gore, who was going with Eric Clapton. Mick came back from America; he had grown up a lot and looked great. He came up and found me in North Wales, where I was having a weekend getaway at a sort of primitive commune run by a boyfriend that I didn't really like. Mick and I went and had breakfast together in the little village, and we decided that we should be together.

A bit later, sometime in 1969, I saw Mick in London. I said, 'Well, you remember that letter that you sent me? About getting married?' And he said, yeah. That's how we decided to get married. He went straight off to Ireland with the band, and I stayed with Sally in Kensington Church Street, waiting for him to get back. But I was happy, I think, to have made up my mind. I had got to the point where I said, it *must* be Mick, because I didn't find myself feeling the same things for anyone else. It was like a feeling of the home I didn't really have. I knew him so well. It was a comfortable thing.

We got a flat in Kensington Church Street, opposite Sally and John Jesse, and we lived together for almost a year before we married. And things were slightly different than they were when we had been together. Mick had been through a lot, and so had I, and there were times I felt I didn't know him. It frightened me sometimes, like being separated from a brother and then not knowing him as well. So we lived together again and got reacquainted. I kept saying, well, aren't we going to get married? And he kept fobbing it off. 'Don't want to ruin the image, y'know.' So I waited . . .

Jenny wanted to get married, and so did I, but as 1969 dawned we had all decided that Fleetwood Mac's true mission was to conquer America and make our fortune that year. With Danny Kirwan duelling and duetting with Peter, Fleetwood Mac was at the top of its form; we knew we were playing better than we ever had. We were eager to bring the new lineup to America and work as much as we could. To this end, Epic Records, our American label, released our second album in the States, having declined to release *Mr Wonderful* the year before. This new American release was titled *English Rose* and featured a cover shot of me done up in a blond wig and British barmaid drag.

English Rose was really a sort of pastiche, composed of the best cuts from *Mr Wonderful*, 'Black Magic Woman', the hit single 'Albatross', and four tracks written by Danny Kirwan. In support of this album, we returned to America and opened Fleetwood Mac's third tour of the United States on 1 February at the Fillmore East in Manhattan. Again our show was divided into two sets. The first consisted of Jeremy's slide replications like 'Madison Blues' and 'Telephone Blues', interspersed with Danny's new stage material. Jeremy would then retire and Peter and Danny would launch into long acidic jams that would weave in and out of various styles including Pete's proto-metal ode to masturbation, 'Rattlesnake Shake', plus improvised explorations for two guitars and a rhythm section. This usually drove our thoroughly stoned audience bananas and we'd take a break, coming back onstage a half an hour later having had the one or two beverages in the interval. Then it was time for Jeremy's oldies set. He'd come out in his gold lamé suit and we'd be introduced as 'Earl Vince and the Valients' and off we'd go. Jeremy was brilliant at this, strutting across the stage like the King of Rock & Roll, hair greased back, snarling and spitting out 'Great Balls of Fire', 'You Keep On Knocking', 'Jenny Jenny' and 'Tutti Frutti'. This parody set usually went on as long as there were still people in the audience and as long as we could stay on our feet. At the very end, sure enough, Harold would make his obscene entrance with all the attendant hilarity. Rubbers would then be filled with beer and thrown at what few customers remained.

We went on like this for a couple of months. Our agency, Premier

Talent, didn't have us fully booked for this tour, and we always tried to fill in dates whenever we could. Sometimes we'd sit around for two weeks waiting for gigs to materialize. One such ten-day stint in a motel in Dearborn, Michigan, was particularly demoralizing. The nice part of this period was that Jenny was with me, having come along so she could hear us play for the first time. She was there on the disastrous night we opened for the Grateful Dead in New Orleans.

The gig was at a new venue called the Warehouse, the night the place opened. Owsley had been up to his tricks. Both bands were flying on acid, and the whole audience had been 'spiked' on Owsley's special electric Kool Aid. ('Peter couldn't even play that night because he was so high,' Jenny remembers. 'Danny was weird too, and Mick looked like a goblin playing drums. It was a very freaky evening.') After our gigs with the Dead, we usually went back to their hotel to socialize, but that night we were too trippy so we went back to our own hotel. Thank God, because after the show the Dead's hotel was raided. The police were after Owsley, and they got him and arrested everyone. It turned out some kid's parents had complained when their child got home from the show tripped out and saying he was Jesus or whatever. Back luck for the Dead, but good luck for us, because we'd have been jailed and deported if they had busted us too.

Another incident from those days reminds me how much I owed to Peter Green back then. I think of it as the time he laid his hands on me. I used to get very confused with the on- and off-beat, especially during the long jams on 'Rattlesnake Shake'. During one show I got lost riding the on-beat, unable to get back and turn it around, just blindly going on and beginning to panic, recalling terrible days at school when I couldn't seem to learn. But Peter saw that I was in trouble and simply walked over and got hold of my hand long enough to put me right again. I was embarrassed, but it felt so *right*, and so typical of Peter's spirit. I apologized profusely after the show, but wonderful Pete made a joke out of it. Eventually I learned how Pete would turn 'Rattlesnake Shake' into a long tangent and be able to come round again by some sort of miracle, back to where we started. Occasionally I'd forget to come back, but eventually I learned and it became second nature.

Our next single, Peter Green's 'Man of the World', was recorded while we were in New York and was released in Britain in April 1969. Like 'Albatross' it had little to do with the blues, owing more to the music that the Beatles and Stones were doing at the time, opening acoustically and then turning to a harder rock feel. Most of all, 'Man of the World' was sad, even abject. In retrospect, we should have seen it as a warning of what was to come. Singing softly, Pete's lyric was ominous: *'Guess I've got everything I need, I wouldn't ask for more/And there's no one I'd rather be, but I just wish that I had never been born'*. Looking back, we now realize just how disillusioned Peter was becoming with rock stardom and the pursuit of material wealth.

Despite its sharp air of sadness, 'Man of the World' was a hit, reaching number two in Britain, a tribute to the esteem in which Pete was held by our British fans. But for us, 'Man of the World' was the end of an era, because it came out not on Mike Vernon's Blue Horizon Records, but on Andrew Loog Oldham's Immediate label. This was the result of financial hassles between Vernon and Clifford Davies. Some of us were happy about leaving Blue Horizon, and some were not. 'I was the last to agree to leave Blue Horizon,' Pete told a reporter. 'I was quite happy there and I didn't like leaving just for money. I said to the rest of the guys, "Watch out. There'll be a comeback from this."'

The break with Vernon meant the end of Fleetwood Mac's 'live in the studio' style of recording. From then on we began to produce ourselves, editing and overdubbing as much as possible.

The British music press was full of Fleetwood Mac's business affairs that spring. As we were about to sign a long-term contract with Immediate, word came that John Lennon was interested in signing us to the Beatles' new label, Apple Records. (The Beatles loved 'Albatross' and recorded 'Here Comes The Sun King' as a tribute to Pete.) Clifford broke off negotiations with Immediate and told *Melody Maker*: 'The Beatles have heard our new album and have become very friendly with us lately. We may sign with Apple if we can get a reasonable deal, but we are an independent team – we write and produce and record – so we may conceivably form our own label.'

Eventually all this fell through, and we signed with Warner Brothers Records. The new album Clifford mentioned, (whose first title, *Bread and Kunny*, was rejected by the label), was released a few months later as *Then Play On*.

Then Play On had to be different – and better – than anything Fleetwood Mac had ever done. We didn't want to release any more records with Jeremy singing Elmore James, so Jeremy didn't even play on the album. The original plan was to issue an EP of Earl Vince's parodies along with *Then Play On*, and we recorded an album's worth of tracks with Jeremy. This parody album was performed as a complete show, with different bands and a vulgar MC. On different tracks we were an acid band, then a blues band, a jazz group, and a fifties teen band backing a Fabianesque Jeremy, whose gifts of mimicry were sorely tested and technically perfect. The record company thought the whole thing was a wank, but we took it seriously.

Then Play On was assembled by Pete from several different sources. First were Danny's songs. Pete could have done all the writing himself, but instead he informed a shocked Danny that he was responsible for half the album. It was another example of Pete trying to shake the Green God image.

Anyway, Danny approached his assignment very cerebrally (much like Lindsey Buckingham would later on), and came up with some good music. He couldn't write lyrics very well, but we figured, so what? It was Peter's own songs that set the tone of *Then Play On* anyway. The playing was sublime, and the lyrics reflected the depressed, even morbid state he was sometimes in. To say Peter Green was disillusioned with our success would be a gross understatement. 'Closing My Eyes' was full of sorrow and self-pity. *'Is it asking too much/When the question is what to do with the life I've had?'* This was followed by 'Show Biz Blues', a sort of Carnatic slide guitar masterpiece that asked our audience, *'Tell me, everybody, do you really give a damn for me?'* Pete's extraordinary dual nature came out on what was perhaps his best song ever, the epochal 'Oh Well'.

The first version was written for the stage and had two parts. There was an aggressive side to Pete's personality; he could check a person out and really know him. *'Don't ask me what I think of you,'* he warns. *'I might not give the answer that you want me to . . . Oh well.'* An air of resignation gives way to a hard rock segment that in turn becomes 'Oh Well Part Two', almost nine minutes of concerto for guitar, cello and flute (which was played by Pete's girlfriend Sandra). This was the other side of Pete's persona, that of the reflective, spiritual musician whose hair was now down below his shoulders and who had taken to wearing flowing caftans and burnouses onstage. 'Oh Well Part Two' was full of Gurdjieffian sonorities and Hispano-Moorish arabesques. Pete had also been listening to the English soundscapist, Ralph Vaughan Williams, whose influence is in here as well.

Pete's best known music from *Then Play On* is the studio version of 'Rattlesnake Shake', his ode to masturbation as a cure for the blues. The song is also about me. *'Now I know this guy, his name is Mick/ Now he don't care when he don't got no chick/He does the shake, the rattlesnake shake, to jerk away the blues.'* And then – blast off! Pete's chainsaw guitar lick, hard as nails and as immediate as a dog's bite, really defined our sound in those days. When the record came out, I took a lot of teasing about the lyric, but I didn't care. It had the frankness and ring of truth of everything that Peter Green did.

Fleetwood Mac would jam for hours in the studio, and after we finished Peter went in with a razor blade and we had an album. Three segments of *Then Play On* came from these marathons. 'Underway' was in the moody 'Albatross' groove; 'Searching for Madge' (assembled from seven separate jams) and 'Fighting for Madge' were hard rock blazers dedicated to Fleetwood Mac's consummate English fan. Madge was an early fan from Darlington, who would turn up in the four corners of the British Isles to hear us play. To this day I've never seen anyone so faithful to a band. Madge wasn't a great-looking girl; in fact she was a rather large lady, but she was a real character. She had a girlfriend who was her physical opposite, a very frail and sickly blonde girl. They'd turn up in these Godforsaken places and would end up sleeping on hotel floors because we couldn't turn them out. They were real young and totally in love with the music. Madge was always treated top notch by Fleetwood Mac. After all, she was . . . *Madge*!

Then Play On ended with Pete's doomy blues dirge, 'Before The Beginning', with a guitar solo that cried like a man in great pain. It gradually became clear to the rest of us how unbearable that pain was becoming.

The album was released in Britain in September 1969, and in America the following month. Pete decided to release 'Oh Well' as a single, with the symphonette 'Part Two' as the B-side. McVie and I thought that this was a mistake. We felt that 'Oh Well' was a bit of a bummer, and we each bet Pete five pounds that the record wouldn't even make the charts. Two weeks later, 'Oh Well' exploded to number two in Britain, and John and I dug into our wallets and paid Pete off.

Then Play On proved to be Fleetwood Mac's next big hit. It reached number five in Britain and was our first American release to sell more than a hundred thousand albums. We were *huge* in Europe. Yet the whole band knew that we were in trouble. Peter Green was unhappy and guilt-ridden. He had really lost interest in the group and wanted to quit even before 'Oh Well' was released, but was persuaded to stay on by Clifford only for the sake of his friends in the band. I'd talk to Pete about the band and he'd say, 'Mick, I wasn't cut out for success. I can take this business or leave it.'

'But it's a shame,' I said, 'to leave while the band is so big.'

'Ah, there's nothing in it to hold me,' he said. 'I'm sick of playing the same fucking thing night after night. I want to jam, Mick. I gotta move on to something new.' Pete was also talking a lot about religion at the same time. A dozen LSD trips had rendered him a spiritually burnt-out case. He had shunted his Jewish heritage aside and become a messianic Christian, which lasted only several weeks. One night backstage after a show, he told me he was giving up clubs and girls forever. 'Mick, I want to find out about God. I want to believe that a person's role in life is to do good for other people, and what we're doing now just isn't shit.'

'But Pete,' I said. 'We're doing a job. We've got to live if we're going to be good for anything.'

But it was like he didn't hear me, or didn't want to hear. His eyes were boring into me. 'I don't want to waste my life,' he said softly. 'I don't want to die thinking I haven't fucking done anything for anybody.'

I didn't know what to say, and we sat in silence for a while. Then Pete got up to leave. 'I just don't know, Mick,' he sighed. 'Sometimes I think music is everything, other times I don't think it's anything. I don't give a shit about the money. I'm in a terrible state of "don't knows" right now.'

To capitalize on the success of *Then Play On* in late 1969, Blue Horizon released two albums, *Blues Jam at Chess* and *Fleetwood Mac in Chicago*, much to our annoyance as this was the material we had cut almost a year before. 'The bulk of our fans won't like it,' Pete somewhat petulantly told the press, 'because a lot of the blues fans have dropped us because we've been on television and have had some hits. I'm pretty angry at this old release coming out just now.'

Yet it was our old fans who were responsible for Fleetwood Mac's solid showing in the traditional end-of-year polls in the music press. *Melody Maker* named us number one Progressive Group for 1969 (the Beatles were number one Pop Group, an important difference in those times), while Pete was voted number three composer, behind Lennon –McCartney and Jagger–Richards.

But success was bittersweet. Although Fleetwood Mac entered 1970 as one of the biggest groups in the world, out-selling both the Beatles and Stones in Europe the year before, we were forced to confront Peter Green's disaffection and increasing disgust with the world. I remember how upset he was by the news of starving orphans who were victims of the Nigerian civil war in Biafra. He used to cry in front of the TV news. At one point he sent more than £12,000 to various charities like

Save the Children. Then Pete became fixated on the idea that Fleetwood Mac should become a charity band. The whole group used to sit around all night in American motels and talk about it until dawn. 'Come on,' Pete would say. 'We can keep working, keep enough to pay expenses and live simply, and give the rest to starving people. We could still be a band, but our lives would be *dedicated* to something.'

'Look Pete,' I'd say, 'what would you do without money? You like to have plenty of cash around and people looking after you.'

'Yeah, but I can walk away from it,' he said. 'I don't *need* it. I'd just feel much better about playing this music if we could give what we make to the poor. There's so much poverty. Maybe we could make a bit of difference.'

We looked at each other and shook our heads. It seemed like the visionary excursion Pete had taken with LSD was affecting his judgement. The rest of us were more into boozing and smoking than frying our brains with acid. We were mystified. I guess that John and I were too middle-class to understand the urgency of Pete's obsessions. We didn't want to be a charity band, but we tried to compromise anyway. One night at the Fillmore East we were playing our set. Pete always walked around to the back of the drum kit while Jeremy was doing his act. 'LOOK,' I shouted at him. 'LET'S START AN ORPHANAGE. FINANCE IT WITH THE BAND'S MONEY. BUT LET'S KEEP SOME OF THE MONEY WE MAKE!'

Pete leaned in close and yelled into my ear, 'LET'S GIVE IT *ALL AWAY!*'

Then Pete began to get a little crazed. He appeared onstage in white robes and caftans, wearing his hair and beard very long. A big crucifix hung from his neck. He did long interviews about his search for God and suffered terribly when they were published. 'That's not how I meant it,' he'd say, after reading some outrageous distortion. I told him he was just giving the press ammunition by trying to evangelize. It was dangerous to expose your innermost feelings to reporters, I told him, unless you researched how you were going to express it.

Eventually there was a showdown over the charity band issue. I told him, 'Pete, it's not gonna work for Fleetwood Mac. It's a pipe dream. We're not really making great fortunes, just a good living, and nobody in the band except you wants to be a pauper. Jenny and I live in a third floor flat. We want to get married and find some place to live. I don't want to work for nothing.'

'Well then,' Pete said, 'I'm going to leave. That's it.'

I think Peter Green saw me as materialistic and insecure. But I wanted to have a family and he wanted to have a cause. McVie felt like I did, although there had been a moment or two where we saw the beauty of Pete's plan. 'We were in some hotel,' John remembers, 'and Pete came in and said, "C'mon, let's give everything away." At one point I even said, "You're right!" But when he left the room I had to shake my head and come to my senses. I said, "Whoa, hang on, pull the reins in here. Has this guy been eating too much acid?"'

We were very sad. Pete had been an extremely together guy, our leader and the ultimate arbiter of style and substance both in the group and in our circle of friends. To see him diminish, as we saw it, and change was extremely depressing. To our shock and amazement, 'Greenie' (as we called him back then) appeared to be going down.

In February 1970, Fleetwood Mac embarked on a European tour, playing to sellout crowds at every venue. When we arrived in Munich in early March, we lost Peter Green for good. Munich was the beginning of the end for the original band.

Somehow Peter had been surrounded by a bunch of rich German hippie brats, a group we called the Munich Jet Set. They had a commune in a big old house with a lot of LSD floating around. During our stay in Munich, Pete was whisked out there and spent all his time getting stoned. We never even saw him, except for the gig, and to this day, John and I always say that was it. Peter Green was never the same after that.

After Pete had been there for a few days, our road manager Dennis Kean and I went out to this commune to try to get him back. Pete was tripping but lucid. He told us he wanted to stay and live in this commune with these Germans. We could see these brats were taking advantage of Pete and were succeeding in pulling him away from us. Appealing to his sense of duty, we persuaded him to come with us and finish the tour. But that night, back at the hotel, he told us he was finished. He said he was in a panic, that he couldn't handle the money, that he was just a working-class person, and he was going to leave Fleetwood Mac as soon as possible. When Clifford Davies told him that the band was committed through May, Pete agreed to stay with us till then. After that, he insisted, he was through. He was very responsible about it. He'd play out his days with us, and that was it.

We returned to England later in March, and tried to carry on as best we could. The German kids had followed Pete home to London and continued to work their dangerous trips on him, which only fed into his terrible guilt about what he called 'unclean money'. Late in April,

Fleetwood Mac headlined the 1970 Pop Proms, supported by Hookfoot and a great young writer and piano player who called himself Elton John. It was around that time that Peter Green cut his last record with Fleetwood Mac. It was a song he had written about the Devil, and he called it, with heartbreaking self-recrimination, 'The Green Manalishi'.

It was the last Fleetwood Mac single with Pete in the band. A sinister throb, majestic blues chords, and a howling banshee guitar powered this appalling song about the temptation to descend into madness – the relentless hellhound on Peter Green's trail. The song was full of weird wails and chilling sound effects, as Peter bemoaned the insidious influence of the Green Manalishi with the two-pronged crown: '*You come creeping around, making me do things I don't want to do . . ./ Can't believe that you need my love so bad, sneaking around trying to drive me mad . . .*' This descent into the maelstrom was written after a terrifying nightmare, Pete told me. He had woken up in the middle of the night, transfixed with fear, unable to move or breathe. Later, recovering, he wrote out the Manalishi just as we cut it. It was Peter Green's awesome valediction, his way of saying goodbye to Fleetwood Mac.

One of Pete's last gigs with us was a BBC radio broadcast we did in the middle of May. Then a club date in London, after which Pete appeared as a solo with the Grateful Dead a few days later at a music festival in the country. A week later, on 25 May, we played London's Lyceum along with the Grateful Dead. It was Pete's last official appearance with Fleetwood Mac as a member of the band. (There are those who were at this show who remember Pete, crazed on acid, trying to burn the amps backstage, but I don't remember this.)

Meanwhile, the press was having a field day with our misfortune. 'MAC LEADER QUITS', read one headline. 'CLASH BETWEEN MUSIC BELIEFS AND BUSINESS'. '"I'M NOT SOME KIND OF RELIGIOUS NUT"'.

In an interview with *New Musical Express*, Pete laid out his agenda for the public, for the first time. He said he didn't want money, that he wanted to be with people who thought like he did. He complained of no rest on arduous tours, and said he felt 'cut down' by Fleetwood Mac's three-guitar lineup. He said he felt that his leaving would bring more out of Jeremy, whose uproaring personality had been eclipsed once Pete had got his sense of leadership of the band. From now on, he said, he just wanted to jam with different people and not be confined to rigid tours and playing the same thing all the time. Pete wanted his freedom. There was no trace of bitterness in his remarks, just more of the nobility we always associated with him. 'You see,' he said, 'it's been a great thing for me to be brought up in the East End with all the violence there and manage to live through that kind of upbringing and then find God and people who think the same way. I just want to give that feeling to as many people as I can.'

The press was also full of interesting rumours about Fleetwood Mac's next steps, if any. Another Euro tour, set to begin 1 June, had to be cancelled, and there were stories published that Fleetwood Mac was distraught over the loss of the Green God and would break up.

Not true, but it was, as John McVie has said, Trauma City.

From *Disc*, dated 23 May 1970: 'Rumours that Christine Perfect would join her husband, John McVie, in the Fleetwood lineup were dismissed this week by the group's manager Clifford Davies.

'He told *Disc*: "Fleetwood will continue as a four-piece group. There is nobody of any race, colour or creed joining them. They go to America on 31 July where they have been booked as a four-piece group – and that's how they'll stay."'

'The Green Manalishi' was released in mid-May. It was our fourth straight hit single, reaching number ten on the British charts by the time Peter Green left us. It would be another six years before Fleetwood Mac had a top thirty record in Britain.

CHAPTER FOUR

Trees So Bare and Beautiful

So Greenie left us, and we thought, oh shit! There were mutterings in the ranks about breaking up the band, but I never understood why. It never occurred to me to quit. I simply thought that we were too stupid to do anything else. McVie and I were a bass player and a drummer and we needed a band.

As John McVie says: 'It's called hanging on by your finger-nails.'

You simply keep going if you're a musician. The whole philosophy McVie and I had (and still have) regarding Fleetwood Mac is, if someone pulls out, we're still here.

But this was cold comfort to Jeremy Spencer and Danny Kirwan during the summer of 1970, at Fleetwood Mac's new country seat, Kiln House, in Hampshire. Pete was gone and Jerry and Danny were deeply affected: they were now fronting the band, and their morale was low. We were *all* depressed and nervous because we had been abandoned by our supreme leader.

To try to muddle through, I took over leadership of the band from Pete. And John and I got our front line some help. She was the best blueswoman and the prettiest musician in England, as well as being John's wife: Christine Perfect McVie.

Christine was from Birmingham, born in the war years like my sisters. Her father, Cyril Perfect, was a university professor and musician, whose own father had played the organ at Westminster Abbey. Her mother, Beatrice (she was known as Tee), was a frustrated musician, but then she had a different sort of touch. Chris's mum was a psychic and healer. She could heal warts overnight with the touch of a finger. Once, when a dear old friend of Cyril Perfect was diagnosed with leukemia, Tee wore white kid gloves to bed for a few nights and the friend was cured. Chris grew up thinking it weird that her mother went ghost-hunting with the local psychic research society. Chris would ask, 'Why can't you be an ordinary mum?' And her mother would just smile to herself.

The Perfect household was full of music, and soon Chris was playing guitar and singing. At age sixteen she and a girlfriend snuck down to London and stormed every talent agency in town, warbling Everly Brother songs. Someone eventually said OK, and their career consisted of a one-song pub appearance, backed by The Shadows, before they were discovered by their parents and dragged home. So, like many of the best musicians of our generation, Chris went to art college, in Birmingham. At a Tuesday night meeting of the college's folk music club, she met a handsome German literature scholar from Birmingham University named Spencer Davis, and the two fell in with each other, busking on tops of buses around Birmingham with guitars for the odd shilling or two. They fronted the university's jazz band for a while, but they soon met a fifteen-year-old schoolboy who played blues piano at the Chapeel Pub at lunchtime. Stevie Winwood.

As soon as Davis met Winwood, they formed the Spencer Davis Group and took off. Nobody could believe this kid could yell out the blues this way. His voice gave Chris goose flesh the first time she heard it. They honed their act in local clubs like the Golden Eagle and the Whiskey A Go Go, and they were *hot*. Chris would trail around after them religiously, but soon wanted to play with a band of her own. In 1964 she joined another local band, Sounds of Blue, playing keyboards with Andy Sylvester on bass, Stan Webb on guitar, and a lineup that included Chris Wood on sax. Sounds of Blue lasted only a year, but they played material no one else was doing in the Midlands at the time – Mose Allison, Ray Charles, Amos Milburn. Leaving school a trained sculptress, Chris went off to London to try her luck, leaving music behind completely. She found a job as a window dresser at Dickens and Jones, working with a lot of bitchy people, and spent a year bored to death. That was when Andy Sylvester called and asked her to join the new band he was forming with Stan Webb. 'At which point I said yes,' Chris remembers. 'I said yes, I will. I'll do it, anything to get out of this.'

Chris continues: 'I didn't know how to play blues piano very well, so on Andy's recommendation I rushed out and bought a whole bunch of Freddy King records. I listened hard to his piano player, Sonny Thompson, and learned to copy his licks. That's where my style comes from.'

Chris began to sing the blues as well. Even though the new band, Chicken Shack, relied heavily on the stage persona of madman guitarist Stan Webb, fans soon took notice of the deep feeling, plaintive and somehow knowing, that Christine Perfect brought to her interpretation of the blues. Few women got involved in the British blues scene, and Chris made Chicken Shack stand out as something different.

In 1967, Chicken Shack was discovered by Mike Vernon and became Fleetwood Mac's Blue Horizon stablemate. (When Mike went up to see the band after hearing a demo tape, he literally found them rehearsing in an old chicken shack in Kidderminster, where they lived.) Mike was particularly elated to discover the beautiful Christine Perfect; in fact I can remember him telling Peter Green that Fleetwood Mac better take care, because this new girl from Birmingham was going to take our breath away at the Windsor Jazz Festival.

And she did.

Mike recorded Chicken Shack right away, and the band had to take its lumps on our circuit. Chris put in her hours of drudgery and dues-paying – freezing in the equipment van, sleeping on the gear, five sets a night at the Star Club in Hamburg, carrying and setting up her own kit. Chris and I met around then. She still tells me that she felt awful when she met me for the first time, in the Marquee dressing room after a Fleetwood Mac/Chicken Shack gig. She tells me she was terrified. I said, what did I do? You didn't do anything, she says. It was like I wasn't there.

I can be totally . . . drifty. Especially during a gig.

John had lived in Ealing until he married Chris in August 1968. Now the pair set up in Dorchester Street and rarely saw each other. If Fleetwood Mac wasn't on the road, Chicken Shack was. They moved to Chalk Farm, then back to Dorchester Street. Chris was getting tired of touring and wanted to be a housewife, so she left Chicken Shack to be able to bask in some of the fun Fleetwood Mac was having during our big year, 1969. 'It was extremely romantic,' she says. 'A little bit of the glamour of what Fleetwood Mac was in those days rubbed off. It was almost like someone marrying a Beatle. You married one of the links in the chain, and you were part of them.'

But the music business wouldn't let go. Mike Vernon talked Chris into sessions for a solo album in the autumn of '69. In the studio she cut songs by Howlin' Wolf, Chuck Jackson, Etta James, Danny Kirwan and five of her own songs in a bluesy style that anticipated soft rock music. A month later, 'When You Say' was released as a single. Then

Chicken Shack had a huge hit in Europe with Chris's lead vocal on 'I'd Rather Go Blind'. That December, she won the *Melody Maker* poll for best female vocalist. 'I was coerced to return to my public as a result,' Chris says. 'I wasn't keen on giving up my life of leisure as a housewife, but then I did like being able to earn money independently.' So auditions were set up at the Lyceum, a band was hired, and a tour followed that Christine considered disastrous. So she quit the business again, just as her solo album, *Christine Perfect*, was released. (It would win her another Best Female Vocal award in 1970, the only time the same person won it two years running.) CHRISTINE PERFECT HAS QUIT ran headlines in *New Musical Express*. 'Christine Perfect has quit the music business. The girl for whom a great future was predicted when she left Chicken Shack . . . has announced she is giving up singing altogether . . . Her withdrawal from the music scene takes immediate effect. She told the *NME* this week: "I shall be doing no more live dates, and making no more records."'

Fortunately for Fleetwood Mac, Chris's retirement lasted all of two months.

Earlier in 1970, before Pete left the band, we had picked up and moved to the country. I had felt for a long time that we should live together communally in a country retreat. Danny had been living in Brixton, Jeremy in Paddington, me and Jenny in Kensington, and it was a drag just getting together to rehearse. Plus it was very much the thing in those days to spurn the evil vapours of the city in favour of the purifying zephyrs of the countryside. So, from a friend of my sister Sally's we rented an eccentric old oasthouse near the village of Alton on the border between Hampshire and Surrey. We lived in two adjoined kiln houses used for drying hops and now converted to domestic use. We moved into this wonderful menage – band, wives, children and roadies. It was me and Jenny, who was pregnant; John and Chris; Jeremy, Fiona and Dicken; Danny and his girlfriend Claire in the attic, and our road crew, Dennis Kean and Dinky Dawson. We were in Kiln House for less than a year, but it was a wonderful time. The summer in the country landscape was inspiring. We worked on the next album in the half-converted kiln room, trying to be a four-piece Fleetwood Mac. We were smoking lots of hashish in chillums. Great blocks of the stuff lay about. There was one long table in the farmhouse room; when we ran out of hash, one could run a fork between the planks and roll joints out of the dust.

It was my pleasure to marry Miss Jenny Boyd on 12 June at the

Alton registry office. Peter Green was supposed to have been our best man, but he had gone off by then and we were shedding many tears over him. So we had Dennis Kean instead. Then we went home, sat on the grass and smoked some joints. That was our reception.

While our summertime at Kiln House was nice, we were under enormous pressure as a band. Pete was gone; we had to prove we could stand as one of Britain's more progressive bands. This gave us terrible cases of nerves, and long evenings were spent quelling mutinies and threats of disintegration. We were really leaning on Jeremy to emerge from behind his personae and write about his life. Same with Danny Kirwan, who now had the burden of replacing the Green God as lead guitarist in Fleetwood Mac. The pressure was on to record the successor to *Then Play On*, and it made us sick. I felt strongly about keeping the band together, and I felt I had to fend off all challenges to our unity. There was one terrible night at Kiln House when everybody decided they wanted to leave. Not only did Jeremy and Danny not want to front the band, but John McVie, after some mischievous indulgence, said he was sick of playing bass and wanted to just be a roadie for a while. But I felt a kind of soldierly duty to somehow *carry on* in the face of hippie lassitude and hash torpor. It took me four hours that night, but, one by one, I talked everybody back into the band.

Jenny can confirm this. 'That's right. I was there that night at Kiln House. They had had it, but Mick talked them back in. He would *not* let go. He will *never* let go of Fleetwood Mac.'

Although Fleetwood Mac was officially a four-piece band when we cut *Kiln House*, we had help from the retired Christine Perfect. Not only did she draw the cover art, but she also sang and played on some of the tracks.

Kiln House opened with 'This is the Rock', Jeremy's gentle and laid-back rockabilly tribute. 'Station Man' was Danny's tasty little 'sticky fingers' lick. 'Blood on the Floor' was a country music send-up, followed by Jeremy's version of Fats Waller's 'Hi Ho Silver' (which had also been covered by rockabilly hero Johnny Burnette). 'Jewel-Eyed Judy' was for Judy Wong, a song that both Jenny and Chris had worked on. Side two started with 'Buddy's Song', a tribute to Buddy Holly that sounded like a medley of his songs. 'Earl Grey' was a Danny Kirwan instrumental. 'One Together' represented Jeremy's sole attempt to write a love song. Danny finishes *Kiln House* with a good rocker, 'Tell Me All The Things That You Do' and 'Mission Bell', his take on the old American hit.

By the time we finished *Kiln House,* we were about two weeks away from a three-month tour of America, which began the first week of August 1970. We were worried because we were used to a three-man front line and our sound was thin without Pete. So, at the dinner table at Kiln House one night in late July, I asked Chris, 'Do you wanna join the band?' She knew we needed to fatten our sound and she knew all the songs anyway, having been forced to listen to them endlessly in rehearsal. So she came with us on the *Kiln House* tour. Her first gig with Fleetwood Mac was at the Warehouse in New Orleans on 8 August 1970. We did all the stuff on *Kiln House* on our little Fender twins, and for the second part of the show Jeremy would play blues and some oldies. It was our first tour without Pete; with Chris singing and playing keyboards the volume was down, but the shows went over great and helped the album do respectably when it came out in September. In Britain the music press duly noted that Chris had joined us, despite various business encumbrances from her solo career, and that she wanted henceforth to be known not as Christine Perfect but under her married name Christine McVie.

It was on this tour that Jeremy's impersonations of Elvis began to get really uncanny. He wouldn't do Elvis every night, no matter how much we begged him to don the lamé suit the band had bought for him, no matter how well it had gone down with the audience the night before. Jeremy had to be in the *mood* for Elvis, because a drastic change of personality came over him, as if he were in a trance. Impersonation is too sorry a word to describe what Jeremy did; he really seemed to *become* Elvis in his mind. An example: before we left England we played a gig. With Jeremy offstage, Fleetwood Mac went into a straight version of 'Viva Las Vegas', breaking off midway through so I could announce, 'Here for your entertainment tonight, all the way from Las Vegas . . . ELVIS PRESLEY!!' Out bounded Jeremy in his suit with his hair slicked back in an obscene pompadour to complete the lyrics to the song. He was really into it when some kid in the third row got up to use the toilet. In a flash Jeremy/Elvis snapped his fingers and killed the music behind him. He pointed towards the embarrassed kid and delivered the killing thrust: 'Nobody . . . BUT NOBODY . . . leaves the room . . . *when Elvis is on stage!!*'

Our poor customer collapsed under this abusive scorn, but that was Jeremy. Yet these performances took a lot out of him. They were like shamanic transformation rituals, and he had a steadfast rule about not impersonating Elvis too often, as if the magic wouldn't work if it were forced and routine.

Actually, Jeremy was getting quieter. Fiona had another baby at Kiln House, and she and Jeremy spent hours reading their Bible together, talking about religion. Fleetwood Mac would be spending the rest of the year on the road and our families were none too thrilled about the separation. Jenny was pregnant and was unhappy as she packed to stay with her mother in Devon while I was on the road. 'Mick,' she said one day, 'I don't feel part of things here.' And I knew what she meant. She didn't really know John and Chris and the hard-core Fleetwood Mac crew that had moved to the country, lock, stock and amps. Jenny was ethereal and spiritually-minded while we were entertainers. She went to bed early while the rest of us stayed up, caroused, made music.

'Jenny, what should we do about it?' I asked.

'I don't know,' she cried. 'I thought about coming with you, but I can't with the baby.'

I was puzzled. 'I thought you hated hotel rooms and rock tours.'

'Well, I do,' she said. 'But I'm afraid for us. When you're gone for months on end and I don't see you, you come back changed. It's natural. And I change too. It can't be helped if you're committed to making the band work, but it feels like we're in danger of drifting apart.'

I didn't know what to say, because I knew Jenny was right.

Fleetwood Mac returned to England late in October, with only a few days to prepare for a November tour of Europe. We were sad and mystified to hear Peter Green's solo album, *The End of the Game*, which had just been released. Freeform acid-rock jams wove in and out of each other, meandering this way and that. It made me wonder what had gone wrong with my dear old friend.

As soon as we got back from Europe, things got really hectic. We embarked on a British tour that December and, the lease on Kiln House having expired, bought a nearby country house called Benifols.

Our new house was a unanimous vote of self-confidence for the band. We felt that we'd weathered Pete's departure and survived five months of constant touring. Christine was a smash, Jeremy and Danny were relieved, and it felt like we were a band again. We had found a routine that suited us: touring, working hard, and coming home with enough money to be comfortable. (We were making maybe £30,000 a year each. Clifford Davies had an offshore tax scheme going on the Isle of Guernsey, but nobody in the band understood it.) So we survived, we lived well, and tried to keep it going.

When the lease on Kiln House ran out, I said I wanted us to stay together. Secretly I felt that the band would fall apart if we weren't with each other all the time, but it also made sense to pool the band's record advance and buy some land. So, for £21,000 we purchased Benifols, a secluded mansion on a hill, just past the Devil's Punch Bowl near Haslemere, in Hampshire. The somewhat ramshackle house came with seven acres of forest and a decrepit tennis court, and we thought it was paradise. We moved in with our retainers and E-type Jaguars and assumed the life of the hip country squire. I *loved* it. We had a full-sized billiard table and a music room where we could rehearse. The place was chock-a-block with kids, dogs, relatives and lots of visitors.

It was heaven, for the first year we lived there. The house dated from early in the 1900s and had been divided into three parts. We never really lived communally, since everyone had separate quarters. Jenny and I took the spacious servants' quarters and the kitchen, and John and Chris got the other side of the staircase. There Chris made a beautiful home, very cozy with antiques and soft lamplight. Jenny used to be cross with me because she said I spent all my time in the McVies' flat, talking about Fleetwood Mac. I remember many long unhappy walks through our woods with Jenny, who was blue because she was pregnant, lonely and felt left out of our intense musical lives. Both Jenny and Judy Wong felt a little intimidated by the awesome powers of our newest member. They saw that Christine could write music, play piano, sing like an angel, rehearse all day with the men, and cook a big dinner without batting an eye. In addition Benifols was neat as a pin and spotless, and Chris was a superb artist and sculptor. She was down to earth, very pretty, and attractive to everybody. People were amazed. What kind of superwoman was this?

We were on tour in Scotland in mid-January 1971, when I got an urgent call that Jenny had gone into labour and it wasn't going well. Come quickly, I was told, because they may not live much longer. I sat in the plane in total panic and prayed. In fact, Jenny's mother had already told her sisters to go home and get the flowers. Our daughter Amy was born on 17 January, by Caesarian section, while I was en route to the hospital. I was there when Jenny woke up from the anaesthetic, and we were overjoyed to see each other and hold our new Amy. What a moment!

But the band was still on the road. I dashed back to Scotland on the next train and my mother came down to Benifols to take care of Jenny and the baby.

Since Clifford Davies kept us booked and working as much as possible, there was barely time for me to get to know Amy before Fleetwood Mac was due back in America for a three-month tour that began in February. This tour almost killed Fleetwood Mac for good.

We arrived in San Francisco for our first show at the Fillmore West, and things were great on the surface. *Kiln House* had done much better in the States than in Britain, and was getting played on all-important FM radio along with Santana's new hit version of 'Black Magic Woman', which they had transformed into a Cuban meringue with a big acid-style jam at the end. It was a great showcase for Carlos, and Greg Rolie's vocal was as true to Peter Green as possible.

But as soon as we got to California, I could see that something was going wrong with Jeremy. He and Danny had taken some mescaline upon arrival, and Jerry, as we called him, didn't seem to come off it for a long time. Since I roomed with him on the road, I just knew he wasn't doing all that well. He was always a dreamer to begin with; lately he had been immersed in the Bible and all kinds of books on philosophy and changing your life. I could see something might happen. But he was also getting lazier and had to be begged and cajoled to do his act. Ironically, he was playing near peak. At the Fillmore he did his Elvis bit and had the whole place off the ground. That night he played with a kind of visionary fire we had never ever seen from him before, and it was stunning. It was also his last gig with Fleetwood Mac.

While we were in San Francisco, Los Angeles was rocked by a devastating earthquake, one of the worst this century. Dozens died, buildings disintegrated, bridges toppled. We were scheduled to fly into LA the following morning to do our sold-out shows at the Whiskey A Go Go.

Jeremy didn't want to go. 'What do you mean, you're not going?' I asked him. It was very late at night, in the motel room we were sharing in San Francisco.

'I can't explain it,' he said. I looked at cynical little Jeremy and saw he was almost crying. 'It's like I have a foreboding of something fucking awful happening.'

I said, 'Look, nobody's crazy about flying into an earthquake down there. Is that what's bothering you?'

'It's not only that, Mick: it's like LA is an *evil* place. When I'm there I can feel like a *pall* of bad vibes. And it frightens me. I'm really scared of going there this time.'

I asked if he was feeling OK otherwise. 'Yeah, man,' he said, 'but I'm homesick. I miss Fiona and the kids. I should be at home with them. Shit, I don't want to go to LA! Something bad's gonna happen, Mick, you wait and see.'

I thought I should try to minimize Jeremy's irrational fears. '*Of course* Los Angeles is an evil place,' I agreed, 'but we don't have to be part of that. We're professionals, we're going there on a job. It's like we have a mission. I think it's possible to go there on a job, do the gigs, and come out again safely without touching on all the evil elements.'

When I finished my speech, Jeremy looked at me as if I were the most pathetic of squares. 'Oh fuck it, Mick. I'll go, but I'm telling you I don't feel right about it this time. Something's gonna blow for sure down there. You'll see.'

Somehow we got him on the plane. John McVie: 'I'm sitting next to him, and we're coming into LAX. He's in the window seat looking out; he turned to me and said, "What the hell am I doing here?"'

Indeed we all wondered what the hell we were doing in Los Angeles in the middle of considerable post-cataclysmic seismic activity. Indeed, the earthquake was still happening when we got there. Everything was very still and very weird. The stench of ozone was thick in the hot, heavy atmosphere. The sky shone a sickly yellow. Jeremy walked out the back of the PSA 727 and I snapped a picture of him, looking rather strange.

We were booked into the Hollywood Hawaiian. After a few minutes in our room, Jeremy said he was going out. 'Hey Mick, just going down to browse. I'll be right back.' I asked where he was off to, and he said he was going to check out a bookstore on Hollywood Boulevard that he'd visited before. He seemed a bit less freaked out than the last few days, and I didn't think anything of him going off.

I should have, because Jeremy never came back.

We waited for him for hours. We looked at each other and worried all day. When he didn't return to the hotel by six o'clock, we cancelled the gig that night. Someone stayed by the phone at all times, but it never rang. We made excursions to the bookstore, which turned out to be a headshop. They had never seen Jeremy. With mounting anxiety

71

we tried to calculate what had happened before we called the police. First, we knew that this was totally unlike the Jerry we knew and loved. We boiled it down to two scenarios. Either he'd been bopped on the head and taken somewhere against his will, or – and in the back of our minds we knew this was the one – he had gone off with The Process or the Children of God or one of the other hippie Christian sects that proselytized along Hollywood Boulevard. They had already stopped us on the street to hand us leaflets and say, Come with us now, brother, the end is at hand, soon it will be too late. Something along those lines anyway. We knew that Jerry was fodder for that stuff. He was ripe for the picking.

This went on for four days. Clifford Davies went to the police when Jeremy didn't show up the next morning. The police told us about these cults, how they would harangue young kids on the street, herd them into buses, and take them to headquarters. They'd be thrown into locked and darkened rooms and held without food and water for four or five days until they renounced their former selves and were subsequently 'reborn' into a life of new ideals. We didn't know if this was happening to Jeremy, but it was the freaky background against which the search for him took place. Most of the people who found their way into these groups were already lost causes, mostly gullible young runaways. Could Jeremy have been talked into joining just like that, off the street? Was he really that unhappy? We were so shocked that he'd left us, in part because of how great he had been doing onstage, holding the audience rapt with the theatricality of his Elvis recreation. 'He had so much power over the audience,' John McVie would say. 'That's what I can't understand. If he wanted to spread his religious beliefs, surely he could've used that power and tried to do it through the group instead.'

'Yes,' Christine agreed, 'but it was "Elvis" who had all the power. Jeremy had no power at all.'

The worst part was not knowing. He was our friend, and in our way we loved him. We hired a famous psychic who tried to trace Jeremy. Our road managers Dennis Kean and Phil McDonnell combed the streets looking for him. Jeremy's picture was shown on TV, and the FBI and Interpol were alerted. We got several tips on where he might have been taken, and every one was checked out. With the help of moderate local Christians who were knowledgeable about the sects, we kept up our search. I remember one search party we made with a girl who worked at the Whiskey. She came along as an interpreter because this group we were visiting would only answer questions by quoting

Biblical texts. Dusk was falling as we drove through the epicentre of the earthquake out in the valley. Freeway overpasses had fallen over into twisted rubble, and the atmosphere was thick with murky grey smog. All felt wiggy and screwed-up. As we approached the house an awful feeling came over me. This group had recently been forced out of Los Angeles by the police for kidnapping children.

They wouldn't open the door, or give us any assistance. They said they didn't know anything about any missing English guitarist and asked us to leave. No hastier retreat was ever beaten, and I took away with me the haunting image of the bland expressions and horribly pallid complexions of the people staring at us through the chained door.

At the end of the fourth day, we got a tip that led us to the Children of God's locked and guarded warehouse in downtown Los Angeles. Whoever called said we would find Jeremy there under another name.

I didn't go. I was still freaked by my last little visit. So Clifford Davies and Phil McDonnell arrived at the warehouse at 11:30 at night, demanding to see Jeremy Spencer. At first, the Children of God denied he was there and refused to let anyone inside. So Clifford bluffed, saying that Jeremy's wife Fiona was seriously ill back in England and something had to be done. That lie got them into the building. An hour of shouting with leaders of the sect finally produced Jeremy, who stepped quietly into the room. His appearance was a shock. His long hair had been shorn down to his skull, and he was dressed in what appeared to be dirty clothes. He now answered to the name Jonathan.

For nearly three hours, they listened to Jeremy quite reasonably explain that he no longer wished to work; that the earthquake presaged the end of the world, and that he felt he had to put his soul in order before anything else. He had been approached on the street by the brethren, and had been talked into their bus by a brother named Apollos, who had shown him a way to a new life. Jeremy showed no concern whatsoever for the band, even when Davies pointed out that the tour would have to be cancelled and that would probably mean the end of Fleetwood Mac. Jeremy said he didn't care: he knew if he had made contact with us, we would have talked him out of the action he had taken. What about his wife and children? 'Jesus will take care of them,' he answered. All the while two disciples were seated on either side of him, rubbing his arms and chanting, 'Jesus loves you'. Other sectarians crowded around, glowered, and told Clifford Davies that he was the devil trying to take Jonathan away from them. And Jerry, according to Davies, was just like a star-struck child. His identity and

personality had been brainwashed away. The old Jeremy Spencer was
. . . *gone.*

When Clifford and Phil reported back to the Hollywood Hawaiian
at dawn and told us what had transpired, we were devastated. In the
grey light of morning, it looked as though we were finished. There
were six weeks left to go on our American tour which, in terms of
money and audience response, was the most successful we had done
in the States. A cancelled tour put our whole career in jeopardy. The
lost revenue and lack of support for our album (*Kiln House* was selling
well at the time) probably meant we would have lost a lot of money
and our house as well. As Chris pointed out, everything we had worked
for, for eight years, was tied up in that house. We all knew we were
facing ruin. I remember talk of trying to arrange a meeting with Jerry
the following evening, because I thought if we could just get to them,
everything could be worked out. Our manager advised against it,
saying he feared for our safety.

What were we going to do? Jeremy had been part of the *Kiln House*
material we had been performing, and his blues set and Elvis act were
vital parts of Fleetwood Mac's show. We were faced with six weeks of
gigs we couldn't possibly perform as a four-piece group.

Only one person could rescue us.

There were groans when the idea was broached to call Peter Green in
England and ask him to fly to California and save our hide. The last
thing we had heard was that his solo album had flopped, that he had
given away all his guitars and was working as a grave-digger.

But we were desperate, and Clifford put through an SOS call to Pete
in Surrey later that day. There was no pressure. We explained the
situation and said, look, don't feel you've got to, but if you could, it
would be great. And that was it. He said he had been about to take a
job as a labourer on a farm, but that in the spirit of friendship he would
do it. He really didn't want to play at all, but he did it and it was great.

As Pete was flying in, Jeremy flew out to the Children of God's place
in Texas, where he was joined soon after by Fiona and their son. (Their
youngest was left with Fiona's mother in Benifols.) We later learned
that Jeremy spent the rest of that year visiting branches of the sect,
helping them recruit more lost souls on the streets of America.

Peter Green arrived two days after we appealed to him. Right away
he let us know what he was willing to do. Our set now consisted of
'Black Magic Woman' and about ninety minutes of free-form jamming.
We had no choice. We were absolutely shattered by Jeremy's defection.

Some nights we went on stage with only a vague notion about what we were going to play. 'We'd arrive for a gig,' John McVie recalls, 'and suddenly find ourselves on stage, staring at the audience without a clue what to play. We were just scared stiff.' Even stranger was the fact that Peter had arrived as part of a package deal that included Clifford Davies's brother-in-law Nigel, who was to play congas with us. (He soon freaked out and went home.)

But Peter Green did help us hold it all together. He treated the whole thing as a joke. He didn't speak much on stage, but occasionally he'd amble to the mike, say something like 'Yankee bastards', and have a laugh! Yet – incredibly – the fans would applaud, and the whole act, even the jamming, seemed to go down pretty well. Even though the band was bored stiff by this, we were always called back for encores and, after a few bad gigs, got on with the gruelling task of trying to re-build our wounded reputation. After the eight weeks of the tour had run their course, we could look back and see we had actually done well in terms of money and fame. It was our best tour ever. But the way we felt inside while making it was pretty awful. The fact that Pete played so beautifully made it even sadder, because we knew we would lose him again. His playing raised goose-flesh on my arms on that tour, and yet at the end he renounced it all once again.

The last date of that winter '71 tour was in New York. After that we collapsed and ran for England with all speed. Fleetwood Mac was drained of all energy and reeling from adversity. 'Over the past year,' Christine told *NME*, 'it seems as if we have just been battered and beaten about the head with a giant club.' It was true. Mentally and physically, Fleetwood Mac's morale scraped the bottom.

But we couldn't give it all up just because Jeremy was out. No one wanted to go through the rigmarole of getting a new band together and going out under a different name, as several people advised us to do. Of the original four Macs, only two had left, and the rest felt we had a right to carry on. We had also been following the rancorous public split between the Beatles that had taken place over the last two years, flogged by the press, and no one in Fleetwood Mac wanted that to happen to us. Once we had returned to the safe world of Benifols with its dogs and kids and familiar landscape, we decided to explore our options. After a few weeks, we began to get letters from Jeremy explaining what had happened; while we still hadn't got over the way he had left, both John and I would have taken him back if he had wanted it. Chris was much less enthusiastic about this, rightly so in retrospect. But neither Chris nor Danny wanted to continue without a third writer, and Clifford Davies had booked a British club tour beginning 4 June, which gave us about a month to try and find a new world-class guitarist who could sing and write.

Judy Wong found him.

Bob Welch saved Fleetwood Mac.

We hired him without an audition.

He was from Los Angeles via Paris, and this is his tale. He was born in 1945 and raised in Hollywood. His father was a writer/producer at Paramount Studios, working with Bob Hope and other luminaries of the early TV era. A self-confessed intellectual snob and crypto-beatnik, Bob grew up on Little Richard and the Beach Boys. When he was seven, his dad bought him a guitar, and he later trained as a clarinettist as well. In high school he tried to start groups and auditioned for surf bands at UCLA. After high school, on money saved from summer jobs, Bob travelled to Paris where he hung around bars whose house musicians were the cream of the expatriate brotherhood of jazz legends – Bud Powell, Eric Dolphy, Lee Morgan. With a friend who was into R&B, Bob spent most of his time playing their instruments and smoking hash under the bridges of the Seine at night.

Bob Welch returned to LA in 1963, around the time his father died. He enrolled at UCLA as a French major and worked nights at the jazz club, Shelly's Mann Hole, where he heard the best bands of the day and nurtured an intense desire to be a professional musician. He kept playing music, but he couldn't quite figure out how to bridge the gap between the street and the music business. He got his break in the summer of 1964, when a friend invited him to take a shot at being the guitar player in a six-piece R&B outfit operating out of Oregon called Ivory Hudson and the Harlequins. It was a mixed black and white group that played 'Night Train' and 'Nowhere To Run' all night in the roadhouses of the Pacific Northwest. The band eventually moved down to LA in two cars and rented an apartment in Malibu from a dentist named Dr Frankel. There were eight musicians and their girlfriends, and they rehearsed on the beach. After some scuffling they got their first job at the biggest black club in LA, the Californian. They played the Brass Rail in the heart of Watts during the fierce rioting of 1966, when the white musicians had to ride on the floor of the car on the way to the gig. They played sizzling soul music for pimps in clubs whose clientele all looked like Ike Turner. During 1966–7, they were the regular band at an urbane black club, Maverick's Flat, full of sophisticated bloods and Hollywood hipsters. Steve McQueen and Muhammad Ali would come in all the time. Billy Preston and the Four Tops were regulars. Next the band went to Europe, where they played Aretha's songs in jet-set clubs in France and Italy. Back in LA the band changed its name to the Seven Souls. Honed to a razor's edge by years of playing together, the group was ready to break out. They had a local hit single in southern California and could play their pick of local venues. Yet they had a problem with their manager, who couldn't cut a proper record deal for them. Bob remembers that the Seven Souls played a make-or-break gig at a club called Winchester Cathedral, competing with a hot but nameless new band from San Francisco, led by a Bay area disc jockey, for the affections of a CBS executive. The best band, it was understood, was going to get a record deal. The Seven Souls did their best, but the other band got signed and became Sly and the Family Stone.

The Seven Souls broke up in 1969. Bob and two others formed a trio, called themselves Head West, and headed east, to Europe, where they gigged until 1971. Freezing in the chilly Parisian spring, Bob sold his last guitar. That's when he got a call from Judy Wong. Bob:

She had been my girlfriend in San Francisco. She sold clothes there and that's where I got my introduction to the whole Haight-Ashbury incense thing. When she called I was at the end of my rope, with no money to get back to California. She said Fleetwood Mac was looking for a guitar player, and did I know anyone who might be interested? I had heard of Fleetwood Mac despite my immersion in the R&B world, because 'Albatross' and 'Oh Well' had been on jukeboxes all over France and Spain. I'd also read the stories about Jeremy's departure in *NME* and the other English music papers. Finally Judy said, 'Why don't you come over and meet everybody and play some guitar with them? You're good enough.'

I got on a plane with literally my last franc and went to London to see Judy, who at the time was married to Glenn Cornick, the bass player in Jethro Tull. There were gold records on the wall, and I remember thinking that this whole world was alien to me. I wasn't a white fan of black blues like these English musicians. I thought of myself instead as a player in an R&B band. I was very identified with all that.

Judy called Mick, and soon I was on a train bound for Haslemere. Mick picked me up at the station in a little VW, wearing mirrored sunglasses and long hair way below his shoulders. I didn't know what to expect, but he and I struck up an immediate emotional rapport. He seemed like a very aware person who was concerned over the state of the world, and I admired that in a musician. So I met them all – Mick and Jenny, John and Chris, Danny and Claire; living under one roof, isolated in a country place that had been some kind of monastery or retreat. It was obvious that Mac had enough money to buy the place, but not to refurbish it. The main detail I can recall, though, is seeing Jeremy's old lamé suit hanging lifelessly on one of the doors by itself.

I was there for about a week, hanging out. John and Chris lived on the middle floor, where Chris had her kitchen. Danny was upstairs, and Mick and Jenny had the downstairs. Mostly what we did was sit around Chris's kitchen table. All the important Fleetwood Mac business was discussed there. We drank coffee and wine, smoked a lot of good hash, and talked it out. Most of the conversation was about Jeremy and Peter Green, who'd done LSD, fallen in with a strange crowd in Germany and left the band. Spencer sounded even weirder. They were traumatized because they'd gone from being one of the most successful bands around to having two of their front men leave within a few months of each other. We talked about this exhaustively. They *couldn't believe* that Jeremy had done this. They were also traumatized by the vibes in LA, New York and the United States in general. I identified with this, since I was in self-exile from the same vibes. They felt that what had happened to Jeremy would never have happened in England.

I went back and forth between Hampshire and London for about a month. Eventually they decided we were interested in some of the same things and that I was a nice guy. I wasn't pushy and didn't want to be a guitar star. I had about a dozen things I'd written in France in 1970, but they didn't ask me, Did I write? Did I sing? Was I a great guitar player? It was more like, Did I fit in? I finally went out there for the third time and at Christine's kitchen table, Mick said, 'Bob, we'd really like to have you in the group.'

I can add a couple of things to Bob's account. We actually held auditions to replace Jeremy, the only time in the history of Fleetwood Mac we resorted to this. Bob appeared from Paris after we had heard four or five people play. He brought along some tapes so we knew he could play; more important, we all got along well and decided that he was gonna be in the band. The auditions went on anyway for a while, but one night we went downstairs and started playing and that was it. It

was unanimous. We loved his personality. His musical roots were in
R&B instead of blues, and that was refreshing. We thought it would
be an interesting blend. We knew he could sing; it was sort of talk-sing,
with astute phrasing and timing. Plus he was well trained, as opposed
to us who had just wandered into it. He was one of those guys who
really sat down and played for hours and hours, an artistic chameleon
who fitted in with our colours and somehow inherited a bit of our
history as well. To this day, I think personality is the most important
thing in keeping a band together. I've seen too many impossible
geniuses.

Once in the band, Bob really developed. He meshed well in every
situation, and his songwriting and style became a big part of Fleetwood
Mac in America. Which we badly needed, because without Pete our
career nosedived in Europe.

We also loved having an American in Fleetwood Mac.

Bob Welch continues:

I moved to Benifols, got an advance from Clifford Davies which I
used to buy a guitar. Immediately I began to discover Fleetwood
Mac's unusual organizational methods. I was expecting they'd tell
me to learn these songs and sing this way, but it was nothing like
that. We just jammed for a long time, and played some blues on the
side. I was waiting for them to tell me what kind of band they were,
but instead I realized they expected me to be the band. I was expected
to pull as much weight as anyone else.

We put Bob to work right away. June and July 1971 were spent playing
the various ballrooms, town halls, pavilions and clubs on the British
circuit. We were down a few rungs from our glory days, but we felt
it necessary to build Fleetwood Mac's reputation back up from the
ground. We played gigs in France and Ireland and a few in Holland.
Returning home from a German festival in a vintage chartered aeroplane, we developed heart-stopping engine problems and had to return
to the airport and make an emergency landing, praying our heads off.
A few hours later a jumbo crashed on the autobahn near Hamburg
with much loss of life.

'I was scared to death,' Bob Welch says of his debut with us. 'I had
never sung two or three of my songs in front of an audience before. I
was petrified. But Mick ran a loose ship. Most of the time it was jam
city. We basically got drunk and had a good time.'

In the middle of this hectic summer, we recorded our next album,

Future Games, at Advision Studio in London. We needed fresh material badly, plus a new identity and direction. We didn't want to be a purist blues group or an acid-rock band any more. So we depended on the writers to come up with the goods. Bob:

> We did *Future Games*. I had some songs that fit and they liked them enough to put them on the album. There was no producer; it was up to mutual consensus among Fleetwood Mac to make the decisions. Basically Chris had to like it, then Mick. Danny meanwhile would disappear for days into the attic and eventually come down with a song. He was one of the strangest people I've ever met, very nervous, couldn't look you in the eye, hard to establish a rapport with. But he was also a very intuitive musician and at the age of twenty he played with surprising maturity and soulfulness. There was an idealistic and pure thing about him that was great. At first I didn't think we'd have much rapport together but, for a while, at least, we did.

Future Games was released in September 1971, in time for our American tour. It was the new-look Fleetwood Mac, devoid of past trademarks. Chris's songs, 'Morning Rain' and 'Show Me A Smile' were both sweet, and Bob's new guitar sounded great and propelled us more into a country rock direction. Although Warner Brothers picked Danny's 'Sands of Time' as the single from this album, it was Bob Welch's 'Future Games' that became a staple cut on the FM rock stations that were now sprouting up all over the United States. The album's cover was shot by my sister Sally. It showed her children Kells and Tiffany playing in the river Nadder near Salisbury, and symbolized our own hopes for the future that the record represented to us. On the back were photos of the five musicians, except for McVie, who chose to have one of his beloved penguin pictures in his place. This was because John, in his early days with Christine, lived near the London zoo which he used to visit with his camera at almost every opportunity. As a member of the zoological society he had the run of the place, and soon became fascinated with the resident penguin population. He wasn't exactly talking to them, but would spend hours getting to know the different species – emperor, rockhopper, gentoo, Adélie. On *Future Games* he said no photos of me, use one of my penguin shots. Then he got very drunk and had a penguin tattooed on his arm. That's where all the Fleetwood Mac penguin iconography started. After that we always had penguins plastered on album covers and many other available surfaces.

Thus armed, we prepared to attempt the reconquest of America. *Future Games* was doing great in the States and we were getting top billing at the Fillmore East (where Van Morrison opened for us) and had broken house records for sellouts in some of our stauncher venues. We were thrilled to have survived, helped in part by the fact that neither Jeremy nor Pete had gone out and started another band in competition with us. But there was another factor. Fleetwood Mac was like a family with strong mutual understanding and sympathy for each other. So many groups sink into personal squabbles. Little things grow into abscesses and the fun of making music together flies away. As the putative leader of the anarchic Mac, I decided I'd go to any length to prevent that from happening.

So off to America we went, but not without certain terrors. As soon as we stepped from cozy Benifols into the violence and dislocation of JFK airport in New York, that old petrified feeling returned. As usual we checked into the Gorham Hotel and stayed in our rooms, afraid to walk around the block or get a sandwich. 'It even rubbed off on me,' Bob Welch says. 'I was so identified with these genteel English people that I got into it. But it felt strange to be back because I'd been away a long time myself.'

Tension hung heavy around us all on that trip, sometimes exploding in the halls of the Gorham. John McVie was drinking quite heavily and Chris wasn't happy about it. One night, after a gig, there was a terrible row. I poked my head out of the door and saw Chris shouting at John.

'I don't have to take this bloody rubbish from you!'

McVie had had one or two, and was livid. 'Come off it and get back in here,' he roared.

Chris responded with some sharp remark, and suddenly I saw a big woodworker's awl go whizzing past my eyes. Chris ducked, thank god, and the awl landed in the door jam with a murderous thunk. Then John began to advance down the hall, eyes glowing like coals. I pulled Chris into my room and locked the door. When the hallway was clear, I put my arm around her and took her to the Carnegie Deli for tea and sympathy.

'Jesus, what am I going to do? I love this guy, but when he starts drinking now it can get pretty scary. It's not really him at all, is it?'

'Well, it's been like this since I've known him,' I said.

'Yes,' she said, 'but with all the pressure from trying to keep the band going, it's got a bit worse. You can see it yourself. I know you can.'

I nodded. She was right.

'I still love John,' she said. 'I wish I felt like I could really talk with him about it . . . but he just doesn't want to hear. This is all very painful for him, but I don't know how much longer I want to cope with this.'

Oh God. If Chris left, it would really be the end of the band in all likelihood. But I didn't think she should torture herself either.

'Look,' I said, 'I love John too. We both do. But right now it's useless to confront him about boozing. All I can do is beg you to try to hold on, Chris, because when we get back on our feet with this new lineup, John's gonna be a hell of a lot better.'

Chris realized I was pleading with her.

'I know it will,' she sighed. 'But in the meantime I'm beginning to get pretty sick of this.'

For the next eleven months, through most of 1972, Fleetwood Mac was almost constantly on the road in America and Europe. We opened for Deep Purple on a couple of dozen gigs, and travelled for several months as second on a bill headlined by Savoy Brown, with Long John Baldry opening. During one of our rare weeks off, early in 1972, we cut our second album in six months, *Bare Trees*, in a few days at a studio near Wembley with our usual engineer, Martin Birch. It was a record that reflected Fleetwood Mac's main preoccupations of that time – road fever and longing for home. Chris's 'Homeward Bound' perfectly captured the weary traveller's wish for stability and a night's rest. She also contributed one of my favourite songs of hers, 'Spare Me A Little of Your Love'; the great thing about her songs is that she always finds such novel ways to say 'I love you'. And she was so obviously writing to her husband. Bob weighed in with 'Sentimental Lady', which became an American FM hit (it was written for his first wife, Nancy).

My favourite part of *Bare Trees* closed the album. We had an elderly neighbour in Hampshire named Mrs Scarrot, who wrote poetry in the form of marvellous and utterly Blakeian visionary odes. I brought a tape recorder to her house one day, and she read a lovely strophe on love and the stark beauty of winter. It was exquisite, and so very, very English. She asked that her poem be titled, 'Thoughts On A Grey Day', and it mirrored the mid-winter ambience of our feelings when we made this record as aptly as John McVie's eloquent photograph of bare trees standing guard in the fog.

We were under quite a bit of pressure that winter to finish the album in time for a June release and our next journey to America that summer. Once again we kissed our families goodbye and jetted to New York. Disaster struck immediately when the master tapes of *Bare Trees* were demagnetized and erased by the new X-ray machines at the airport! What a nightmare! We spent a horrible and hectic few days at the Record Plant in New York re-mixing the whole record before we had to hit the trail again.

Bare Trees did well in America, as opposed to Europe, where one critic called it 'another nail in the coffin of Britain's greatest blues band'. But in the States we were rejuvenated by Bob Welch's considerable energy and went over well. Our fans could be counted on to buy somewhere between 300,000 and 400,000 copies of each of our records as they came out, which kept our label happy and maintained Fleetwood Mac as a viable opening act and occasional headliner during these frustrating times of trying to get back on our feet. But as 1972 progressed, Danny Kirwan's behaviour began to become more extreme. He was drinking quite a bit and had become very withdrawn and isolated from the rest of the band. There was a personality clash between Danny and Bob Welch, which didn't help matters much.

Danny had been a nervous and sensitive lad from the gitgo. Quite frankly, he was never really suited to the rigours of our business. On that long tour in 1972 he was quite volatile and intent on rubbing everyone up the wrong way. His personality became so negative that suddenly I found myself the only person in Fleetwood Mac who liked him. We spent much of that year driving around America in a pair of station wagons, and I was the only one who was speaking to him. It was awful.

It all exploded one steamy night in August. For weeks Bob and Danny had been grating on each other. Bob would get mad and I'd have to put myself out to cover for Danny, who would simply withdraw into his own world. I tried to explain to the others that when Pete left the group, Danny went through more torture than any of us realized. Not exactly Mr Showbiz, he had been thrust out front, and the pressure was obviously taking its toll. There were some things that happened that weren't even rational. We were doing a college tour, and one night in the dressing room Danny was being odd about tuning his guitar. We've always been real sticklers for tuning, right to this day. Danny had almost perfect pitch and used it in his playing, which was always very melodic and tuneful with lots of bent notes and vibrato. That night there was a row over Bob getting his guitar in tune; it was something tiny, but it touched off a spark. Suddenly Danny got up, went to the lavatory, and smashed his head on the wall.

Five minutes to showtime, and there was blood everywhere! Danny then grabbed his precious Les Paul guitar and bashed it to bits in the lavatory. We couldn't believe it. Back in the dressing room he started throwing things. Outside, the place was packed to the rafters with hundreds of kids. Danny yelled, 'I'm not going on!'

We said, 'What do you mean, you're not going on?'

'I'm not going on!' he shouted and went totally out of control, throwing stuff. I said, 'Danny, what's this about? The fucking tuning? Why are you overreacting this way?'

I was trying to calm him, but it was no use. We had to go on stage without him, at a moment's notice, and play. We struggled through the set most pitifully. Bob did his best to cover, but it was hard because Danny played all the lead parts. I kept checking the wings, hoping Danny would stop sulking in the dressing room and come join us. We told the crowd that Danny wasn't feeling well, but I felt he'd come out because he could hear us playing, and floundering for the most part. It was the strangest thing. We came off after finishing the set, and there was Danny, sitting quietly. I said, 'Didn't you go back to the hotel?'

'Oh no,' he answered, quite blithely. 'I sat at the sound board and watched you. Yeah, wasn't bad really.'

I thought it rather cruel to see your fellow players going through a whole lot of shit, and sit through it. It would have been one thing if he'd left the auditorium, but it was another thing to stay there and coldly watch us drown. There, backstage, he proceeded to criticize the show. 'Look, Mick, the tempo was really dragging the first couple of numbers.'

I felt like saying, 'Well . . . fuck you!'

But I didn't. Back at the hotel, there was consternation and many calls for Danny's head. But I was loathe to fire him because he played so well. 'Jesus, this is unbelievable,' Bob Welch said. 'Look, Mick, you gotta fire this guy. We can't live this way.' The rest of us were so hurt and insulted by what Danny had done we didn't know what to do. Our manager was back in England, and I was the one who had to make the decision, which would mean pulling out of two weeks of gigs and cancelling the tour. That night I had dinner with Jon Lord of Deep Purple, and in the restaurant he gave me a pep talk. I went back to the hotel, talked to the rest of the band, and we decided that Danny was fired. I was the one who had to do the deed, I felt, out of allegiance to

Danny and the spirit of the past three years. I went straight to Danny's room. The scene was dreadful. No one had ever been asked to leave the band before, and Danny had no idea how alienated from him the rest of the band had become. He was a walking time bomb, carrying all his emotional baggage around with him. It was a major event to even ask him for a cigarette. He didn't like people touching him, wouldn't let anyone hug him or anything. 'This is hell for us,' I told him, 'and it has to be hell for you. It just can't go on any longer. I wish I could tell you how sorry I feel.' He said nothing.

I left his room and went up to John's door in tears. When he opened it, I said, 'The deed is done.'

CHAPTER FIVE

Hypnotized

Things went downhill from there.

At this point – mid-1972 – Fleetwood Mac had spent the past five years either on the road or making records, with varying degrees of success. We had stood both at the top of the charts and looking over the precipice of failure.

For the next two-and-a-half years, we went through hell. In the wake of Danny's departure, we expanded to six pieces, then deflated to five, and finally pared down to a quartet. We made records that were both good and indifferent, and at one point we almost lost the band entirely. It was *that* close. At the same time I nearly lost Jenny, and narrowly escaped losing my mind as well.

It was a crazy and confused time, a period in our collective history that underlines the notion that nothing ordinary ever happened to Fleetwood Mac.

There was no talk of quitting after Danny Kirwan left the band. Although we limped back to Hampshire, we were quite resolute about finding other people and carrying on. We had some time, before a late fall '72 tour of Europe, to retool Fleetwood Mac and try to figure out where we were headed. It was the era of glitter and glam, David Bowie and T. Rex, when English rock musicians dressed in stacked heels and metallic clothes and wore lots of makeup. Fleetwood Mac, on the other hand, was reluctant to dress up and pretend we were gay. We wore jeans and flannel shirts and played blues and liked to jam. We found ourselves an anomaly in England, unwanted and ignored by all but our most loyal, hardcore fans. In America, however, we were crucial members of the college boogie circuit, which really sustained us in those years. We had been touring with Savoy Brown as one of their opening acts, and we couldn't fail to see that they were doing big, big business. Now our manager told us our three-guitar front line was passé and that what Fleetwood Mac needed was a lead singer, a front man, someone on whom the audience could focus. Fleetwood Mac, he said, needed to be more like Deep Purple or Uriah Heep.

So our first step to reconstitute Fleetwood Mac was to steal Savoy Brown's singer, Dave Walker. We had got to know Dave on tour, and thought he was a good guy and a rabble rouser. This pleased Clifford Davies, who thought we needed someone to whip up the crowd. But we didn't think like that. Dave Walker was a bid for the big-time rock/boogie scene, alligator boots and the raised fist in the air. But there were some misgivings about him from the beginning. Bob Welch and Chris both thought he was too blatant, too rough around the edges and shallow as a performer. But he could really put feeling into HOWYADOINPITTSBURG!!

We needed another guitarist as well, so we decided to go out as a six-piece and co-opted Bob Weston from Long John Baldry's band; Bob was a good player and performer. We rehearsed for a month at home to get this line-up – Fleetwood Mac's seventh – as tight as possible for a long road trip that began in Scandinavia in October, continued through Germany, Italy, Holland and England in November, and was followed by an American tour in December.

It was around this time that we hired a new tour manager. Just as we raided Savoy Brown for its singer, so we headhunted their most able roadie, the inestimable John Courage, who has been a key player in the Fleetwood Mac saga ever since.

JC, as we call him, was born in Belfast in 1950, the son of an army captain and a member of the brewing family. He was brought up in Aylesbury, Buckinghamshire, went to prep school and couldn't pass the exams, just like me. So he went to London, a lad from the countryside trying to break into the music business. Sound familiar? No wonder we've been friends for years.

After working first as a curtain-puller in a theatre, then as a stage-hand and stage manager, he was offered a job at The Roundhouse in Chalk Farm as a stagehand. To save money he lived in the rafters. Then he went to work as a roadie, working for Chicago, Noel Redding's Fat Mattress and Chicken Shack after Christine had left. It was on the three-month American tour we did with Savoy Brown that we met him. John remembers:

I used to go see Fleetwood Mac in 1967 in a pub in Godalming, a little town in Surrey, along with Jethro Tull and Ten Years After when they were all starting out. Fleetwood Mac intrigued me because they had one of the first thousand-watt PA systems. It gave them incredible power, more than any other band I can recall from then.

In late 1969 I got a job with Savoy Brown in America for a hundred dollars a week. I stayed with them through that tour we did with Fleetwood Mac in 1972. I noticed then that they needed to get their road trip together. They had an American roadie who didn't understand their English equipment and wouldn't even lift amps. Where are my stage-hands, he'd yell. If there's one thing I had learned at that point, it was: if you want a job in this business, shut your mouth and get on with it.

By the end of that tour, John McVie and Mick Fleetwood had taken notice of me. I remember one of the last shows we did with them, on Boston Common. I had driven the equipment overnight from Chicago. I had been gobbling pills and my brains were befuddled. I felt a tap on the shoulder and found McVie wearing a hideous horror mask. I almost collapsed, but he thought it was hilarious.

When Fleetwood Mac left the tour, McVie said, 'We'll be home in three weeks. Come down to Benifols and check out the scene. Maybe we can work together.' I had always thought highly of them, so it felt like a dream come true. So when I got home I called them. Down in Hampshire, I found them in a gorgeous place in the country. It was the epitome of what a band should be doing, living and working together. You'd see Chris and she'd say, 'Have you eaten yet? Have a sandwich.' The whole thing was beautiful. We'd smoke joints, go round the pub, then back to Benifols where Chris would have dinner ready. *Incredible.* Eventually they said, you can have a job and live here too.

I was speechless, literally, because I had a bad stutter back then. But they were all so generous and easy-going. It was John and Chris, Mick and Jenny, Bob and Nancy, with the roadies in a sort of dormitory upstairs. I was so grateful they asked me to join them. It was like an exclusive but very hip club.

Before I got the job of tour manager, I had to drive up to London and meet Clifford Davies, who I didn't like from the beginning. Our first meeting consisted of a row over Mick's big symphonic gong, which he wanted to take to America. Clifford tried to tell me I couldn't take it because of the expense. I told him I didn't work for him and walked out. Clifford Davies was not an easy man to get along with, and my relationship with him was strained after that.

So off we went on the road as a six-piece band for the first time. Dave Walker did get the crowds going in his Big Boogie style. He had shtick. He was a good singer, we all felt, but he was an interpreter rather than an original. But McVie was close to him on tour, so we didn't say anything. Bob Weston was fine, a solid guitarist and an engaging performer. But we had already entered the oddest phase of Fleetwood Mac, musically anyway. And the most unnatural. Fleetwood Mac had always been a collaboration. It was rather bizarre to now have a stereotypical 'lead singer'.

Off the road in early 1973, we hired the Rolling Stones' mobile studio and brought it down to Hampshire so we could record our next album at home. The result was *Penguin*, an album that Bob Welch terms 'obscure' and Christine describes as 'weird'. Halfway through *Penguin*, we started to wonder about our new singer, who was often drunk and disorderly around the studio. But *Penguin* had some bright spots. Chris's songs – 'Remember Me', 'Dissatisfied' and 'Did You Ever Love Me?' – were solid, and Bob Welch's impressionistic 'Nightwatch' featured Peter Green, who was persuaded to play some far-echo guitar, albeit uncredited. (Around the same time, Jeremy Spencer appeared backstage at one of our gigs somewhere. He'd made a horrible album the year before with the Children of God, and he seemed happy to see us, with apparently no regrets about leaving us. We were delighted to tell our old comrade that all was forgiven; soon after that we heard he was in Argentina. Danny Kirwan, still managed by Cliff Davies, had also made an album and got a band together.)

We went back on the road to support *Penguin*, and the shows were successful. The album sold respectably, although we continued to be plagued by various identity crises. A typical example: March 1973 and we're playing around England. Mike Vernon chose that moment to reissue 'Albatross', which he owned. Once again, four years after the original release, 'Albatross' shot to number two on the British singles chart. Immediately our audiences started to demand to hear our 'current hit' at the gigs. The worst came when *Top of the Pops* played the old 'Albatross' film clip with Peter Green for several million people at home, after which the show's host blithely announced that Fleetwood Mac had, unfortunately, broken up.

As I've already said, it was the days of Roxy Music and the glam people. Fleetwood Mac, more homespun and oriented towards

California country rock and blues, couldn't get arrested in Britain. But in America it was another story. We went on the road there, and *Penguin* was selling our usual 300,000 units without a hit single. We toured endlessly that spring, and I can't even remember where I was when Jenny bore our daughter, Lucy Fleetwood, on 7 April. What I do remember was the riot that occurred three weeks later when 15,000 kids and Fleetwood Mac were tear-gassed by the cops at a baseball park in Stockton, California, where we were playing a festival with Elvin Bishop, Canned Heat and Buddy Miles.

Back at home that summer, we again brought the Stones mobile and co-producer Martin Birch to Hampshire to cut our second album of 1973. Halfway through *Mystery To Me*, we said goodbye to Dave Walker. He had spent most of the sessions down at the pub while Chris and Bob Welch desperately tried to write material Dave could sing on the album. It wasn't really his fault. He was a good guy to have on stage, but when it came to the subtleties of recording, it didn't wash. It was really our fault for bringing him into an untenable situation. After months of quiet agony, it came down to deciding whether we were going to back Walker as the dread 'lead singer' or finally realize that by keeping him on we were throwing away what Fleetwood Mac had been, and that we *weren't* Savoy Brown. After Dave Walker left Benifols, we also had a spasm with McVie, who had enjoyed drowning his sorrows with Dave at our local. Suddenly paranoid about his playing, John decided to take off for France and record his bass parts later. Much begging ensued to get him to stay and finish the album. In the meantime, Chris and Bob had to scramble to rewrite music that had been tailored for Dave Walker.

Mystery To Me was probably the best Fleetwood Mac album since Peter Green left the band three years earlier, and was also the biggest hit we had in the early seventies. Bob Welch wrote most of the record, including the album's best-known song.

'"Hypnotized" was originally written for Dave Walker as a 6/8 blues screamer,' Bob says. 'After Walker was fired I rewrote the piece in Christine's kitchen so I could sing it instead. At the time I was very influenced by the books I was reading, like Carlos Castaneda and material on the Bermuda Triangle – that whole area where the paranormal intrudes upon reality. The other influence on that song was the general atmosphere at Benifols, which was rather spooky and strange, even in the summertime. There was an odd, ethereal mood around those grounds all the time, and a feeling that anything could happen.

I was reading about, as the lyric says, "a place down in Mexico where man can fly over mountains and hills", and one night I had a vivid dream that a UFO piloted by a Navaho shaman landed on our over-grown grass tennis court one moonlit night. That was the feeling that went into "Hypnotized". Chris helped a lot with the new tempo and the mood. I remember listening to the playback with her. She looked at me and said, "It gives me the willies, Bob." I felt the same way, even after a hundred playbacks.'

The album's title comes from a phrase in Bob's song 'Emerald Eyes'. He also wrote 'In The City', 'Somebody', a great tune called 'Miles Away', and 'Keep on Going', which Chris sang. We had another track as well, 'Good Things', but it was dropped for a version of the Yardbirds' 'For Your Love' at Bob Weston's suggestion. We were very laissez-faire in those days, and said what the hell.

Mystery To Me was a good, long album with plenty of music. It was atmospheric and intelligent and we knew it was going to be a big hit. So we had a big tour lined up, lots of colleges, which were our bread and butter in those days. It was an audience that had sustained us for a long time. When we got to the States in September 1973, the album was on the radio all the time and the fans were great. We sensed we were on the verge of a breakthrough and had another real shot at the Big Time in the USA. So we cheerfully embarked on the usual lengthy four-month Fleetwood Mac tour, determined to succeed this time. Jenny and the children were on the road with me, and we worked constantly. For a while it was fun, sharing the hardships of the road with my family.

We did all these insane things to save money back then. The roadies would drive fifteen hours a day to make the gigs. They would go four or five days without a hotel room, grabbing cold burgers while setting up the gear. Most of the time they didn't want to eat anyway because they'd taken a handful of whites to stay awake on the interstate. Or we'd ship the gear by plane without paying for it. John Courage would take our eight plane tickets down to the airport early in the morning and check in twenty pieces of band equipment as luggage. He'd put the tickets in a locker and leave the key with the airline. We'd show up later in the day, retrieve the tickets, and check through our personal luggage as well. Courage used to go right down to the tarmac and supervise the ground crew loading the bulky amps: 'C'mon lads, you can get it in there.' We got away with this for years, until they started clamping down on security at the airports.

The tour went beautifully for the first month. The fans came out in force to see us; *Mystery* zoomed up the charts, and for a while it looked like Fleetwood Mac was on the wing again. Then someone asked me how I felt about my wife having an affair with Bob Weston, and suddenly it all came crashing down.

At first, I tried to figure it out by myself. I realized that, as usual, I hadn't been paying enough attention to Jenny, and she allowed herself to be seduced by Bob, a real lady-killer with all the smooth lines. ('See that one over there?' he'd say to me when we were in some bar. 'Give me five minutes.' Wham! Sure enough, he'd be back with the girl in a moment. That's how he was.) I had noticed that he and Jenny had been taking long walks at Benifols and seemed close on the tour, but I had no idea that anything was going on, apart from the feeling that something wasn't right. I remembered trying to talk to Weston in the hotel bar while we were in Detroit. He seemed real down, and I asked him if he was feeling all right. And of course he was going through hell because he'd been a real buddy of mine, and he hadn't told me what was going on between him and Jenny.

The more I thought about it, the sicker I felt. For years on the road I had done my best to be Mr Faithful. There had been a couple of extremely rare drunken indiscretions that were never quite right, one-night stands that had been either bad or indifferent. I could never see the point of chasing girls. Once, in the early days of the band, a young lady climbed into my bed in Denmark. I touched her, but her skin felt weird, sort of wet and raw like a porpoise. I realized I didn't like her because she wasn't Jenny. I freaked out and asked the girl to leave, and she went over and climbed into bed with Peter Green on the other side of the room.

Eventually, I confronted Jenny, and it all came out. 'Look,' I said to her, 'what's going on with you and Bob Weston? How could this happen?'

She was quite calm about it. 'Mick, I'm tired of feeling like I'm alone – even when you and I are together. Ever since we met you've had this trait of just wandering through things, being aloof, not paying attention to me or your daughters. You're just not that involved.'

My head suddenly felt like it was made of lead, and I put it into my hands. 'Oh God,' I moaned.

'Sometimes,' Jenny went on, 'I think I must be mad to be married to someone who can't even remember my birthday, or the birthdays of our children. At least Bob Weston talks to me, and I can feel like someone else knows I'm there.'

Of course, everything Jenny said was true. For years I had been more married to Fleetwood Mac than to her. And my personality – well, anyone craving a lot of attention from me is in for a lot of trouble. It's terrible, and I know it.

So Jenny told me that she and Weston had become close back in England, and the relationship had intensified when we were on tour. Hearing this in her own words broke my heart.

The result was the traditional stiff upper lip – on my part. I just said, We gotta carry on with this tour, *no matter what*. Jenny and the kids left the tour and went to Los Angeles. I was really hurting, but still trying to keep the band going. I kept thinking that this was a make-or-break tour and that I didn't want to be the one who fucked it up.

So we kept playing. The shows sold out and the album sold well, because we were on the road. I didn't speak to Bob Weston, but I could feel the strain taking its toll on me. I made John Courage show me Weston's hotel phone bills, and tortured myself counting how long he spent speaking with Jenny, and suffered like mad because of it. I schemed, wanting to know about them and dreading it at the same time.

After a couple of weeks I was in real bad shape. I could feel myself starting to crack. I couldn't take it, mentally. I didn't hate Bob Weston, but I was injured. What can you do? You can't hate someone for something like this. I was upset and spent all my energy trying to rationalize the painful feelings that washed through me in a river of anxiety. The final straw came by the pool of the Marina Hotel in LA during a pause in the tour. Weston and my kids were in the pool, playing and laughing. Then he got out and cuddled up with Jenny and began to read poetry to her – right in front of me! It was either completely insensitive or without any thought whatsoever. I felt like I was going to have a breakdown. Why were they rubbing it in my face?

I talked to Bob Welch. 'I can't take this much longer,' I told him. Then I rented a little sailboat and sailed out into the marina, crying my eyes out for the first time in years. My wife! My children! I never lost my temper, but Bob Weston had made a big mistake. He had pushed the whole affair over the edge.

We went back on tour, which lasted until 26 October 1973, when I sat down with the band and said, 'Look, I'm sick about this, but I can't play music with this guy any more and I think we're gonna have to wind this tour up.' We were in Lincoln, Nebraska. John Courage fired

Bob Weston, telling him the tour was over and that it would be for the best if he didn't travel with the band. He was put on a plane and we didn't see him again for years. Then we all gathered in Bob Welch's room to call London and break the bad news to our manager.

We were all there – the band and the roadies. Bob Welch did the talking. 'Clifford? Can you hear me all right? Listen, we've got a big problem. We had to fire Bob Weston and Mick's in a bad way. We're putting the tour on hold for a while until we can get ourselves together again.'

Silence. Then our manager blew his stack. 'Well, Bob, that's fucking it, then, innit? I just want to remind everybody that if you blow this tour like you've blown the others, you'll never get another chance. Not with me in any case.'

Bob tried to calm him down. 'Hey, man, we don't wanna cancel the whole thing, just postpone the tour for a few weeks so we can regroup, that's all.' Bob explained as best he could about Jenny and Weston, but Davies wasn't having any of it.

'You better listen to me good and proper,' he said. 'If you stop the tour it will destroy my reputation with the bookers and promoters I have to depend on to survive in this fucking business, and I swear to you that I'm not about to let myself be dragged down by the whims of a bunch of irresponsible musicians.'

We looked at each other in disbelief. This guy thought we were his slaves!

So Bob Welch tried again. 'Clifford, be reasonable. I told you we're *not* breaking up. We're burnt out and need a rest. We can't continue right now. We're going to take a few weeks off, come back to England after Christmas, and make the next album. That's it.'

'Hey, buddy boy,' Clifford said, dripping with sarcasm, 'you better get something straight. If you pull out of this tour, there ain't gonna *be* a next album, because your careers are going to be over. I'm warning you.'

'What, Clifford?' Bob asked. 'What are you warning us about?'

'I'm warning you that I *own* you. I fucking *own* Fleetwood Mac, and the sooner you bloody well get that through your heads the better.' And he hung up.

But we ignored what he said, not knowing that soon all hell would break loose. Fleetwood Mac temporarily disbanded in Nebraska, and we went our separate ways. Jenny and the kids went to London. Bob Welch, John Courage and Fleetwood Mac's gear went to LA. Chris and I went back to Hampshire, while John took some time in Hawaii. For a couple of months everything was in turmoil and we had no idea what was going on. Clifford Davies sent Bob Welch a letter reaffirming that he hadn't slaved for years so he could be 'brought down by the whims of irresponsible musicians'. Chris and I didn't know what to do. The letter informed us that Clifford Davies was taking over Fleetwood Mac, and we could either be part of it or not.

For the first time, we had an inkling of what was in store. But we never seriously considered that our manager would send a fake band on the road to fulfil Fleetwood Mac's tour commitments. So we waffled for a few weeks, still not knowing what to do. I asked myself if I could take over Fleetwood Mac if I had to. I'd never had any thought of managing a band. In fact I had only stumbled into the role of 'band leader' because Peter Green bowed out and someone had to do it and John didn't want to. So I kept things going within the band, and Bob Welch talked to the record company. That's how it went.

Clifford had been specifically told: don't worry, we're not breaking up. We're *not* breaking up! But he was convinced I had lost my biscuits for the time being. And so he thought he'd take this thing over, and that's what he did, in no uncertain terms. He ran down, registered the name Fleetwood Mac, and sent Danny Kirwan's post-Mac backup band to the United States to play shows as Fleetwood Mac.

But we didn't know that at the time.

It put us out of action for a year.

I remember all this as a period of desolation. I was twenty-six years old, and not a happy man. Everything I'd been working for was in a shambles. My family, our home and the band were all at stake. I tried to pull my thoughts together and drew a blank. I went to visit my parents in Salisbury. Jenny had already been down to see them; they kept to the middle-ground and didn't close her out, since she was like a daughter to them. Every day seemed to bring more bad news. We were vaguely aware that our manager was up to no good, but Chris and I were in the dark and uncertain what we could do about it. I called Bob Welch in LA. 'Mick, we've been threatened,' he told me, 'and we may not even have a right to our name.' We knew something terrible was happening, but we just sort of let it happen to ourselves.

I felt so bad. I said to my father that I just wanted to go away, as far as possible, and forget about bands and lawsuits and try to clean out my spirit. He told me about the son of an old family friend who was teaching at the University of Zambia, thousands of miles away in southeast Africa. It sounded perfect to go visit this guy and collect my thoughts. A few days later I flew to Lusaka.

Zambia is the Heart of Lightness, a vast country south of Zaire, west of Tanzania, Malawi, Mozambique, north of Zimbabwe, which back then was Rhodesia, in the midst of a civil war. In Lusaka I made my way to an address on the university campus, where I was welcomed by a sweet English guy with an African wife. They helped me find a house to rent, and there I was, two weeks on my own in Lusaka. I didn't do much. During the day I tried to make plans, but it wasn't much use. I felt it was better just to disappear rather than mope around and lick my wounds. At night I sat outside and ate insects with the security guards. After a few days, I decided to go off into the bush and see Zambia National Park, which is the second-largest game reserve in the world. I caught a small plane out of Lusaka and flew to this little resort in the middle of the African bush. It was very off-season at this white hunters' lodge, where I found only two other guests besides myself. This proved to be great therapy. I immediately made friends with the African safari guides. We'd spend endless nights drinking beer and drumming on tin boxes under the stars. It was an incredible experience, and those little tapping things they taught me are still with me today. Oh, the feelings that memories of Africa conjure – how small one feels in its giant scale, and how frightening that can be. I remember late at night the hotel would shut down the generator and the lights would go out. I'd light a candle and go to my hut. One night I heard some real deeeep breathing right outside the door. It was a kind of purring of the extremely large pussycat variety. It got louder and louder, right outside the netting, until I was almost dumb with horror and shitting myself. I was about to jump out of bed and climb on the cupboard when the breathing subsided and then faded away. The next morning they said they'd been having problems with old castaway lions who had been shunned by their pride and came to scavenge in camp. They were said to be very dangerous.

I empathized.

Another day, I walked out too far in the bush with my movie camera. I wandered for a mile or two, filming a flock of vultures circling way overhead. I followed their gyres for several minutes, and then came to a strange kind of understanding. *You're the visitor here*, the vultures seemed to say. *You're not part of our world. Have you come here to die? We can take care of that.* Through my viewfinder I could see that the huge, monstrous carrion-feeders were circling closer, and lower. I panicked. It was *me* they were hovering over. It was then that I realized how far I had run to get away from Fleetwood Mac. I had to get back, to the lodge, and then to work. I ran back to the resort as fast as my reedy Englishman's legs could carry me, and made arrangements to return to Lusaka on the next outgoing bush plane.

The day before I left, a bunch of Germans showed up, very macho and drunken. They wanted to go out to film some bull elephants. I tagged along to see how tough they were, along with a very bored safari guide, who knew what was going to happen. As soon as the Germans drove their Land Rover within site of the first bull elephant we found, the mighty thing put its ears back as if to charge. It was awe inspiring. I could scarcely believe how immense this elephant was. The drunken Germans, meanwhile, were shaking with fear. They wouldn't get out of the car. C'mon, says the guide, getting out. *Nein, danke.* They were so scared they wouldn't shoot any film.

Back in Lusaka, there was a telegram from my family, saying to come home. I went back to England, stunned and inspired by what I had seen and learned in a few weeks under African skies. Something in my soul felt cleansed, and I felt recharged and better prepared for the many battles awaiting me just over the horizon.

While I was in Zambia, Jenny had time to think. Our marriage was in her hands, and it was really up to her to decide what we were going to do. She remembers:

Our daughter Lucy was born on 7 April 1973, by Caesarian section. Mick was on the road in America, and I cried because he wouldn't see her for a long time, and I felt so alone. And when Mick came home, he and I didn't communicate. We were very close, but we didn't talk. I felt like I was by myself.

Then Bob Weston came along. At Benifols I wasn't really part of the whole Fleetwood Mac clique and the others didn't speak to me that often. But Bob Weston wasn't part of that. He was very chatty, and I thought, wow, someone to talk to! We had the same birthday and understood each other in a nice way. God! I hadn't had anyone understand me for years! I was alone in the country, tied down with the children, all my freedom gone. So we'd walk the grounds and chat, all very innocent. We went along on tour in America and suddenly I realized that I enjoyed talking to this man. I felt myself coming alive again. I felt young, and I had felt so old all those years. So it became pretty intense, and Mick was upset. Fleetwood Mac disbanded and he went to Africa. I went to England and stayed at Ron Wood's house, the Wick, then with Patti and George Harrison, who also were having an upheaval in their marriage. I drank a lot because I liked Bob but couldn't help feeling that I was violating my sacred friendship with Mick. I was tearing myself up, drinking brandy to numb everything.

Finally I went to a psychic woman near Benifols, who advised me to cool things down. So I sent a telegram to Mick, to get him to come home. I told him that I was willing to try again. I went back to Benifols even though my heart wasn't really in it, but I felt that this was what I was meant to do. I was angry with the gods, because I felt I'd lost all the free will I ever had in life. It didn't seem fair.

Meanwhile, the Fake Mac was on the loose!

Bob Welch started getting the first calls in Los Angeles early in December, while I was still in Africa. A poster had appeared with Chris's picture on it, advertising gigs by 'The New Fleetwood Mac'. Chris, of course, knew nothing about this. Our manager had informed the trades that Bob Welch and John McVie had left the band, which would be carried on by Christine McVie, Mick Fleetwood and new members, who would be available to complete the obligations of the disrupted tour. John Courage saw the whole mess up close:

After the original tour was cancelled, the equipment and I went back to LA. I stored Fleetwood Mac's gear in the garage of my girlfriend's house in Hermosa Beach and promptly got busted for the usual roadie vices – pot, a little coke, and an extremely overdue and unpaid-for Hertz rental car. I was looking after about $2000 of the band's money at the time, which I used to pay a lawyer to get me off.

Soon after that, I got a call from Clifford Davies. He said he was bringing Fleetwood Mac back over and to get the gear and meet them in New York. I said, who's in the band? Well, he said, it's Mick and Chris and I don't know who else is going to join them. When I met the group in New York and saw that it was a bogus band made of various guys in Clifford's stable, I was disgusted and tried to quit. But I was reminded that I owed them $2000 and was persuaded to work it off by staying with the Fake Mac for a month.

The phony Fleetwood Mac went to work in January 1974, and it was horrendous from the first gig. Fleetwood Mac had well-known personalities, which you couldn't replace just like that. When the fans saw strange musicians pretending to be Fleetwood Mac, playing their music, they were outraged. People booed, walked out, demanded their money back. At a few gigs people threw shit at the musicians. I told them I'd do a month, but after a few shows the whole thing was destroying me. Finally, in Chicago, I called Bob Welch. He told me he was working his arse off, and to hold on if I could. The others are coming to California, he said, and it's going to work out. We were in a hotel in Chicago, and I skipped.

Eventually, according to my understanding, the Fake Mac only played two weeks of a ten-week tour. To this day I don't know the names of the musicians involved, and I don't wanna know. Years later, the singer of the group contacted us to apologize. He swore that the musicians had been told that I would be joining them on the road after a few shows, so they went ahead. Eventually they formed their own band and recorded a single, 'Why Did You Do It?', that was said to have some bearing on the case.

All this was in full swing as I returned from Zambia. The fake band was on the road, Bob Welch had the lawyers ready to litigate, and we could see that it was going to get pretty raucous. Bob was frantically trying to persuade Warner Brothers Records that Fleetwood Mac still existed and that our manager didn't own the name. We hired some lawyers who procured an injunction against the fake band in the Chancery Division of the High Court. The booking agency was informed that the Fleetwood Mac they had out on tour was imposters, and the tour was stopped. But the record company was chary. Their deal was technically with our manager, not with us. Clifford signed the record contract; he was the producer and furnished the services of a band called Fleetwood Mac. Our gross monies were paid to him. That was the English system. We were paid a wage. He got 50 per cent of the band's publishing and took 20 per cent of our royalties. The people at our label barely even knew any of us in the band. We had to convince them somehow that we owned our name, or they wouldn't let us make another record, which would truly mean the end of the group. I remember John McVie saying to them, 'This is crazy. It's our *names* – Fleetwood and Mac.' The whole affair was extremely frustrating and would lead to *years* of the usual farce connected with litigation. Clifford thought he had us. He had other acts and could raise money for lawyers. That was his technique. The label immediately put our money in an interest-bearing account and said they'd be happy to pay whoever the judge told them to. He knew that English litigation was an endless process and thought he could starve us into submission. He didn't figure on our ever having the resources to take him on. We were shocked when we discovered how pathetic our situation was. When we looked at things we had signed, years before when we were children, we realized we had a pretty awful situation going. 'You *knew* about it,' their lawyers sneered. 'You *signed* it.' They gave us documents signed back in the sixties, drunk on aeroplanes. 'Here, Mick, just something we gotta take care of.' It turned out we had signed away our song publishing.

It took four years to get all this straightened out. BIG MAC ROW read music press headlines in February 1974, and our reputation promptly went down the toilet once again.

As John McVie has pointed out, every time there was a personnel change in the band, our energy level sank for a few months. This time, we rotted in our house in the country for almost half a year. Suits and counter-suits prevented us from recording a new album in England, and Fleetwood Mac at that point didn't mean shit in Europe. So we were stuck in the country, with almost no money coming in. Our royalties were tied up in court, and we couldn't work to support *Mystery*, which was a hit in America. As Jenny recalls, 'Mick and I hardly had any money at all. To buy a pair of shoes for twenty pounds was a big deal.' We all felt a tremendous sense of inertia and helplessness, a feeling that we had to move or die. But Benifols was our home, and for months none of us was brave enough to overcome the malaise, and just get up and go.

Bob Welch in Los Angeles was anxious to move Fleetwood Mac to California. On crackling phone lines, he worked to convince me we *had* to move closer to our all-important record company, our lifeline to our audience. He correctly saw that we couldn't win our lawsuit in England and couldn't make another record until we somehow proved who we were, and renegotiated our record deal. 'We can't live on air,' he told me. 'We better get this thing going again somewhere else, or we can forget about it and all get jobs.'

I got off the phone and looked around. England in winter seemed dismal, bare and grey. I felt depressed.

Finally I said, look, let's get out of England and go to America. The record company's there, and we have to tell them that we're still here; let's make an album.

Neither Christine or John were keen to do it. I said, let's do it and treat it as a trial period. All we know about America is hotel rooms and gigs and wanting to go home after five months. Let's all get apartments and see what it's like. I said, all we ever do is work over there all the time anyhow. We've gotta get out of England and make a record or we're *finished*. Let's just go over, have a sniff, and see how it is.

This won over John McVie, and Jenny was raring to go to escape the stagnation of Benifols. Still, Chris resisted. She had put a lot of work into her home, she was close to her family, and wasn't all that crazy about California. But I begged her to try it for six months. I swore that we would come back to England if she didn't like it. And, of course, she saw that it was a good thing to do. We were demoralized from sitting at home for months and needed shaking up. We hadn't made any music or gone anywhere. We *needed* this.

So off we went. And I thank Clifford Davies for it in the long run, despite everything, because he was the reason we left. The end result was that everybody loved California and we never went back. We held on to Benifols for several years until it became a tax liability, and then we sold it.

Fleetwood Mac touched down at LAX in late April 1974. We stayed at the Chateau Marmont for a few days, before finding other quarters. Jenny and I moved the children to a house on Fernwood in Laurel Canyon, just vacated by Glenn Frey of the Eagles. John and Chris found a place nearby, at the bottom of the hill. Bob Welch had got married and was living in a little house across town. We found him very pissed off. He was highly strung to begin with, and being Fleetwood Mac's *de facto* manager was more than he had bargained for when he joined the group. We were terribly frustrated, since we all knew that *Mystery To Me* could have been a monster had we been able to properly go out and play behind it.

Fleetwood Mac arrived in the US with $7,200. That was it. No gear, no staff, no record company unless our deal could be renegotiated with a rather diffident Warner Brothers, no manager, and no credibility. Promoters who had been burned by the last tour were rightfully suspicious. Our record company weren't positive we owned our own name. (Around this time dear Bill Graham took the trouble to write a letter to the court in which our suit was being heard, attesting to our identities and our credibility, and explaining the supreme importance of a group's name.) We were deluged with all sorts of contradictory advice. Several Industry Heavies told us bluntly that Fleetwood Mac was finished. Once a group got into court, they solemnly intoned, it was all over. It was going to be impossible to resurrect the old band.

They just said, 'You can't do it, forget it. The only way your band is going to make it is to change the name.' The other thing we were told is that we had to have a manager, preferably someone Heavy.

Well, we didn't want to change our name, which would have been a gross capitulation to Clifford Davies, who never thought for one moment that this group would actually stick it out and fight. And when it came right down to it, we didn't want a manager either. What happened instead was this: in England I had been sitting on one end of the phone while Bob was in LA, trying to take care of the record company. And we took it from there. That's how we inherited the job of managing Fleetwood Mac. We found ourselves fulfilling a function we'd been paying someone a fortune to do. Later, after Bob left, I just carried on, for the next seven years.

We were forced into it, actually. Bob knew a bit about publishing, and the record company said they had to negotiate with somebody. But we didn't want to rush out and subjugate ourselves to some new tyrant. So we formed a company, Seedy Management. I got paid a little, and John got a piece of it too. I enjoyed it, and it was a healthy situation. It had its pitfalls, as we will see, but it was a system that would serve Fleetwood Mac very well, and one that put us in control of our own destinies for years.

Once we got settled, our major task was to renegotiate with Warner Brothers. We needed a lawyer badly, a music business attorney who could talk to these people. Bob Welch knew a guy named Mickey Shapiro, whom I had occasion to visit one day that spring. Mickey recalls it this way:

> I knew Bob Welch because he used to play with the Seven Souls at a bar in Haworth called The Haunted House. I also knew Judy Wong because she had been the secretary at a black club I hung out at, Maverick's Flat on South Crenshaw. Then Bob went off and joined Fleetwood Mac and I didn't see him for a while. Meanwhile I had shifted my legal practice to music. [One of Mickey's first clients was the mid-sixties pop group, the Strawberry Alarm Clock, which started out as the assistant manager of a Safeway and four boxboys. Later he fired the boxboys and hired the guys from the loading dock.]
>
> In June '74, Judy Wong calls to say that Bob's band is coming to LA, and she wanted to bring Mick Fleetwood and John McVie over to see me. Shortly after this, my house was robbed, completely

stripped bare. At this point Judy Wong shows up with Mick Fleet-wood, looking like a drop-out from the Buffalo Springfield, wear-ing jeans, flannel shirt and cowboy hat, along with McVie and two little girls in his arms. I gathered he was having some domestic problems.

Now Mick is not exactly Mr Warmth on the first go, so it took a while to get the story out. He said, 'We're an English band that's come to America. Because of problems with past management, we don't have a one-to-one relationship with anyone in Burbank, and the record company doesn't care about us. We're not getting any attention, and we're almost broke. Do you know those people?'

I told them I knew Mo Ostin, then the president of Warner Brothers Records. They told me they were selling 300,000 albums each time out, and I told them I thought I could get them a deal anywhere. They asked if I could help, I said I'll be happy to, and I was hired.

The next day, Bob Welch comes in, sits on the floor where Mick and John had sat, and said he was gonna leave Fleetwood Mac. He's the American in the group! It seemed like a calamity, because although Mick was the spiritual leader, Bob had been the business manager. So I took them on. I did a little research and found that Fleetwood Mac's last album had sold the same 315,000 copies as their last five albums. It was amazing. The records sold at the same rate, pace and time-frame, to the same people. When I went to Burbank I found Fleetwood Mac suffering from a perceived-value situation. Warner Brothers thought they were a wonderful blues band who couldn't write hit singles. They toured and worked hard, and that's what it boiled down to. To them, Fleetwood Mac was dependable and safe; it was like dancing with your sister. You didn't have to put down paper for these guys when they came to the office. The Warner people said, 'They don't come here and bother us, and we don't bother them. We mail them a cheque and they mail us back an album and we put a cover on it. A nice, obedient band that doesn't make us crazy.'

Mickey helped me renegotiate with the company. I was at every meeting, as band manager. This made them even more wary, since they weren't used to negotiating directly with the band. They knew we had a court case going in England and were suffering from the slow pace of the British legal system, but they demanded to be indemnified from legal responsibility in case we lost. We had no choice.

We started rehearsing our next album, *Heroes Are Hard To Find*, in late June '74, and recorded it the following month at a studio called Angel City Sound in LA. It was our first complete album that wasn't recorded in England, and it also turned out to be the most polished Fleetwood Mac album yet, and the one that was furthest away from the blues. Bob Welch wrote most of it. 'We struggled with material,' he recalls, 'because nobody at that point could really articulate a clear direction. We wanted to do modern, no-cliché music, and had many long philosophical discussions about what we should do.' Chris came up with the title song, an uptempo blues with horns, no less. This was Fleetwood Mac, but very contempo LA. It was a love song, but the subtext was that we desperately needed a couple of heroes to replace the ones we had lost.

Heroes Are Hard To Find was released in September, but not before we had to go to court to beat off an injunction from Clifford Davies that would have prevented the record from coming out – and us touring to support it.

When we finally got on the road, we faced another gruelling tour – forty-three shows ending in early December. Not only did we have to sell our record and Fleetwood Mac to our audience; it was even more crucial to reestablish the band with the industry, the agents and promoters who all said, Well, last time out we really got hurt. The worst bit was that our money went down. We had been used to working for five grand a night. But this time we were forced to take gigs at two grand and even fifteen hundred bucks, just to get back into the business. For us, this was a big drag, after all the years we'd worked. There was much bitterness in those Holiday Inns, many fevered curses heaped upon the deserving brow of our ex-manager. Bob Welch did a great job, however; he took the proverbial bull by the horns and became the front man for Fleetwood Mac, working his arse off every night. We had some personnel spasms when we added a keyboardist, a black guy who was a friend of Bob, but he didn't last long. Then, to fill out the sound, we added another keyboardist in the person of Doug Graves, who'd been an engineer on *Heroes*. He was better, and didn't last either. But after a few gigs, our first in about a year, we settled down and it felt good again. In November, *Rolling Stone* did a positive story on us, called 'The Real Fleetwood Mac Stands Up'. Under the picture of the four of us happily boozing, Bob Welch was quoted: 'I guess it's just not our nature to have an "image". At some point you have to realize that you may never be Elton John. But then again, the point isn't to sell a record to every man, woman and child on earth. The point is to have a career, do what you're doing and do it well. Fleetwood Mac has done just that.'

But down deep, we knew Bob wasn't happy. He had burnt himself out writing the last two albums, and he was actually feeling quite fried. Marital problems aggravated being on the road for him. The album did all right, but wasn't the big success we'd been chasing, and the single, 'Heroes', wasn't a hit. It was at this point, I think, that Bob Welch looked back on all the years and work and began to see a dead end. He'd had enough. We kept playing, but things were strained after a while. It wasn't too serious and nothing was said, but I sensed something was about to happen.

Sometime late in November 1974, while we were home in LA on a break from the *Heroes* tour, I started to look around for another studio, since we expected to make our next album soon after we quit touring. I was just doing my managerial thing. One day I went grocery-shopping at a supermarket in the Valley, and in the parking lot I bumped into a man I knew named Thomas Christian, who mentioned in passing that he was working for a studio in Van Nuys called Sound City. You should check it out, he suggested. So I piled the groceries and the kids in the back of my seedy old Cadillac and went right over to this studio.

At Sound City I was introduced to Keith Olsen, the engineer. To demonstrate the sound of the studio, he played me a track called 'Frozen Love', from an album that he had recorded there.

I thought the guitar sounded great, but my attention had been caught by what I saw through the thick glass that separated Sound City's two recording studios. It was a girl, rehearsing a vocal in the next studio. A piano track was playing, and I could faintly hear her say something to the engineer about wanting to have bird-songs somewhere in the mix of the song she was working on. I even remember what she was wearing – a long, sort of Indian cotton skirt and a little blouse, really pretty. In fact, I thought she was one of the loveliest and most attractive girls I'd ever seen, but I somehow managed to remain nonchalant as I blithely asked Keith Olsen, 'Who's that pretty girl in there?'

Her name, he said, was Stevie Nicks.

Part Two

Englishmen who go to California never recover.

Wilfred Sheed

CHAPTER SIX

Like A Charmed Hour
and A Haunted Song

Let the poet address her as Rhiannon,
'Great Queen'
Robert Graves, *The White Goddess*

I've always felt a sense of depth and destiny about Fleetwood Mac. We always did everything on instinct. Nobody ever auditioned for Fleetwood Mac, and that's one of the reasons nothing ordinary ever happened to this band. Somewhere up there, I've always felt, was a little magic star, looking out for us.

People were *meant* to be in this group.

So: shopping for a studio in the Valley, I saw this girl through a window. But I didn't meet her just then. While I was stomping away to the rhythm of 'Frozen Love', appreciating the impressive guitar on the track, the guy who wrote the song and played the guitar was working in the next studio. He came in, we were introduced, and that was that. I went on my merry way, which was along the back end of the *Heroes Are Hard To Find* tour in late December 1974.

About a week later, Bob Welch announced he was quitting Fleetwood Mac.

It happened after a minor incident. We were playing in Las Vegas and things were strained. It didn't seem that serious, but I could sense that something was in the air. In the kitchen after a gig, Bob sort of snapped and Chris said 'fuck you' either then or later; my memories of this are hazy because it was nothing heavy. Unfortunately, it happened at the end of the tour, as we were about to make a new album. Bob simply said that he was leaving, and it wasn't a massive surprise. Bob says:

> I felt like we were just going around in circles. Fleetwood Mac was floundering then, and the essential creative freshness had faded. I thought I needed to strike out on my own and find another context. They felt all they had to do was to add new blood. I could've stayed, but I felt that if I didn't test myself now, I'd never do it. I remember John McVie said, 'Bob, it's rough out there; you don't realize what you're throwing away for some possibility that doesn't exist.' I knew what he meant. Fleetwood Mac is a marriage – you don't give it up easily. Mick tried to convince me to stay, but . . .

It was almost New Year's Eve when Bob left the band. There was some upset over the latest defection – John Courage destroyed an amp when he was told, emblematic of the crew's frustration with the foibles of musicians – but I just said not to worry, that all would turn out well.

I rang up Keith Olsen over at Sound City and asked: What was the name again of the chap whose music and guitar-playing I had liked when I visited the studio?

Lindsey Buckingham, Olsen said.

I told him I wanted Lindsey Buckingham to be the new guitarist in Fleetwood Mac, and what did he think?

Olsen replied that Lindsey was part of a team, the other half of which was his girlfriend, Stevie Nicks. They had a band called Buckingham Nicks and were very much a pair. Keith said he didn't think Lindsey would be interested in joining Fleetwood Mac without Stevie.

Without hesitating, I told him that I wanted them both. Then I called Mickey Shapiro and said, 'I met these guys and am asking them to be in the band.'

The girl who sang just like the sweetheart of the rodeo was, indeed, a daughter of the great American southwest. Stevie was born in Phoenix, Arizona, in . . . well, let's just say she was born after the war. She'd like it better that way.

Her father, Jess Nicks, was a successful business executive, and as he got promoted, transferred and headhunted by various companies, the Nicks family moved around a lot during Stevie's childhood – Arizona, New Mexico, Texas, Utah, Los Angeles. I remember her telling me that as soon as she and her younger brother began to make friends in a new place, their father would get a new job and off they'd go.

One of the strongest influences on Stevie's childhood was her father's father, Aaron Jess Nicks. A. J. Nicks was a country singer and musician. By the time his granddaughter was little more than a toddler, he had taught her to warble the female parts of classic country duets, like 'Are You Mine' by Red Sovine and Goldie Hill. He lived in a couple of trailers up in the mountains in Arizona and played his guitar, fiddle and harmonica in dry gulch saloons all over the state, occasionally taking little Stevie along for the ride. She'd sing along and dance on the bars of the gin mills he played, and the customers loved it, this old man and his tiny angel.

But it didn't last. When she was around five, A. J. wanted to take Stevie on a little tour, and his son said no. A. J. was mad. He'd been paying Stevie fifty cents a week to practise her guitar, and he insisted she was going to be a big singing star someday. But Stevie's parents wouldn't let her go, and A. J. stormed out of the house in a rage. He stayed away for two years after that. Nobody saw or heard from him. Stevie was very upset. A. J. always wanted to be a famous country star himself, but he was a bit eccentric and never was able to get much of a career together.

Stevie had her first group, The Changing Times, while she was in high school and the family was living in Los Angeles. She wrote her first song when her parents gave her a new guitar for her sixteenth birthday: it was called 'I've Loved and I've Lost and I'm Sad but not Blue'. It was a song about the unrequited love she felt for a popular boy. One day he looked at her, and she went home and wrote this song. It was then she learned that she could experience things by writing songs about them.

Jess Nicks soon moved his family again, to the suburbs south of San Francisco, between Stevie's sophomore and junior years of high school. At Menlo-Atherton High, Stevie was an instant hit, voted runner-up for Homecoming Queen her first year in the school. Then on to San Jose State, where she majored in speech communication before leaving to tour with her first professional band, Fritz, in 1968.

Fritz was a quasi-psychedelic band that played San Francisco Sound and worked as an opening act between 1968 and 1971. It was a guitar-organ-bass-and-drums quartet with what was then known as a 'chick singer' – Stevie Nicks. The bass player was an acquaintance from high school – Lindsey Buckingham.

They had met by chance at a weeknight musical gathering for kids, whether at church or school nobody remembers. Stevie was there with her guitar, just to get out of the house. In walked Lindsey, a year older, slender, with curly black hair. He sat down at the piano and began to play 'California Dreaming'. Stevie wandered over, and they sang a couple of songs together. When the thing was over, they went their separate ways and didn't see each other for two years.

Morris Buckingham, known as Buck to family and friends, owned a coffee plant, lived in the well-to-do suburb of Atherton and belonged to the Menlo Country Club, where his three sons learned to swim, and swim hard. Lindsey's brother Greg won a silver swimming medal at the 1968 Olympics. Lindsey, more motivated by love of music than by aquatics, quit his college water polo team (after a churlish coach told him he'd never amount to anything) and joined the local rock and roll band instead.

Lindsey picked up his first guitar at the tender age of seven, and taught himself to strum along to his older brother's collection of early rock & roll 45s – Elvis, Buddy Holly, the Everly Brothers, Eddie Cochran, Chuck Berry. These avatars were Lindsey's formidable first teachers.

By the time he was thirteen, he had fallen under the sway of folk music, especially the flat-picking style of the Kingston Trio, who were almost local heroes since they were based in San Francisco, only a few miles north. He spent most of his early adolescence teaching himself the various picking styles he was hearing, hours of delicate fingering on his acoustic guitar. A few years later, like most American boys of his age, his musical ears came under the influence of Brian Wilson, the emotional, harmony-weaving leader and composer of the Beach Boys.

When it was time for Lindsey to join a rock & roll band, he discovered that intricate finger-picking was no substitute for the raunchy rhythms of rock. So he joined Fritz as the bass player. For the next three years Fritz gigged around the Bay Area a good deal, occasionally opening shows for the more famous San Francisco bands – the Jefferson Airplane, Big Brother and the Holding Company, Quicksilver Messenger Service, the Charlatans, Moby Grape and the rest. Fritz never managed to break out of that local scene, but they had some fun and gained a lot of experience. Stevie once told me about a show when Fritz opened for Big Brother in Santa Clara: 'Janis Joplin got up to sing, and for the next two hours my chin was on the floor. I mean, you couldn't have pried me away with a crowbar. I was, like, *glued*. Mick, you know most of the stuff I do when we're onstage? That's who I learned it from. It wasn't that I wanted to be like her, because I had my own thing, but I figured that if I ever get to be a performer of any value, I've got to create the same kind of feeling that's going on between her and the audience.'

There was something going on romantically between Stevie and Lindsey even back in the days of Fritz, but neither of them wanted to admit it. The band had a tacit policy: *hands off Stevie Nicks*. Stevie, ever sensitive, thought no one in the group liked her because they thought she was too ambitious. But it was really that nobody wanted anyone else to have her. If someone started paying attention to her, the other musicians let him have it. 'These guys didn't take me seriously at all,' she once laughed. 'They thought I was only in it for the attention. To them, I was just a girl singer, but they hated the fact that I got a lot of credit.' What really galled the four male members of Fritz was that they would spend days practising and working on songs only to have people call up and say, 'We wanna book that band with the cute little brownish-blonde girl.' It drove them mad.

Eventually Fritz got a manager, and he tried to get them a record deal in Los Angeles, but LA and Fritz couldn't relate to each other. By mid-1971, Fritz broke up. Stevie and Lindsey stayed together to work on songs; they had shared the lead vocals in Fritz and knew they were good together. Stevie was drawing and writing verse all the time, and Lindsey was just about sleeping with his guitar in those days. That they were a potentially great song-writing team was undeniable. Within a few weeks they were romantically linked as well.

So they decided to try their luck as a duo. Calling themselves Buckingham Nicks, they resolved to move to Los Angeles to be closer to the music biz. Just then, however, Lindsey was felled by an attack of acute glandular fever and spent about nine months in 1971 and 1972 laid up. Although it was a frustrating period, the two made use of the time off. They mostly sat around and worked on songs and ideas for songs. Lindsey got hold of an electric guitar and taught himself the art of lead playing. He also bought himself an Ampex 4-track reel-to-reel tape recorder, which changed his life; he set it up in his father's office in Palo Alto and taught himself the craft of audio engineering. That's where all his early songs, like 'So Afraid', come from. He'd slave for hours with his 4-track, his headphones and one little microphone, putting all this music together obsessively, until he got it right. Learning this way, I feel, is what made him such a brilliant record producer later on.

Eventually, in 1972, Buckingham Nicks arrived in LA. They moved in with a record-producing friend, Keith Olsen. Through him they signed a deal with a small new label called Anthem. The two guys who had the label had a distribution deal with United Artists and the original idea was for Stevie and Lindsey to go to London and record an album at Trident Studios. But this plan fell apart when Anthem's partners split up. Eventually one of the partners got a deal with Polydor Records, and that's how Stevie and Lindsey came to record their album, *Buckingham Nicks*, at Sound City, Keith Olsen's studio in the valley.

The assistant engineer on those recording sessions was Richard Dashut. Eventually he became Fleetwood Mac's esteemed co-producer and one of my dearest friends. He enters our tale here in his role as Lindsey's main conspirator in the studio.

He was born in West Hollywood in 1951, and studied philosophy at that temple of wisdom, the University of Las Vegas. He remembers being turned on to the parallel dimensions of rock and reefer in 1969, heavily influenced by two albums from the great late-sixties British blues revival: John Mayall's *The Turning Point* and Fleetwood Mac's *Then Play On*. He left college and came back to LA wanting to get into the movie business. Instead he got his first job as a janitor at Crystal Sound in Hollywood. It was lowly work – he wasn't even allowed in the control room except to vacuum and empty the ashtrays – but he got to see the big stars of the day under working conditions: Joni Mitchell, Jackson Browne, James Taylor, and Crosby, Stills and Nash. One day Graham Nash and Industry Heavy David Geffen invited Richard into the control room and asked what he thought of a mix. Richard recalls looking down at the mixing board, a 16-track with these huge Dolby units they used to have, and thinking that it looked like the instrument panel on a jumbo jet.

Richard knew Keith Olsen, and got a job doing maintenance at Sound City in early 1973. After a week he shifted to assistant engineer, and that's when he met Buckingham Nicks. 'They were staying with Keith Olsen,' he remembers, 'and cutting their album. Lindsey and I were friends five minutes after we met that first day of work. We went out back and smoked a joint. I met Stevie and twenty minutes later we decided to get a place together, since I was looking and they had to move out of Keith's. So we moved to North Hollywood, near Universal. I'd come home after twenty hours working with Keith in the studio and trip over Lindsey's microphone cables. He'd be up late working with his 4-track. Various guitar players – Waddy Wachtel and Warren Zevon – would be passed out on the floor. Sometimes I'd find Stevie sleeping in my bed because she'd had a big argument with Lindsey. It wasn't a very easy life; you had to be resilient, and we were young.'

After months of hard work, Polydor released *Buckingham Nicks*, in November 1973. Listening to the record today, with all the hindsight of what was to follow, is fascinating. It includes 'Frozen Love', the only joint composition on the album, seven minutes of orchestration and good guitar. This, as I've said, was the track that Keith Olsen played for me when I went to visit Sound City a year later. I remember hearing that guitar and thinking: this guy reminds me a little of Danny Kirwan.

Buckingham Nicks was dedicated to Stevie's grandfather, A. J. Nicks. It featured a provocative cover, with an obviously bare Stevie looking over the equally bare shoulder of Lindsey. This didn't play well with Stevie's family. The album didn't play well with the record-buying public either, and soon Buckingham Nicks found itself without a record company. They played a few gigs, opening shows for Mountain and Poco in, among other places, Birmingham, Alabama, trying desperately to interest people in their record.

When it stiffed, they were back at square one, almost completely broke.

Richard Dashut: 'I had moved out to a one-bedroom apartment near Fairfax. After *Buckingham Nicks* bombed, Stevie and Lindsey ran out of money, so they moved in with me. Back went the 4-track, the cables, the stoned musicians sprawled on the floor, and we worked on demos for the next Buckingham Nicks album – 'So Afraid', 'Monday Morning' and 'Rhiannon'.

They were lean, lean times for our lads.

While Lindsey and Richard worked on the group's demos, Stevie worked cleaning houses and waitressing at Bob's Big Boy to keep food on the table. She remembers:

I was cleaning the house of our producer Keith Olsen for $50 a week. I come home with my big Hoover vacuum cleaner, my Ajax, my toilet brush, my cleaning shoes on. And Lindsey has managed to have some idiot send him eleven ounces of opiated hash. He and all his friends are in a circle. They smoked hash for a month, and I don't smoke because of my voice. I'd come in every day and have to step over these bodies. I'm tired, and I'm lifting their legs up so I can clean up and empty the ashtrays. A month later all these guys are going, 'I don't know why I don't feel very good.' I said, 'You wanna know why you don't feel so good? I'll tell you why – because you've done nothing else for weeks but lie on my floor and smoke and take my money.'

Money was so tight that occasionally Lindsey and Richard would take turns bouncing cheques at the local coffee shops. Richard remembers that the people who worked at the IHoP and the Copper Penny knew they were working on a record with no money, and let rubber cheques go by with a wink. Lindsey also had a short-lived job soliciting ads over the phone for some agency, and there were occasional session gigs as well. Early in 1974, he went on the road with Don Everly's band, which Warren Zevon had organized after the Everly Brothers split up. It was a short club tour, but Lindsey got to sing some of Phil Everly's vocal parts and got a lot of experience. When the tour got to Nashville, Lindsey met and jammed with some of la crème de la crème – Roy Orbison, Ike Everly and Merle Travis.

Lindsey was away for about six weeks. During that time Stevie got a new job waitressing at a place called Clementine's, a Roaring Twenties-style restaurant in Hollywood. She had to wear a sort of flapper outfit for the job, which she and Richard found hilarious. 'Stevie is so friendly and such a good woman,' Richard says, 'and we laughed all the time when we weren't out slaving.'

When Lindsey returned, work resumed on the next Buckingham Nicks album. Richard: 'The owners of Sound City now told us they would let Lindsey and me cut an album there, for free, without a record deal, and shop it around to the labels afterwards. This was unheard of, but we had so much faith in what we were doing that some of it must have rubbed off.' Indeed, it was purely faith in themselves that got them through hard times. Stevie and Lindsey had serious offers to form a Top Forty showband to ply the steak-and-lobster circuit on the west coast. These managers called them up and told them the money and all the gigs they could handle were there – if only they'd play Top Forty, because *nobody*, they said, would pay to hear Buckingham Nicks play their own songs.

Years later, Lindsey said that he and Stevie knew that if they became that kind of band, playing that kind of music, they would forfeit their artistry and lose what musical direction they had. Not wanting to prostitute themselves, they hung up on those offers and, as a result, got no gigs. They continued to audition for record labels at the same time as they worked on their album. Lou Adler, the boss of Ode Records, listened to half of one song and said thank you very much. A big producer at 20th-Century Records thought they were a smash act but couldn't persuade anyone to sign them. In the midst of this rejection, they kept working. Stevie wrote 'Landslide' and recorded it. She wrote 'Rhiannon' on a piano, and Lindsey had already worked out the dramatic opening chords. These were the songs, they felt, that along with 'Monday Morning' and the others would make them stars.

They were right.

Stevie's family, meanwhile, were beginning to have some doubts about her career. When she went home to visit in the spring of that year, 1974, they saw that she was getting very skinny. She wasn't eating and was obviously unhappy. Her parents had been sending her a little money here and there, but what they really wanted was for her to finish school. Her father, who Stevie loves dearly and respects, advised her to start setting some time limits on her career choice. A few months later, he was rushed into open-heart surgery; when Stevie couldn't reach his bedside before he was wheeled in, she was filled with remorse that she might lose him before he could see what she had made of herself.

On New Year's Eve, Stevie and Lindsey were having a little party at their house and wondering if 1975 was going to be a better year for them. Then Keith Olsen walked in and said, 'Hey, I've got some news . . . Fleetwood Mac want you to join them.'

And Lindsey was so surprised, he recalled later, that you could have knocked him down with a feather.

I repeat: I wasn't consciously shopping for anything other than a guitar player when I called Keith Olsen. Ever since Peter Green, I've been a sucker for guitar players. Who was that guitar player? That's what stuck in my mind from my first visit to Sound City, even though I was aware there was a girl singing. Lindsey's guitar stuck in my mind.

Only later did it become apparent that Lindsey was with Stevie. They were together. Their ambitions and hopes were as a unit. They had been working for years, I was told; they were hitting brick walls but were determined to keep writing together. Later Stevie would give me a hard time. 'Aaahhh, if I hadn't been with Lindsey you wouldn't have wanted me.' And like that.

Keith Olsen called me back and said that Stevie and Lindsey were interested, and so we set up a dinner meeting at a Mexican restaurant called El Carmen. Lindsey came up to our house on Fernwood, off Laurel Canyon. Judy Wong was there too, and we soon adjourned to the restaurant to meet John and Chris who were driving in from their house at the beach. Stevie Nicks was waiting for us, still dressed in her flapper's outfit from her waitress job. 'I saw Fleetwood Mac drive up in these two old clunky white Cadillacs with big tail fins,' she said years later, 'and I was in *awe.*'

We settled in at our table, ordered dinner, and then started smiling. There was something magic in the air, and we all felt it. We also got drunk on the margueritas. Lindsey offered to play an audition, and we explained we didn't think that would be necessary. We chatted for a bit longer so Chris could suss out the situation. When I first asked her about having another woman in the band, I knew she had some natural reservations, even though she didn't say anything. Being the lady in the band, a lady who first and foremost was a musician – and one of the lads – she just said, 'Do me a favour; as long as me and Stevie hit it off everything will be fine, 'cause there's nothing worse than having a couple of ladies in the band who don't like each other.' But at this dinner I saw that Stevie was extremely sympathetic, and that the two girls were hitting it off real well. Before the dessert came, I simply asked them: 'Want to join?'

Stevie and Lindsey looked at each other, and said, 'Yes.'

I said, 'We'd love to have you in the band.' And that was it.

Being without much in the way of cash, Stevie Nicks and Lindsey Buckingham were almost immediately put on a salary, $200 a week each, as new members of Fleetwood Mac. We may have paid a little of their rent as well, but I can't remember. No one really had much money then; we were just surviving at that point. Everything of Fleetwood Mac's was still in Bob Welch's name because we had no green cards that would let us work and earn money in the States. I remember that the $200,000 record advance from Warner Brothers to me, John and Chris went directly into Bob's bank account and that years later he got a *hell* of a tax bill.

And so it came to pass that we hired Stevie and Lindsey.

Within a day or two, Christine returned to England to see her family and take care of some business, while John McVie and I began to rehearse with Lindsey in a garage on Pico Boulevard in Santa Monica. Thus was Fleetwood Mac reborn as a garage band: the Dynamic Trio. And it went great: we bashed around for hours, happy just to be playing. When Chris returned, the whole band convened in the basement of International Creative Management on Beverly where our agent, Tom Ross, sort of adopted us, gave us space to rehearse, and watched us take off from there.

Christine: 'That was my first rehearsal with Stevie and Lindsey. They were in the band, but I'd never played with them before. I started playing "Say You Love Me" and when I reached the chorus they started singing with me and fell right into it. I heard this incredible sound – our three voices – and said to myself, "Is this me singing?" I couldn't believe how great this three-voice harmony was. My skin turned to goose flesh and I wondered how long this feeling was going to last.'

Several things were obvious from the start.

Fleetwood Mac once again had a front line of three singers and songwriters, but more powerful than ever. Those early rehearsals reminded me so much of the energy that exploded when Peter Green brought us together with Jeremy Spencer for the first time. And right from the gitgo, we could tell that this was gonna *play*. Lindsey was a brilliant player, and Chris and Stevie sounded as lovely as falling water. Plus, the vibes and energy were shimmering. I also found Stevie to be the most endearing combination of Beatnik poet and cowgirl. From the beginning, she was determined to bring a mystical quality into this version of the band. Right when she and Lindsey joined, she asked me for a set of Fleetwood Mac albums so she could look for a theme or a thread that ran all the way through the weave. She sat in her room and listened to all of the music and came up with a word – mystical. She later reminisced: 'Since I have a deep love for the mystical anyway, this really appealed to me. I thought, this might really be the band for me because they *are* mystical, they play wonderful rock and roll, and there's another lady, so I'll have a pal.'

Yet the truth must be told: neither Stevie nor Lindsey were ecstatic about joining Fleetwood Mac. They had laboured on the songs for their second record with the zeal of true believers, and now that music would be presented to the world as a product of Fleetwood Mac. Lindsey wasn't really familiar with our music to that point, except for *Then*

119

Play On. But he knew we had a tradition of good guitars, and they were dead broke, so they did it.

But Buckingham Nicks enjoyed one last gasp. Right after they joined us, someone in Birmingham, Alabama called up and asked them to headline a show. Twice in the previous year Buckingham Nicks had opened shows there; the local radio played their album, which enjoyed strong local sales. So they flew off to Alabama with three other players and discovered that Buckingham Nicks had sold out a 6000-seat hall! And the audience went *nuts* when they came out. Their minds were completely boggled. Unknown in LA, unable even to get a cheap gig somewhere, they were local heroes in Birmingham. They played several dates on this great Buckingham Nicks Farewell Tour. At the last show, Lindsey announced that they were joining Fleetwood Mac, and the audience could only gape, silently. What, Lindsey Buckingham wondered, were they getting themselves into?

But their luck had turned.

Years later, Stevie confided: 'We fell into the American Dream out of nowhere. We were just nowhere.'

John and Chris had, in the meantime, moved out to the beach, a three-room apartment in Malibu, where Christine set about writing her songs for the next Fleetwood Mac album. She wrote 'Over My Head' and 'Say You Love Me' there, on an old portable Hohner electric piano, overlooking the Pacific Ocean blue. She had two other strong tunes as well, the lover's lullaby 'Warm Ways' and a blues called 'Sugar Daddy'. I first heard these when I went over to their place the day that Stevie and Lindsey brought their demo tapes over for a listen. It was clear to us that their songs were tremendous, and had already been completely worked out. Lindsey had been labouring over the harmonic guitars of 'I'm So Afraid' since at least 1971. 'Monday Morning' and 'Landslide', Stevie's wistful take on ageing and changing, were intended for the next Buckingham Nicks album. Same with 'Rhiannon'. They proposed that Fleetwood Mac re-record Stevie's 'Crystal' from *Buckingham Nicks*, but with more production, and to this we assented.

We worked on this music for several weeks, getting more excited all the time. We were hot. Lindsey was the most creative guitar player we'd had since the days of the Green God, and as I watched Stevie dance around the rehearsal room I had a feeling that audiences were going to devour her.

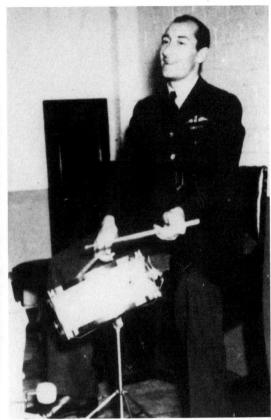

Top left My mother, 'Biddy' Brereton Fleetwood, Hayling Island, 1938 *(Fleetwood Collection)*

Top right My father, Wing Commander Mike Fleetwood at the drums, 1945 *(Fleetwood Collection)*

Left Mick, age three, in Egypt in 1950 *(Fleetwood Collection)*

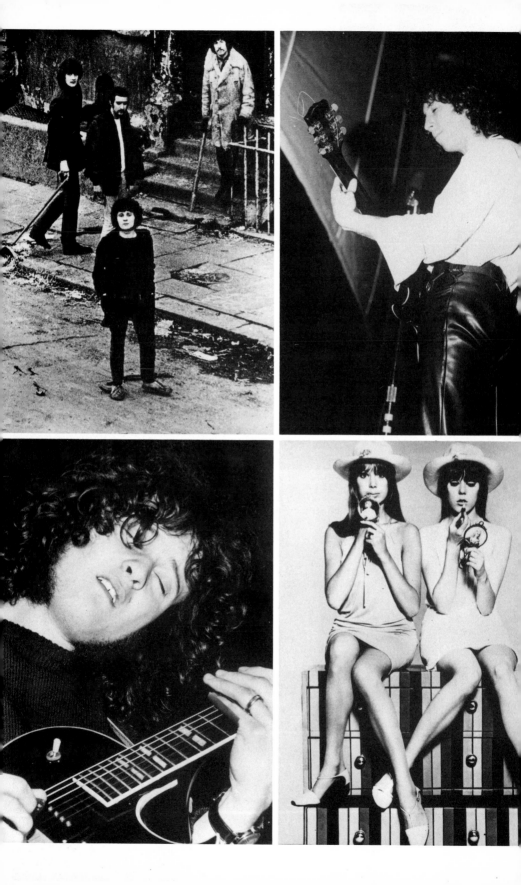

This page: left The enigmatic Danny Kirwan, 1969 *(Zuma Archives)*

Centre We pose with Cliff Richard after a television appearance, 1969 *(Zuma Archives)*

Bottom Peter Green in his final days with Fleetwood Mac, 1970 *(Zuma Archives)*

Opposite page: top left Earliest Fleetwood Mac photo, in the streets outside the Nag's Head pub, Brixton, 1967 *(Zuma Archives)*

Top right Peter Green, 1968 *(Zuma Archives)*

Bottom right The glorious Boyd sisters, Jenny and Patti, pose for a *Vogue* layout, circa 1966 *(Jenny Boyd Collection)*

Bottom left Jeremy Spencer, 1968 *(Zuma Archives)*

This page: above Christine Perfect, 1970 *(Zuma Archives)*

Top right The *Kiln House* band with Jeremy's son, Dicken, 1970 *(Zuma Archives)*

Bottom right Fleetwood Mac at Benifols, 1973 – Christine, Mick, John (sitting), Bob Weston (standing) and Bob Welch *(Warner Bros Records)*

Opposite page: top left Fleetwood Mac, 1975 – me, John, Chris, Lindsey Buckingham and Stevie Nicks *(Warner Bros Records)*

Top right and bottom left Mick on the road, 1978 *(Warner Bros Records)*

Bottom right Chris and Stevie, 1978 *(Zuma Archives)*

Right Lindsey, 1979 *(Warner Bros Records)*

Below Me and Mum after a cake fight on the *Tusk* tour, 1979–80 *(Fleetwood Collection)*

Left Mick, John Courag Mike Fleetwood, Bel Ai 1978 *(Fleetwood Collect*

Above Stevie, 1979 *(War Bros Records)*

Left The Blue Whale, Little Ramirez Canyon, Malibu, 1984 *(Zuma Archives)*

Centre Drumming with the Super Adzo Group, Star Hotel, Accra Ghana, 1981 *(Zuma Archives)*

Bottom Me, Jerry Lee Lewis and Keith Richard, 1983 *(Richard Aaron Photo)*

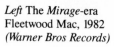

Left The *Mirage*-era Fleetwood Mac, 1982 *(Warner Bros Records)*

Right Peter Green, 1987 *(Syndication International)*

Left The *Tango in the Night* band, 1987 *(Warner Bros Records)*

So in February 1975, we went over to Sound City to record, with Keith Olsen as engineer. In the studio we added two songs to the album. 'Blue Letter' was a fast country rocker written by the Curtis Brothers, a good group working the same vein as the Eagles and other legatees of the Byrds and Buffalo Springfield. They were making demos at Sound City while we were there. I heard 'Blue Letter' and thought, that's a *good* song. (Fleetwood Mac still plays it today.) 'World Turning' was written in the studio; it came out of a jam between Chris, Lindsey and me. Based on an old Peter Green song, it would later develop as my solo showpiece in concert.

There was a lot of cocaine around, and we recorded our album in a somewhat Peruvian atmosphere. Until then, Fleetwood Mac hadn't had much experience with this Andean rocket fuel. Now we discovered that a toot now and then relieved the boredom of long hours with little nourishment. The Devil's dandruff, in those days, was still the musician's friend.

And all did *not* go smoothly in the studio. Lindsey was full of ideas about how his new band should sound. He's a record producer at heart, and felt strongly about the way the music should come across. He'd sit down at the drums and suggest rhythms and parts. 'Hey Mick, try this . . .' But when he started doing that with John McVie, he ended up in a whole heap of troubl̥. John has always been a bit over-protective of his own ability, and never liked suggestions. So John and Lindsey were straight away at loggerheads. That was the start-off, and of course Lindsey couldn't win. McVie is a consummate game-player, and Lindsey just didn't know. If he wants, McVie can get me on my knees, exhausted, begging for him to stop. Bloody-minded, John would growl, 'I'm not sitting here being told what to do by someone who's just joined the fucking band!' There was a pecking order, and Lindsey had to be taught some tact or McVie would attack him. John would say, 'Hang on a sec, you're talkin' to *McVie* here!'

All this was very healthy in the long run. At one point they told each other to fuck off, and that was it. After that, there was a balance between their personalities. Lindsey was confronted with the fact that, although he had been dominant in Buckingham Nicks, now he was in a band, one which did things by consensus. Fleetwood Mac has always been a democracy.

We finished recording and mixing the new album in June 1975, and called it *Fleetwood Mac* for the sake of continuity. The whole organization gathered to listen to the playback of our first record with our new line-up. 'Monday Morning' led off with a hard attack, followed by 'Warm Ways', 'Blue Letter', 'Rhiannon', 'Over My Head' and the new version of 'Crystal'. The second side began with 'Say You Love Me' and went on with 'Landslide', 'World Turning', 'Sugar Daddy' and the guitar-army crescendos of 'I'm So Afraid'.

I remember thinking: *this record could be a monster.* All we had to do was convince our record company of the same thing. At that point John, Chris and I had been making records for Warner Brothers for years. Our joke with the company was that the usual 300,000-unit sale of our albums paid their lighting bills. It was always, 'Oh, Fleetwood Mac's got a new album out, it'll do fairly well, they'll tour and that's it.' But we knew this album was different from the rest. Everyone felt something exciting. For years we had been floating, without much direction. But this new band had chemistry. Biochemistry, even. We were *enthused.* I thought, let's go down and talk to Mo Ostin, the president of Warner Brothers, and let Mo know that this time we really want the record company behind us.

So I went to see Mo. Mickey Shapiro came along. I told him, 'Look, we really feel something here. We don't want you to think of this as just another Fleetwood Mac record. And if you and the company aren't excited about this record, then we prefer not to be on the label. We're not unhappy, but this means enough to us to say *please*, let us go if you don't love this record and think of us as a new band.' Mo smiled in his avuncular way, and assured us things would be OK. At that point, nobody at the label had even heard the record. But we wanted to let them know that this project was very special to us.

Of course, various calamities attended the rebirth of Fleetwood Mac anyway. First the master tapes to the new album were misplaced at one point. They were found, after a period of bowel-loosening panic, in a pile of tapes about to be erased.

Then we discovered that, as I had feared, the attitude of Warner's execs was decidedly ho-hum. Maybe it was hard to blame them. Indeed, our sales had been static, and they thought of us as a solid opening act who broke up and disintegrated and changed personnel with every new album and tour. This typecasting drove us mad. Mickey Shapiro took our tape to Joe Smith at Warners and played it for him. Joe's ears pricked up. 'Hey, this is a good record!' he said. 'Maybe we could do *350,000!*' He wasn't being flippant; he thought that was our limit. The thought of selling millions of Fleetwood Mac records occurred to no one but the band, and record executives were used to the inflated fantasies of musicians. They heard them all the time. 'Maybe,' Smith told Mickey, 'we could move an extra 50,000 albums if we had a hit single.'

Concerning the need for a single, Joe Smith was dead-on. We had *never* had a hit single in America, and our last in England had been five years earlier. So we set about looking for some help. At that point, no one knew which song to pick as a banner we could wave on the radio for our fans.

Another conflict with our label was over touring. I was determined that we had to take our music to our audience, even before the album was out on the streets. This new band had never worked on stage as a unit before. And Fleetwood Mac has always been a working band; that's where our whole line of action has come from. Now I knew that our fans, the people who buy the records and come to the shows, were going to be faced with what essentially was a new band. I said, we've got to risk going out and playing as a band. No one had seen Stevie and Lindsey before, outside of Alabama. I thought it would be a great training ground for when the record came out.

Warner Brothers thought this was stupid. They didn't want us to tour prior to the album release date, and they didn't want to advance us any tour money. They'd seen too many Fleetwood Mac break-ups on the road. They thought we were committing suicide by playing without new music to sell. They told us we couldn't go out on the road without a manager. I told them we'd had nothing but problems with managers, and that we had Mickey Shapiro looking after us and felt it was fine. One exec, Bob Regehr, was adamant about not touring the group. 'Mick, you're crazy,' he told me. 'You haven't even got an album out yet!' I said the hell with it and made plans to do a few shows anyway. I was so discouraged that we made discreet inquiries to other companies, notably CBS and Arista, to see if they wanted us when it came time to renegotiate at the end of the year. Our low status in those days was confirmed when our label took out an ad in *Billboard*. In the photograph Stevie was identified as Lindsey and vice versa. We were not amused.

And so, against all advice and conventional wisdom, the new Fleetwood Mac began its career as a touring band on 15 May 1975, in El Paso, Texas. We gigged all around the Lone Star State – Amarillo, Abilene, Dallas, San Antonio, Austin – before flying to Detroit and playing all over the midwest and northeast through June. We'd rehearsed ourselves thoroughly, and I felt we sounded and looked great from the gitgo. Stevie, wearing her tight jeans and filmy blouses, immediately assumed her role as Fleetwood Mac's sensuous gypsy dancing girl. She and Lindsey had been working together for six or seven years at that point, and onstage their unity was apparent to me as never before. We opened with 'Station Man' and various numbers from *Kiln House* and *Bare Trees* for the old Fleetwood Mac fans. Lindsey did Peter Green's 'Oh Well', which earned a cheer. We played 'Crystal', 'Rhiannon' and 'Blue Letter' from our unreleased album, which went over surprisingly well, especially the emotional explosion with which Stevie finished 'Rhiannon'. I turned 'World Turning' into my solo spot, emerging from behind my drum kit to dance with my big African talking drum; a Nigerian friend of Peter Green's had made it for Pete in London years before, and I took an instant shine to the incredibly expressive instrument which had a language of its own. Eventually, Pete made me buy it from him.

We played almost any decent gig we could get, mostly 3000-seaters: the Paramount in Seattle, the Arena in Milwaukee, the Celebrity in Phoenix, the Albuquerque Civic auditorium, the Century Theater in Wichita. We opened for Loggins and Messina all over the place. We opened for Ten Years After in Minneapolis and all over Western Canada. We opened for the Guess Who? at the University of Montana at Missoula. We were making $3000 a gig, but often, if we didn't sell out a hall, John Courage and I used to give back money to promoters in the dressing room after the show, so they'd stand by us when we needed them later. The people who were coming to these summer gigs were our hard-core fans who'd been with us since 1968. At every stop, we told people about our record, and said we'd be back to play for them again, after they'd heard it.

Almost from the beginning, touring exacted a toll on the band.

One of the first things to break was John and Chris's marriage. John McVie was drinking heavily to cope with the pressure of launching the new band, and his moods began to blacken. He could be combative and quite frightening. And at that point, Chris decided she'd had enough. We were in San Francisco, playing the Oakland Coliseum, when the word went out that John and Christine were no longer occupying the same rooms in the hotel. This was all handled very low key, and there was no talk of breaking up the band. They both knew it was too late for anyone to back out of Fleetwood Mac now, since too much was at stake – especially our pride. I know that Chris felt very bad about it because she hadn't really stopped loving McVie. As a parting gift she had a huge golden ring, emblazoned with a noble penguin, made for him to show John that she still felt for him. So despite the heartbreak, especially John's under the circumstances, we all soldiered on.

We knew we were in trouble in terms of getting on the radio. We could kill ourselves on the road for the next year, and it would be a total waste of time if we couldn't get our new stuff on Top Forty radio and the FM rock stations. If our label wasn't going to go after airplay full speed ahead, we had to hire an independent promo man to help us. To this end, we hired Paul Ahearn to break *Fleetwood Mac* on the radio. Paul and Glenn Frey of the Eagles had been living as room-mates in the house Jenny and I moved into in Laurel Canyon when we came to Los Angeles. When Glenn moved out to their next abode, his suite was taken over by music writer Ben Edmunds, who introduced me to Paul when I started to look for help. Paul Ahearn:

> Mick was kinda shy about looking for help. They'd had such bad experience with management before; now they knew they had a good record but didn't know who to turn to. Warners merely expected to see the usual respectable Mac numbers, but they didn't really know who to get after on a new record. They figured Mac sold enough to keep them on the label, mid-charts, but no big numbers. So they made me 'tour co-ordinator' on that first tour by the new band. But actually I was working the record, calling stations and using my contacts to get them to actually play the thing.
>
> The big thing was, they didn't have a single. I put them together with Deke Richards, who had produced most of the early hits by Michael Jackson and the Jackson Five. They remixed 'Over My Head' so it would sound good on a car radio, and FM stations started picking it up right away.

The new version of 'Over My Head' was very 'high-end', with a new guitar intro and different vocal harmonies. It was a hotter mix that sounded great on the radio, and it began to hit almost as soon as Warners released it in September. But not without some resistance. Back then American radio was much more polarized into FM/good guys/albums versus AM/crass/singles. Whereas FM radio took to the single right away, AM was slow because commercial radio had the same expectations – 'just another Fleetwood Mac record' – as the label. We would call stations and people would have us confused with Savoy Brown. But once we got going on the road, we had a big break-through every week, with some important station adding our record to its playlist. The stations later saw local sales continuing strong and kept playing the record. That's how our momentum began to build. After only a month or so of this, we had sold 400,000 records.

To this, our beloved label said 'far out', and refused to pay an $86 bill for promotional balloons at one of our gigs.

Fleetwood Mac spent the rest of 1975 on tour, driving between American college towns in a pair of rented station wagons, beginning on 9 September, in El Paso again, and ending ninety gigs later in December.

And I *loved* it. For me, this was it. A band live is what a band is. Making records – twelve songs in eighteen months – is not what a band is. We were brought up to believe in playing live, and if you sell a few records, you're lucky.

But it was the sound of this band that killed me. Chris and John were at the top of their form despite Chris giving John the elbow, as he so succinctly phrased it. For most of the show Chris was really fronting the band, with Stevie and Lindsey definitely playing support-ing (but still crucial) roles. And it was totally fascinating to watch our new members blossom into their own. Lindsey was incredibly fluid as a live guitarist, and I was immediately impressed with the amount of obsessive thought that went into his art. It was hard to get him away from the music, even. He wasn't outgoing, and on the road we had to drag him out of his room to have fun. He had very strong opinions, and was completely involved and committed to what we were doing. Lindsey, I soon learned, was really a musical alchemist, sitting for days on end with his tape recorders, just working. Being with us now, he was really forced to change his personality in some ways. Before he had been in control; now he was in an established band and had to tread a bit more lightly than he might have wanted to. And I could even see, as the first days of the tour turned to weeks, that the long-term Lindsey-Stevie relationship was beginning to change as well. When they first joined the band, he had control. Very slowly, he lost that control, and he didn't really like it. After we made that first record, Stevie began to come out of her shell and talk as a person in her own right.

What was she like? She had a sore throat a lot and liked to melt into a corner, wrapped in a shawl, with a cup of tea, to write and draw.

She was charming and funny and very candid which nicely balanced Lindsey's reluctance to air his feelings.

Did I fall for her right away? I don't know, but she immediately felt like a soul mate. There was a bond. I'm an old drama queen, and so is she. What I liked most about her was the feeling of being comfortable enough to be silly and stupid.

These thoughts trigger the following memory. On that first tour of the new band, we were staying at the original Holiday Inn, the oldest one, somewhere in Texas. It was a dump. I ended up in Lindsey's room after the gig. It was the first time I ever sat around and got stoned with Lindsey, man to man. We were just hanging around, and got to talking. I had stopped smoking years before, and needless to say I got hammered on this joint we shared. Remember, this is in the earliest days of the new band. We're both sitting there, and straight out of the blue he turned to me and said, 'It's you and Stevie, isn't it?'

I was in a terrible condition, but I remember this hitting my psyche like a bolt of lighting. I really didn't understand. I could only stammer, Whaddaya mean? But he didn't really answer. It merely appeared to him that there was something between me and Stevie Nicks. The moment passed, and it was never mentioned again.

The other thing I also liked right away was that Fleetwood Mac actually *sounded* better, mostly because Richard Dashut had come on board to mix the band in concert. John Courage had been mixing us for years at that point, but from the first tour rehearsals, in a theatre on Sunset, Lindsey was looking for something different.

Richard: 'After they finished their album, which I'd not worked on, much to my dismay, Lindsey called and said, "How would you like to go on the road with Fleetwood Mac?" I looked at my four walls and said, yeah, I'll go. The first gig was in El Paso. I'd never done live sound in my life. I was nervous, very nervous.'

John Courage: 'So I got the roadies together and said, "Listen, Lindsey and Stevie are insisting that this *worm* do the sound – a *studio* type. We gotta show him what the road's really like. *Keep him up all the way to El Paso!*"'

Dashut: 'Courage threw me into a big Winnabego Executive with four or five of Fleetwood Mac's hardcore roadies. To me, they looked like cut-throat bikers on acid. "Get to know the fellows," Mr Courage advised. The result was forty-eight hours of heavy doping, with no sleep. They smoked tons of joints, and consumed mounds of blow. I was a virgin. They kept me up, and I was a zombie when it was time to go to work.

'I found out there was very little art in the band's live sound. The feeling was, as long as everything's running to levels and there's no buzz, it was good sound. So I learned to do "live mix" by trial and ordeal. Mostly ordeal, since my job description also included driving the band and handling their luggage as well. There wasn't much money and we mostly travelled in station wagons. Later there would be thirty people in the support groups, but that first tour was just Courage and me. Lindsey and I would be in the lead wagon with the luggage, smoking joints with the windows rolled up and listening to the radio. Loud. It was like a Cheech and Chong movie. Courage would be driving the rest of the band behind us. We'd arrive, dead tired, and the band would collapse into their rooms, but I had to do the luggage. And of course the road crew loathed me because I got to ride in the comparative comfort of the band cars and the occasional limo. One night, early on, I was initiated with a thoroughly wrecked room. But I was too tired to complain.'

Days and weeks on the road blurred together. Southern Illinois University at Carbondale. Purdue Hall of Music, Lafayette, Indiana. Next day, drive 180 miles to Cincinnati. Fly to Chicago, pick up car, drive to La Crosse, Wisconsin. Next day fly Mississippi Valley Airways to O'Hare, change to Ozark flight 559 to Moline, pick up cars and drive to Davenport, Iowa, for that night's show at The Orpheum. Next day drive 150 miles to Bloomington to play Illinois State. Then over to Kent State. Next day fly to Detroit to play the Michigan Palace. Next day, Busch Stadium, Indianapolis. Next day, Columbus, Ohio.

That was just one week in September.

John Courage: 'I set up this system to avoid the nasty-looking cocaine dealers who hung around the bands and sold them bad drugs. The band kept telling me they needed coke, and eventually I said, "If you need coke, I'll get it for you." Because I was afraid they'd get busted in some little town by some derelict coke dealer with the narcs on his heels. So I would procure large quantities from reliable sources – and of course it caught up with me in the end. But I felt my job was to make sure there were no more disasters on the road. I felt protective. And the system was safe; it worked as long as it was expected to.'

'All right, get those broads off the stage.' That's what Loggins and Messina's road manager, Jim Recor, used to shout to John Courage as Fleetwood Mac finished our show. Other macho bands didn't see how we could tour with two women, and McVie and I took a lot of ribbing at the bar over this issue. But instead of being a problem, it was the opposite. We bore up a little more. John Courage remembers the change when Stevie and Lindsey joined. 'They were young, good-looking, friendly and fun to be with. Bob Welch was serious and moody and he went through depressing times with us. But now I saw John and Chris and Mick laughing and enjoying themselves again. It seemed idyllic, after what we'd gone through.'

And so we laboured, through that whole autumn, pushing our record in every college town in America. Or so it seemed. There were some pretty rough times for the whole band, but Stevie Nicks especially went through a period of anxiety and self-doubt after getting some pretty heavy negative reviews. This was a new band to the critics as well, and we were consequently reviewed as if we were unknown. *Rolling Stone* said that Stevie's singing was 'callow', and many reviews said something like, '. . . the raucous voice of Stevie Nicks and the golden-throated Christine McVie, who's the only good thing this band has left.' Stevie is extremely sensitive, she would go to pieces when she saw these things. She began to think we only hired her because she was with Lindsey, part of a package. And I'd say no, we *love* what you're doing, and the audience loves it too. This was true. I couldn't take my eyes off her when she was onstage. But she had a hard time believing it, and confided that she was beginning to think she wasn't that good. There were other factors as well. Somewhat fragile to begin with, the grind of the road – four gigs in a row, one day off – began to beat her down. Driving around, we were all cold all the time, and without any catering, decent meals were extremely rare. Young Stevie Nicks proceeded to lose weight she didn't have in the first place. She again alarmed her family when they saw her while we played Phoenix late in the year, and I know there were a few bad moments when she seriously considered leaving the tour and the band.

I'd say to her, 'C'mon Stevie, you've got to eat and stay fit. You're an important part of this band now, we *need* you.'

'Mick,' she said, 'when I joined I hadn't a *clue* it would be like this. No one told me, and I didn't know me and Chris would be sleeping on amps in back of trucks. But I've decided that I'm going to make it through, and that no one's going to say, "Oh she can't cope, she should give it up".'

No one ever did say that about Stevie Nicks.

She also felt a lot better after 'Over My Head' jammed into the American Top Ten in November 1975. Stevie's harmonies were a crucial element in that record's sound, so the airplay and good sales gradually invalidated the banal jibes in the press. In fact, like many artists, she was able to turn her blues into something creative and beautiful. I have a strong image of her during that first tour, sitting backstage and writing the lyrics to 'Sisters of the Moon' in her notebook, working into her art some of the torn and frayed feelings from those earliest days on the road.

Other memories: playing in front of a sold-out stadium in Anaheim, with Rod Stewart headlining. Backstage we got drunk with Rod and laughed about our old band, the Shotgun Express. And after the last date on 22 December, I gleefully watched Courage and Dashut wreck our two rented Impala station wagons by playing bumper-cars on the ice-coated parking lot of our last Holiday Inn for at least a few weeks.

We took a break at Christmas, satisfied that we had done our duty and done it well. *Fleetwood Mac* was awarded a gold record that month. We had sold a million and a half records and were pleased to discover that there was a new attitude in Burbank towards Fleetwood Mac. Now Mickey Shapiro and I spoke to Mo Ostin every week. He was very helpful, taking an interest in the band, aiding us in our ongoing legal battles with Clifford Davies in England. Bright and knowledgeable, a wonderful listener, Mo was crucial when it came time to renegotiate our contract. And he was generous. Fleetwood Mac got a big raise in royalty payments, a substantial cash advance on our next album, and Mo let us know that Warner Brothers believed in the band. We in turn renegotiated with Stevie and Lindsey, making them partners in the band.

Over the years I've heard many theories why this was the version of Fleetwood Mac that got to be so successful.

All I know is that Stevie Nicks and Lindsey Buckingham really brought something to the band, projecting an aura of hip California glamour to the audience for whom we were playing.

Fleetwood Mac was also, according to the critics, the first adult rock album, attracting an audience that had given up on teen-oriented pop and disco music.

And all I know is that Christine McVie's talent really exploded. Three of the four hit singles from that album were her songs.

Here's the truth. It was a fucking accident, really. It was a matter of keeping ones ear's open. I heard them in the studio, and I *knew*.

CHAPTER SEVEN

Piggy in the Middle

Ah, cruel Fate! Bitter Destiny!

As Fleetwood Mac crawled and clawed our way back to the top, the gods were laughing at us, and having sport. As *Fleetwood Mac* inched its way to the summit of the charts, our lives were snarled by disharmony and pain. In the year it took us to make our second album with the new lineup, the record that would change all our lives forever, we all got divorced.

The whole band. Chris and John's seven-year marriage was already over by then. Stevie and Lindsey's relationship, four years old, dissolved when Stevie walked out. And Jenny and I . . . well, the story follows shortly.

In the past, events like these would have killed Fleetwood Mac. But not now. We all knew it was too late to stop. So we kept the band together, continued to work, and proceeded to make the best music of our career in the form of a record that would become one of the biggest-selling albums in the history of commercial recording.

But the hell we all went through in that year of 1976 really cannot be adequately described.

Yesterday's gone. Thank God.

I blame myself for the situation that led up to Jenny and I ending our marriage.

It all began when we started the new band, and I became so immersed in managing Fleetwood Mac and seeing it succeed that I began to neglect Jenny again. We had moved to a rented house in Topanga Canyon. It was like the Laurel Canyon house, but more in the country. Topanga is a glorious and scenic place, where the Santa Monica mountains crash down to the sea, but it's also forty-five minutes from

Los Angeles by car. Soon Jenny started to feel rather cut off, and we started having some real problems at home. I wasn't seeing anyone else, but I was either in the studio or on the road and she felt ignored. Jenny is always in search of the Grail, and I suppose she was asking herself, Is this my lot in life? In frustration she had a fling or two. I didn't know much about it, but I said, OK, let's get through it and carry on.

Jenny is better at this sort of thing than I, so I'll ask her to continue:

I always had an absolute fear of Mick becoming famous and wealthy. I felt that if that happened, I knew we'd break up. This fear that things would change was heightened when we visited a numerologist during this period. She predicted that the next Fleetwood Mac album would be very big and that Mick would be a millionaire. But success didn't impress me. The children and I never saw Mick, and we felt abandoned in Topanga. Yet Mick and I couldn't verbalize to each other. Our feelings were pent up.

I had something of a breakdown then. It happened at a barbecue at our house. I was feeling a bit crazy. John Courage was teasing me about something, and I just snapped. I began to punch and pummel Mick in front of everybody. I was screaming and hysterical. I looked up and saw that Mick had a helpless look on his face. He didn't know what was wrong because he didn't know how unhappy I was. All those years of waiting for him had worn me out. So I snapped. They put me to bed, and I started having convulsions. It was a major-league breakdown.

When I felt a little better, I told Mick that if we didn't separate I might do myself in. Once again, there was almost no reaction. So I moved out into a little flat and we had almost no communication. Then I had a car crash, and Mick was furious with me. I don't blame him, but I was quite crazy at the time. Eventually, Mick said he wanted a divorce and we did it. So I took the girls and went back to England. And as soon as my feet touched British soil I felt better. It was so wonderful to be away from the crazy world I had been living in.

The divorce didn't really hit me too hard at first, because I just kept working on the band. It finally got to me when I realized I had to ask Jenny to return the little silver balls my sister Sally had given to me years ago. I had put them on my key chain, and soon they became dented from being thrown out the window so visitors to our flat in

Kensington Church Street could get into the house without us trekking down the stairs. When we divorced, Jenny took the car and with it the keys. So when I had to ask for my balls back, that was the point when it hit me that we weren't together any more, and it was my own stupid fault. It was a terrible feeling.

The McVie's marriage cracked apart for good while we were living in a rented house in Florida, having taken some time off from touring. We decided to use the vacation to rehearse and write for the next album. It was a strange house, a run-down place with overgrown grass and frogs in the green swimming pool in which we half-expected to see William Holden floating face down. There was barbed wire around the property and a rather odd atmosphere. Our big equipment trucks were pulled up in the driveway, and we stayed there with the roadies and their girlfriends. 'Go Your Own Way' and a couple of other songs were written there.

John and Chris were only nominally married at that point. Actually, she'd been seeing our lighting director, Curry Grant, in secret whilst we were on the road. John suspected something was going on. He'd say to me, 'He's doing her, you know.' And I'd say, 'No, no, no, John, it's all in your mind.' Soon Curry started having trouble with the rest of the crew; they saw what was happening and didn't like it. It got so Curry couldn't ride in the van with the rest of them. Colonel Courage would berate the roadies, and they'd say they hated Curry 'cause he was messing around with Christine. So the colonel and I confronted her, and she told us it was true. John was very upset, and we fired Curry because it was disrupting the band. Chris was told it had to be that way, and she understood.

That was our attitude. No matter how awful things became, the band had to come first. It was do or die. But it made touring very, very hard. John and I became very close to each other again because our marriages were both failing. We rode around the USA in our station wagons and talked and talked. That's how we got through. When that part of the tour was over, Chris moved out of the house she and John had bought in Topanga. After Chris left John lived there with another lady, but it didn't work out. By then, John didn't fancy the idea of living in a house anyway. When we were all living in England at Benifols, he and Bob Welch used to go to the boat shows in Portsmouth and Southampton. So when we got back, John went down to Marina Del Rey, bought a fibreglass ketch he named *Adélie* (after his favourite family of penguins), and lived on it for a year.

Stevie and Lindsey broke up as well. To this day, I don't really know how it happened. I remember that Stevie went into the sessions for the new album as a single woman, as did Chris. At the time, she said something in a joking way about Lindsey being more interested in his guitar than he was in her, and she got tired of it and left. There was some conflict, I recall, about the 'crackin' up, shackin' up' line in 'Go Your Own Way', which Stevie felt was unfair and Lindsey felt strongly about. Much later, Stevie made her perspective clear to me:

'Suppose Lindsey wasn't playing well on a particular song or something,' she said. 'As his girlfriend, I should be a comfort to him, right? You Know: "Who cares about it? You're great anyway!" I mean, that's what old ladies do for their men, right? But I couldn't, because I was also frustrated and saying, "Look, if you could just get your guitar part tight, we could put the vocal on." I'd be pissed off at him too. There was no way we could get any comfort from each other about what went on in the band. There was no love, because everybody was too nervous. And while we were travelling all the time, none of us had other friends to talk to . . .'

Stevie has also said that the relationship between her and Lindsey was already a bit rocky when they joined the band. As Stevie started to express herself more, as she became a star, things didn't get any better.

These were the less-than-ideal conditions under which Fleetwood Mac began to record our next album. People who knew us were agog. After all, it isn't so unusual for a couple in a band to break up. But both couples? And me? It was ironic.

We were all in a state of total weirdness. We needed to be apart from each other in the worst way, but at the same time we had to work together. We were trying to let go personally and cling to each other professionally at the same time.

Breaking up the band was never even discussed. It was never an option. We just carried on. I can't remember one moment when it was suggested we not carry on.

We came off the road in January 1976, just after 'Rhiannon' had been released as a single and started to climb the charts. My next task was to find a *sympatico* studio to follow up *Fleetwood Mac*, which was about to be awarded a platinum album. I wasn't sure where we were going to record, but I knew that we should get out of town and not do it in LA. I've always been in favour of throwing people into new situations; it's healthy for any artist to change scene during a time of enforced creativity. No one objected to this plan; whatever I arranged, we did.

I'd heard good things about a studio called the Record Plant, in Sausalito near San Francisco, so I decided to go up and take a look at the place. At the time I was seeing a very young blonde named Ginny who I had met on the road in Texas. Actually, Dashut had met her first, but I had taken a shine to her because she had freckles and reminded me of Jenny. So John Courage told Richard to hand her over – orders from the colonel – and I flew her in to LA from her hometown (on which occasion our crew played a nasty trick on me; someone called and threatened to have me jailed and deported for transporting an underage girl across a state line for immoral purposes!). We stayed at John's house in Topanga for a few days, then I borrowed Christine's Datsun and we drove up to Sausalito to look at the studio. It seemed like a good place to work, and it came with a house we could live in, up in the Berkeley Hills, while we were recording. So I booked the studio for nine weeks and returned with the whole band plus assorted friends and helpers early in February to begin work.

Sausalito – that's where the real Fleetwood Mac craziness started. *Fleetwood Mac* had been recorded in a quick three months. This new album would take us almost a year, during which we spoke to each other in clipped, civil tones while sitting in small airless studios listening to each other's songs about our own shattered relationships. I mean, it was heavy. We all felt so fragmented and fragile.

While we were at the Record Plant, Stevie and Christine lived in a rented apartment in the nearby marina; we lads were in the Plant's house in the hills. Immediately rumours began to fly about who was seeing whom after hours. And the studio itself proved to be a bizarre place to work. The centre-piece of the place was what was referred to as Sly Stone's Pit. This was a sunken lounge, heavily carpeted in thick, revolting bordello-like burgundy shag, in which Mr Stone would seclude himself when he was using the facility. The pit was acoustically dead and boasted its own nitrous oxide tank. We didn't really use this room (it was usually occupied by people we didn't know, tapping razors on mirrors), but some of us did go in there to pray from time to time.

These sessions were almost indescribably difficult, from the beginning. Let's let Richard Dashut set the tone:

They started out recording with the Record Plant's own engineer, but then they fired him after four days for being too into astrology.

I was there, basically keeping Lindsey company, and Mick takes me into the parking lot. 'Guess what?' he says with a smile. '*You're doing it.*' You can imagine how I was both excited and scared. I hadn't even worked on their last record. Since Fleetwood Mac had always produced their own records with an engineer, here I was being asked to co-produce this crucial second album. At that point I wasn't sure I could handle it, so I brought in a friend, Ken Caillat from LA, to help me, and we started co-producing. Mick gave me and Ken each an old Chinese I Ching coin and said, good luck.

The band had brought some great songs with them, but they needed arrangements and a unified sound. All I can say is that it was trial-by-ordeal, and the craziest period of our lives. We went four or five weeks without sleep, doing a lot of drugs. I'm talking about cocaine in such quantities that at one point I thought I was really going insane. The whole atmosphere was really tense, with arguments all the time and people storming in and out. To relieve the tension we'd look for sexual release, but even that didn't help much.

The only refuge was in the music. Music was the only release we could find. At one point, things got so tense between us all that I remember sleeping right under the sound board one night because I felt it was the only safe place to be. The workdays would drag on for eighteen to twenty hours, and eventually the amount of cocaine began to do damage. You'd do what you thought was your best work, and then come back next day; it would sound terrible, so you'd rip it all apart and start again.

And yet – I turn on the radio today and they're *still* playing that album. It took a long time, but our system worked for us. Our attitude is: if that's what it took, so be it.

The work itself was difficult enough. Trying to pull it all together in the midst of an emotional holocaust was really outrageous. John and Chris were only barely speaking to each other. Stevie was upset and confused, because she was the one who had walked out on Lindsey, who in turn was pretty down until he decided he didn't want to be unhappy and alone and started getting some girlfriends together. This upset Stevie even more. There were many ill-concealed arguments and floods of tears. Then John took up with Sandra, who had been Peter Green's girlfriend, which bothered Chris who still had feelings for John. Oh God, it was a real bloody soap opera, I'll tell you. And I was piggy-in-the-middle, the grand mediator between the warring parties, and the father figure whose job it was to urge on the troops. 'We must carry on,' I could hear myself saying. 'C'mon, let's be mature about this. Let's sort it out. We've got work to do.' Yet piggy had raw feelings of his own, because Jenny had come back to Los Angeles and taken up with our old friend Andy Sylvester, who had been the bass player in Chicken Shack, my flatmate back in Ealing, and then our room-mate in Kensington Church Street. Later Andy had migrated to Los Angeles, and when Jenny returned she and the kids moved in with Andy near Fairfax. Ah, the pain I felt. He was one of my best friends. It was like she had left me for my younger brother. I remember talking to Andy on the phone from Sly Stone's pit. 'Andy, whatever you do, take good care of them.' The same old lines that people say in these situations. I was terribly upset, not doing well at all. I got off the phone and was called back into Studio B to lay down a drum track.

And the atmosphere kept getting nuttier. It was like a cocktail party all the time. The studio was full of weirdos we'd never seen before, partying with each other while we tried to work. And we were certainly doing our fair share of the old powder. There was one coke dealer who kept us supplied with high-grade Peruvian flake, and we were so grateful to him that I considered (in my state of dementia) giving him some kind of credit on the album jacket. Unfortunately he got snuffed – executed – before the thing came out.

Then there was the Thousand Dollar Cookie Session. Stevie's girl-friend Robin had prepared some fresh hashish brownies. Be careful, they said, these things are really strong. But the band ignored the advertised potency and gobbled freely. We spent the night in such a bent condition that not a note was played and the engineers went home. John and Stevie spent hours huddled in a corner, giggling like mad over a copy of *Playboy*.

We spent two months completely obsessed with getting it right. At one point we wasted four expensive days *trying to tune a piano*! It seemed that the piano in Studio B wouldn't stay in tune, and Fleetwood Mac had always been picky about tuning. So we called in a guy we dubbed the Looner Tuner, a man with all these tattoos who somehow couldn't manage to get the thing the way we wanted it. We got even more obsessive and brought in a blind guy to tune the thing, and it still didn't sound right. Then we went through about nine different pianos, and then we ended up not using any of those piano tracks anyway. Another time we spent days working on the drum sound, at one point gaffer-taping two bass drums together into one long tube in an attempt to capture the tone we were searching for.

Then there was Jaws. This was a nickname that we gave to a tape machine that acquired an appetite for eating (and destroying) fresh takes. And yet there were some triumphs in all this. I vividly remember the night Stevie cut 'Gold Dust Woman'. We'd been in Sausalito for a month, and were beginning to get urgent phone calls from Warner Brothers, who were wondering how we were doing. We didn't want to tell them that we were beset by romantic turmoil and that the only thing holding us together was a thread of Mac family cohesion. For me it was Stevie, physically the most fragile of us all, who exemplified the drive to create and prevail. I recall that she did her first vocal track of 'Gold Dust Woman' in a fully-lit studio. The song needed both a mysterious power and a lot of emotion. As take followed take, Stevie began to withdraw into herself, reaching inside for the magic. The lights were dimmed; a chair was brought in so she could sit, saving her strength at three in the morning, and she wrapped herself in a big cardigan to ward off the pre-dawn chill. An hour later she was almost invisible in the shadows, elfin-like under big headphones, hunched over in her chair, alternately choosing from her supply of tissues, a Vicks inhaler, a box of lozenges for her sore throat, and a bottle of mineral water. Gradually she gained total command of her song. On the eighth take, exhausted but exalted, she sang the lyric straight through to perfection.

After nine weeks of this, we were all ready for the asylum. Lindsey was getting frustrated and agitated about the state of the sessions. He had strong ideas about how he wanted us to sound; there were major disagreements about who was running things. (The truth was that no one was running things.) Late one night I sat him down on the floor of the studio and talked to him. I said, Lindsey, it comes down to this: either you're in a band or you're not. It's neither good nor bad. If you accept the fact that you're working with other people, then that's great. But if you don't accept that fact, then you shouldn't be in the band. We looked at each other hard for a long, long moment. I know that, to each other, we both looked haggard and burned out. But the matter was resolved, and we continued.

There was one incident above all that convinced me our time in Sausalito had to end. Everyone was completely fried, but it was John McVie who showed me the way.

We used to get up at eight o'clock at night and make our way to the studio. One night I arrived and found John there on his own, trying to get a bass part right. I looked carefully, rubbed my eyes, and could not believe what I saw. There was tough, brutally cynical John staring at this picture of the notorious teenage guru, 'perfect master' Maharaji. He was kneeling down in front of the console, concentrating on this guru and trying to nail his bass part. This, I thought, is not our John at all. He's snapped. His mind has finally left him. John McVie – playing and praying at the same time. I took this as a guiding signal. We'd been in Sausalito long enough. It was time to take our tracks, get out, and go home.

Just before we left the Record Plant, I had a strange premonition. We were sitting around the studio, playing the rough cassette mixes of the work we'd done. *Fleetwood Mac* had gone platinum, and there was the usual concern and fear about whether this follow-up would do as well. When the tape ran out, I said that this new album was going to do much better, that it could even sell as many as eight or nine million copies if our momentum held. The others laughed, and someone touched wood.

The strange thing is that this turned out to be a very conservative guess.

Exhausted, the torn and frayed members of Fleetwood Mac filtered back to their homes in Los Angeles and took a few days off. When we gathered again to listen to the tapes of the work we'd done in Sausalito, we were aghast at how awful they sounded. The tapes sounded . . . *strange*. We tried switching speakers and then switched studios, but they still sounded bad to us. It was suggested that the cursed 'Jaws' tape machine had somehow ruined them, and deep depression set in. For a while it looked like we were going to have to start all over again.

Then someone found a mixing room in the Hollywood Boulevard porno strip where the tapes sounded . . . well, good enough to work with. It was there, between sleazy theatres playing films like *Dick City* and *Squirm*, that the new album was moulded. All the Sausalito tracks were stripped down to the drum tracks and we started to dub new instrumental parts and vocals. Once again, the inaudible sound of breaking hearts filled the psychic air. The three writers – Chris, Stevie and Lindsey – continued to communicate with each other via their new songs. 'It was very clumsy sometimes,' John McVie remembers. 'I'd be sitting there in the studio while they were mixing "Don't Stop", and I'd listen to the words which were mostly about me, and I'd get a lump in my throat. I'd turn around and the writer's sitting right there.'

This time, though, to achieve some of the intimacy required to edit and mix what would become an extremely intimate album, we closed the studio doors to friends and foes alike. We also postponed a fully-booked tour to allow the creative process ample time to mature. This process began in mid-March of 1976. By early June we were hip deep into the project, and the end was not in sight. 'The Chain' was still a hodge-podge of several different riffs and songs. 'Don't Stop', written for John by Chris, was half-finished. 'I Don't Want to Know' was rerecorded at Wally Heider's studio. Chris wrote 'Oh Daddy' for me, the only dad in the band. 'Songbird' was recorded in an empty university auditorium in Berkeley with a mobile unit. I said it should sound like Chris is sitting alone at the piano after a concert, when everyone has gone home.

At that point, we had to leave off recording for a while and go out on the road for most of the summer. *Fleetwood Mac* was *still* climbing the charts, a year after release, and it looked to us like we could give our chartbursting fellow British blues exile Peter Frampton a run for his money if we had another hit single and our summer tour with the Eagles did well. To this end, we released Chris's 'Say You Love Me' in June (the flip was 'Monday Morning') and it too went right to the top.

Rehearsals for the summer tour began on 4 June and lasted ten days. Six months of studio frustration and claustrophobia were unleashed, and the band roared as I'd never heard it before. Off we went on 18 June, opening at Royals Stadium in Kansas City. This leg of the tour consisted of three acts – us, Henry Gross and Jeff Beck. Then to the Omaha Arena, the Iowa State Fairgrounds, the Pine Knob Music Theater in Michigan, then all around Wisconsin, Minnesota, North Dakota, and Illinois. On 29 June we played Busch Stadium in St Louis with Jefferson Starship, Jeff Beck and Ted Nugent. Then to Riverfront Colosseum in Cincinnati.

A bunch of big outdoor shows supporting the red-hot Eagles began on 2 July at the Greensboro Colosseum. The next day we played the Omni in Atlanta. On the American Bicentennial – 4 July 1976 – we played Tampa Stadium with the Eagles; this was truly a gig I'll never forget. As I looked out into the crowd that packed the massive field and stands, I beheld hundreds – no, *thousands* – of girls dressed exactly like Stevie in black chiffon dresses and top hats; Stevie's stage costume. At the point in our set when Lindsey began to play the guitar intro to 'Rhiannon' and Stevie walked out and intoned, 'This is a song about a Welsh witch,' these girls went mad, swaying and singing and giving themselves to the music, to Stevie, and to the spirit of the ancient Celtic goddess. By now, with the success of the single, 'Rhiannon' had become one of the focal points of the set. Graceful and mysterious in her diaphanous chiffon, Stevie's dance sent us into a dimension that can only be described as mystic. I would look at her, dancing with her eyes closed, and I could see *she was in heaven.*

By reading our reviews I could see that a lot of people were jumping in and reading all sorts of stuff into this performance. Only nine months earlier, Stevie's reviews were so bad she thought about leaving the band. But now the critics were calling her the most compelling woman in rock music. And I felt the same way. I began to develop a real rapport and friendship with Stevie, and did all I could to spend as much time with her as possible.

In any case, people got very excited about 'Rhiannon', and it stopped the show every time we performed it.

After another show with the Eagles in Jacksonville, we took a week off to do more work on our new album at Criteria Studios in Miami. We arrived just after Bob Marley had finished mixing his *Rastaman Vibration* album there, and the studio still smelled of sweet Jamaican ganja smoke.

Here my private life began to get very confused. I was very friendly with Stevie, and at the same time I began to regret my split with Jenny. I missed her familiar presence and her warmth, and when I contemplated the distance between me and my daughters I began to feel ill. So I called Jenny and begged her to bring the girls to Florida for a holiday. To my great relief, she said she would come. We had a nice family reunion, and although few of our differences were resolved, we joked that our divorce might fail the way our marriage had.

My parents, Mike and Biddy, came over from England to join the tour as well. By then I had made about a half-million dollars from the success of *Fleetwood Mac*, and one of the ways I enjoyed these riches was to fly my parents over to see me and then send them on to Hawaii for ten days. That's really when it began to hit me that we were doing well, that we were 'making it'. Mike and Biddy loved being on tour with Fleetwood Mac. They had always been a family of gypsies, moving about, and they mucked in right away, taking care of people and picking up bags and luggage. Having them on the road made the road feel like it was home.

We spent the rest of that summer on tour. The Spectrum in Philadelphia. The Brown County Arena in Green Bay. Mile High Stadium, Denver. Three Rivers Stadium in Pittsburgh. We played a lot with the Eagles and Loggins and Messina, as well as the Beach Boys, The Band, Steve Miller, Firefall, (the late) Tommy Bolin, and Santana (they played 'Black Magic Woman', we didn't). Mostly things went great.

We had a hot record, the audiences were wonderful, and we knew we had a big winner in the can. However, I do remember that the tension between Stevie and Lindsey was very real. They were still negotiating their personal adjustments to each other while touring in a band and making a record. Oh, the sparks, and how they did fly! Feelings were running so raw between those two that the slightest word or look could set off an emotional cyclone. In those days Stevie was still quite dependent on Lindsey to provide musical direction and settings for her songs, and she resented this dependence.

'Well, *that* doesn't work,' Lindsey would comment sarcastically when she tried something of hers that didn't sound right to him. 'Why don't we do it *this* way.' He'd play something on the piano, and she would just glare at him furiously. I'd try to intervene, 'Stevie, what's the matter?'

'Oh, nothing,' she said. 'I just feel like my music has been hijacked, that's all.' Lindsey would lose patience and storm out of the studio, or he'd say something caustic and Stevie would leave in a flurry of recriminations and tears.

It all boiled down to Lindsey's lingering resentment that Stevie had left him, while Stevie feared that her music would lose its appeal without Lindsey's guiding hand. In addition, Lindsey felt jealous, since new men were being drawn to the now-single Stevie like honeybees to a gorgeous, pollen-laden blossom. And the fact that Stevie was being courted by the Eagles' Don Henley didn't really help matters. He had called earlier, asking to meet her. They talked on the phone a few times, but hadn't met when Fleetwood Mac played our first show with Henley's band. So we get to our dressing room in Greensboro and are told the Eagles are in the next dressing room. Stevie, who is quite shy, wasn't at all the type to go over and introduce herself. So when she enters the dressing room she sees a huge bouquet of roses and a card, which read: 'The best of my love . . . Tonight? Love, Don.'

Stevie was furious. She thought it was the least cool approach anyone had ever made in the history of romance. They hadn't even met! She was really pissed off, flushed with anger. She didn't notice me and McVie, collapsed in the corner with hysterical laughter. Finally, Christine had to take Stevie aside. Don didn't send that note, Chris said. Mick and John did. It was a while before Stevie felt like talking to either of us again.

The San Diego Sports Arena, Wednesday, 25 August 1976, 10 p.m.

Rick Roberts and Firefall have finished their set. The houselights dim and we take our stage positions in darkness. A shower of bright light, and we open with our current hit single, 'Over My Head'. Then John steps to the stagefront and blasts out his classic punchy bass line to 'Station Man'. From behind my drum kit I try to crack him up with weird faces, but he pays no attention. Lindsey, in jeans and a cream-coloured kimono top, takes the lead, filling in his usual sparkling, folkish riffs. The crowd loves his playing, and applauds every lick.

Halfway through the show it's time for the dance of Rhiannon. A spotlight catches the foxy tinted-green streak in Stevie's hair. The billowy, ultra-feminine dancing is really only part of it. Lindsey's screaming lead guitar is just as important in establishing the mood of ecstatic, pagan romance the song conveys. Stevie's howling voice competes with the guitar, and usually wins, leaving her sated and temporarily spent.

Now Chris takes over with 'Why' and 'You Make Loving Fun'. Then Stevie moves behind my kit, while Lindsey works out Peter Green's vintage 'Green Manalishi', which he and John turn into a rocking duet of their own. Now it's my spot, 'World Turning'. Chris steps out from behind her keyboards, playing maracas and singing the chorus with Stevie and Lindsey. I polish off a quick beer for courage, and suddenly I'm out in front of this big hall, a gangly figure in my black vest and usual plus-fours, making the talking drum rumble and squawk, pounding the rhythm with one stamping foot. I look up to see the kids swirling in front of the stage in their own oceanic dance as 'World Turning' picks them up and sweeps them along.

Suddenly, the show is over. We've been playing our brains out for ninety minutes, but it seems like half that. (Other nights it seems like twice that!) The two encores are 'Don't Let Me Down' and 'Hypnotized'. Bob Welch is in the audience tonight, and I hope he likes the way we do his song.

Backstage after the show. We refresh ourselves, as John Courage keeps admirers at bay. A few minutes later I see Stevie trying to slip away, stopping to speak to several ardent fans, as she always does. One girl presses five turquoises into her hand and whispers, 'For everyone in the band.' Another girl slips a large silver bracelet onto her wrist. Then Stevie settles into a waiting limousine and is gone, on her way to our hotel on Harbour Island. Other fans, waiting outside, run after her car, hoping just to touch it. That girl, I say to McVie and Courage, is going to be a very big star.

Finally, on 4 September 1976, *Fleetwood Mac* inched ahead of *Frampton Comes Alive* and emerged as the number one album in *Billboard* magazine's chart. At last! After fifty-six weeks on the chart, the last few at number two. We stayed on top for one week, but it was all we needed to feel like we were the greatest. It gave us immeasurable confidence, and provided all the more reason to finish our new album, which we had decided to call *Yesterday's Gone*, after a line in 'Don't Stop'. Like everything else on the face of the planet, this too would change.

Here a word about Seedy Management. This was the company established by John McVie and myself to look after Fleetwood Mac. Located at 1420 North Beechwood Drive in Hollywood, this office, run by Judy Wong and several other employees, was the nerve centre of the band and the parent company of Penguin Promotions, which oversaw touring; Limited Management, which handled other artists; and our publishing business, Gentoo Music and Rockhopper Music.

I derived endless satisfaction from knowing that our self-managed success was the hardest thing for people in the music business to accept. Before, the Industry Heavies would come up and say, 'You'll never make it without us.' Now they'd say, 'You *really* need us now, you can't possibly keep it up without us.' And I'd laugh, because I knew that if we had gone through our recent calamities under the 'guidance' of some disinterested party, the band would have split. With the band running its own show, we couldn't take sides. The band was responsible to itself, and we were too smart to commit suicide. No manager could have stayed out of what we went through. I took pride in all this. We ran a doctored photo in the music trades showing a smiling Fleetwood Mac standing around me and John dressed in pimp hats, pinky rings, and zoot suits with large bills sticking out of the pockets. The caption said that the band was proud to be signing with Seedy Management. Another prank photo showed me and John standing outside a pawn shop, having lost our pants, carrying our gold records to trade for quick cash.

Later that month we participated in a nationally televised event, Don Kirschner's Rock Awards. The whole set-up was very Hollywood, all glitter and hype, but we'd been on tour for months and I thought it would be okay for us to get a little public recognition. This event hit different people in different ways. After getting awards for Best Group and Best Album, we went to a party at some hotel and stayed about half an hour. In the limo on the way to the hotel, Chris looked at me in disbelief and asked, 'Does this mean we're stars?' The question was so innocent and sweet, and so full of disbelief.

Stevie Nicks, she told me later, was scared. Why? I asked. She said that after the show, she got in her limo with her brother Chris and drove home. We'd just got these awards, just been on television, just got a lot of applause and everyone was singing our praises. And what did all this make her feel?

Lonely, she said. She said she knew how Marilyn Monroe must have felt.

Meanwhile, our record company was clamouring for our new album. They wanted it badly.

As manager, I took these calls. I explained that the basic tracks were finished, and that the material was very strong; but we were now working on making what was good even better, and then better and better. And the company was very good about it. They called and asked to hear some of the tracks, and I told them, quite firmly, that they weren't hearing anything until we had finished. They asked, do you realize how much money you're spending? And we did. We were completely aware that we were spending a *fortune*. And that, to my mind, was the advantage of not having an outside manager. If we had someone hustling us, and hassling about the money, we would have been too intimidated to wait until we had got it right. As musicians and players, we did it our way.

As the recording sessions began to wind down, we took ten days off in October 1976 and went to London for a week with the European Press. Waiting for us as we straggled into the lobby of the Montcalm Hotel was a scruffy and unattractive character with wild long hair. He was carrying a big cassette player blaring disco at top volume, had a beer in his hand, and seemed to know us. We looked closer. It was Peter Green.

We were shocked. No one had seen him in years. The one-time Green God had turned into a flabby ex-hippie, dissolute and dishevelled. 'Aren't you embarrassed?' Chris asked him.

'Naw,' Pete said. 'I mean, fuck it. What the hell.'

We couldn't believe it. We didn't quite know what to do, so he stayed at the hotel with us for a few nights. He'd knock at your door, sit on your bed, and not say anything. We were *so* brought down by this, and appalled that in our time of triumph we should be so terribly reminded of the fragility of life as we were living it. There, but for fortune . . .

But not since the heady days of Fleetwood Mac's meteoric success in 1969 had we been so fawned over by members of the European press – which was nice because they had been resolutely ignoring us ever since. We huddled with French, Dutch, German and Scandinavian journalists and radio people, all of them quite enthusiastic. It was a good omen that the reborn Mac had an audience outside the United States.

But we – at least the English members of our little troupe – were in for a rude awakening when we staggered groggily off our night flight from London, back at LAX. There the immigration authorities put us through hell and scared the daylights out of us. John, Chris, Colonel Courage and myself were still British subjects who had arrived on tourist visas years earlier. It's no exaggeration that we barely got back into America. They almost deported us.

So Mickey Shapiro had to embark on the process of getting us our crucial 'green cards', which would confer immigrant status on us and allow us to work legally in the land of the free and the home of the brave. This proved to be a substantial problem. Some of us had juvenile marijuana arrests back in England. We couldn't lie about it, as it would violate the statute and cause immediate deportation if it were discovered. So a tremendous paper shuffle occurred. First Jenny and I had to get married again, so she, Amy and Lucy would be legal as well. Neither of us was exactly thrilled at this prospect, but we were dutifully re-wed, six months after our divorce, with Lindsey Buckingham serving as best man. Actually, though Mickey had insisted that we follow this course only as a legal formality, I was happy to be reunited with my family. We bought a lovely house high up over Topanga Canyon – my first real plunge into the *Fleetwood Mac* bootie – that featured a stunning view and plenty of privacy. To this we added a couple of new rooms, a little recording studio, and a miniature house for the girls. We were starting to make some real money now. It was nice to be able to bring in a top decorator and tell her, quite breezily, to do this and that and bill my business manager.

Fortunately for our immigration problems, Mickey Shapiro happened to know Senator Birch Bayh, the powerful Democratic committee chairman from Indiana. Mickey persuaded the good senator that Fleetwood Mac was a decent and hardworking bunch, and the senator said he'd be happy to put in a good word for us to the proper authorities. Indeed, around that time John and Chris and I attended a nine a.m. meeting in Senator Bayh's chambers in the Old Senate office building in Washington. We were in our stage clothes, having not yet been to bed from the previous night.

We were ushered into the office and introduced to a brace of nervous and awestruck senior immigration officials. And not long afterwards, the green cards came through. We were, of course, elated at having been spared the long and demeaning process of immigration hearings in Los Angeles. By then, we'd been off the road for three months, but we still wanted to show our gratitude to our friend. So, after two days of rehearsal at Pirate Sound on North Beechwood Drive, we embarked upon what we called 'The Penguin Country Benefit Safari'. This was a 5 December Fleetwood Mac show at Market Square Arena in Indianapolis in aid of the senator's campaign debt.

Meanwhile, as 1976 drew to a close, our career began to accelerate. In November our three-year-old album *Mystery To Me* went gold; sales had been substantially goosed by increased airplay of 'Hypnotized'. Then, as we wrapped up our new album, John McVie came up with a new title for the record.

Rumours.

It was brilliantly apt. It seemed at the time that everyone in the music business in southern California had the exclusive inside dope about the secret lives of Fleetwood Mac, and no one hesitated to circulate the most scurrilous tales. They said that Stevie was sleeping with me; that Christine had run off with Lindsey; that Stevie was seeing both John and me on alternate Wednesdays; that violent fistfights were commonplace in the studio; that Stevie was definitely leaving the band next Friday; that Stevie had left us months ago and this was the reason the new album had been delayed; that we were all crippled by massive quantities of alcohol and cocaine; that Stevie practised black magic and led a coven of witches in the Hollywood Hills; that Fleetwood Mac was a burnt-out case. Tales of flamboyant infidelity and dementia circulated like polluted air. So rampant were the rumours that sometimes we heard them fifth hand, got worried, and had to call each other up to make sure we were still sane and in touch. So we thought to call the album *Rumours* would have a nice touch of allure, interlaced with a healthy dose of irony.

In the studio, we had been overdubbing so much that our master tapes literally began to wear out. Lindsey and Richard Dashut and Ken Caillat fought constant battles against the music's 'high end' dropping out after hundreds of hours of over-dubs.

By the time the album was finished, all the original parts had been replaced except for the drums. Yet our production team managed to perform this technical wizardry with such skill that the finished record sounds seamless. The most blatant example of this process was a song that originated back in Sausalito. Pieces of unrelated music were spliced into verse, chorus and bridge, for which Stevie wrote the lyrics. This number later became known as 'The Chain'.

In early December, we sequenced the album. Lindsey's 'Second Hand News' opened, followed by Stevie's 'Dreams', Lindsey's 'Never Going Back Again', Chris's 'Don't Stop' (written for John), Lindsey's aggressive 'Go Your Own Way' and Chris's 'Songbird'. 'The Chain' opened side two, followed by Chris's 'You Make Loving Fun', Stevie's 'I Don't Want To Know', Chris's 'Oh Daddy' (written for me), and Stevie's 'Gold Dust Woman'. We also had several tracks that were left off *Rumours*, including Stevie's mysterious song 'Silver Springs'. This we released as the B-side of 'Go Your Own Way', the first single from *Rumours*, issued just prior to Christmas. By early 1977 American radio was playing the shit out of the record, which quickly made the top ten, and then our lives began to change forever.

We shipped 800,000 copies of *Rumours* to record dealers in February 1977. At the time, it was the largest advance order in the history of Warner Brothers Records. The cover depicted me and Stevie in our stage clothes, she in black chiffon and ballet shoes, me with my wooden balls hanging. In my left hand I hold the same crystal ball juggled by McVie on the cover of *Fleetwood Mac*.

Had that crystal brought us good luck? *Fleetwood Mac* had by then been on the charts for eighty weeks, sold four million copies and become the company's all-time best-selling album.

Within a month, helped by massive airplay on the new soft-rock FM radio formats that were springing up around America, *Rumours* began to climb the charts, and the press began to spotlight some of the traumas and travails we'd been undergoing. *Rolling Stone* put us on its cover in bed with each other. Chris and Lindsey were snuggled together under a sheet. Stevie and I cuddled in the middle. John kept his jeans on and is seen perusing a nudie magazine. Even though there was much heartbreak at the time, we still somehow managed to laugh at ourselves.

In the meantime, we at Seedy Management [Penguin Promotions division] had been planning our conquest of the planet on behalf of *Rumours* for some time. To that end, Fleetwood Mac convened at a rehearsal hall on Cahuenga Boulevard on 4 February and rehearsed every day for a month. The shows on the *Rumours* tour would begin with 'Say You Love Me' and run through songs from both albums. Lindsey would perform 'Oh Well'. 'Go Your Own Way' would begin the encores, and the show would close with 'Songbird'. Despite emotional hardships, psychic ju-jitsu, and not having played regularly in months, the band sounded great. Stevie's voice was a little raw; she had shredded her vocal chords singing the shit out of 'Rhiannon' the previous year, and the fragility of her throat caused us to cancel several weeks' worth of gigs later on.

We spent the month of March playing around America, mostly big halls that seated from ten to fifteen thousand. Audiences were rabid in the West and the South. The Jefferson Colisseum in Birmingham, Alabama, former Buckingham Nicks stronghold, had sold out in an hour. Likewise the Spectrum in Philadelphia, the Nassau Colisseum, the Hartford Civic Center. Everywhere we encountered Stevie's adoring fans, lovely girls in chiffon and witchy hats, who swayed and waved and sang along with Stevie on all her songs. One of the craziest audiences we encountered was a hall of 9000 naval cadets at Annapolis. When they saw Stevie walk on stage, the roar was *inhuman*.

By the end if March, *Rumours* was a platinum record, having sold a million copies in its first month of release.

On April Fools' Day, we released our second single. 'Go Your Own Way' had been a top ten record. Now Stevie's song 'Dreams' would go to number one and help to launch *Rumours* into the ionosphere.

That same day, we flew to England for a series of shows in mid-sized 3000-seaters, only half-prepared for what we would find, Fleetwood Mac having been forgotten by British rock fans these past several years. Instead we found enthusiastic old fans and a newer gang turned on by Stevie and Lindsey. We also found that Peter Green had been committed to a mental hospital for a heavily publicized incident the previous December.

For the previous five years, since leaving the band, Pete had been receiving about £30,000 a year in composers' royalties. Now he wanted the money stopped (as he later told a magistrate), because he wanted to remove all vestiges of his former life. So Pete took a pump-action rifle and went to see Clifford Davies, who was now doing business under his real name, Clifford Addams, in Paddington. Pete marched into the office and told Clifford that he wanted his royalty payments suspended and threatened to shoot out the windows. Addams called the police and Pete wound up in prison. In January, his doctors filed reports that convinced the judge to send him to hospital rather than back to jail. All we could do was shake our heads, having already spilled enough tears over Pete. We felt we'd done our share of crying.

So, early in April, the 1977 Penguin Country Safari roared through some of Fleetwood Mac's ancient native venues – Birmingham, Glasgow, Manchester, Bristol. Sure enough, when we reached London to play the Rainbow Theatre on 8 April, there waiting for us was Pete. But it wasn't the Peter Green we had known.

Coming home to London and playing for our original fans was extremely special and very moving for John and Chris and myself. Stevie and Lindsey were very aware of our feelings, acknowledging onstage that this was a magical moment for the veterans in the band. Two years after we had left our familiar lives in England to take our chances in California, we returned home with banners waving and heads held high. Peter Green was even persuaded to attend the victory party that our label threw for us, although our founder couldn't bring himself to attend the concert.

While we were in London we also put out feelers for Jeremy Spencer. Back in 1975, he'd been seen in London with the Children of God, selling literature on the street and telling strangers he'd once been in a band called Fleetwood Mac. We'd also heard he had put together a band he had called Albatross. We sent out people to look for him, but Jeremy couldn't be found; later we received word that he was still with the Children of God at their headquarters in Italy.

And then we were off again, to France, Holland, Germany and Sweden, places where the name Fleetwood Mac still meant the blues. It was our pleasant duty to show them our new tricks and change their minds.

We took ten days off after our European sojourn and scattered to our homes. Jenny and I were still sharing restive domesticity up in Topanga Canyon. John brooded on his 41-foot boat in the marina. Chris was living with Curry Grant at her house above Sunset. Stevie was in her new house on Doheny, while Lindsey and Richard Dashut shared a house in Beverly Hills. Then it was back to work on the second leg of the *Rumours* tour, twenty-five cities in the mid-west and northeast. By this time, most of our troupe *hated* being on the road. As we hopped from Arena to Coliseum to Bowl to Dome to Stadium to Garden to Civic Center, we devised all sorts of ways to lighten the heavy psychic load of performance on little rest. Each band member had his/her own limo. Even Dashut and Grant had their own limo on this tour, as befitted their exalted responsibilities of *son et lumière*.

Our contracts with promoters carried an exhaustive refreshment rider, specifying in minute detail what kind of food and drink we required backstage. It was on this tour that Fleetwood Mac acquired its image of being a *de luxe* organization; yet it was a reputation we cultivated without apology, and it was true that whenever possible, we went first class all the way.

The high hopes and countless hours we had poured into *Rumours* were completely validated when the album slipped into the number one position on 21 May 1977, displacing *Hotel California* by our colleagues and friendly rivals, the Eagles. *Rumours* stayed at number one on the *Billboard* and *Cashbox* charts for the next eight months, a total of thirty-one straight weeks. During this period we stayed on the road, advertised heavily, and kept releasing irresistible singles by Christine – 'Don't Stop' over the summer (which got to the top three) and 'You Make Loving Fun' the following autumn (also a top ten record). Suddenly, as manager of the band, I found myself described in the press as the sullen and menacing svengali of Fleetwood Mac. I tried to explain to interviewers that nothing could be further from the truth. Fleetwood Mac, I'd explain, was more a way of life than a business. To us, success came as a pleasant surprise, not a vindication after years of worry over low sales figures. We never cared about how many records we sold, we just wanted to get out and play. I'd explain that it was just like going to the office for us, and that our job, *our duty*, had always been to play through all the ups and downs. That's how I felt in 1977. I still feel that way today.

During a June break in the tour, we again took time off to indulge in some extra-curricular activities. Lindsey and Stevie had worked on an album by their friend Walter Egan, and were currently helping guitarist Warren Zevon with his. (Both John McVie and myself played on Warren's record.) I had decided some time before to take Bob Welch's career in hand. I felt strongly that Bob was a wonderful musician whose best work hadn't surfaced in Paris, the name of the trio he had formed after leaving us two years before. Bob had written twenty songs and collaborated on three more while he was with us between 1971 and 1974. There was no doubt in my mind that, given the right presentation, he could have a hit record and take part in some of the rewards that were now coming our way after such hard travail. This was the heyday of Fleetwood Mac – full-on work, touring, airplay, success. We felt like we were on the old coaster heading up, and I wanted Bob to be in on this ride.

We had earlier set up a Seedy subsidiary called Limited Management, to look after Bob and a couple of other fledgling clients. A record deal was procured, and Bob proceeded to make *French Kiss*, which indeed became a hit when released that autumn. Containing some great songs ('Outskirts', 'Danchiva', 'Hot Love, Cold World') the record also had a new version of 'Sentimental Lady' on which Lindsey played while we were working up in Canada.

We went back on the road on 25 June, playing a month of massive outdoor shows with the Eagles, Boz Scaggs and others. I loved this part of the tour, because my parents came along and their enthusiasm – 'The Wingco's here!' – cheered us all up. My father was especially taken with the extravagance of the tour. He was quite amused by our spending thousands on a giant inflatable penguin, full zeppelin sized, which was supposed to float over the band at these big outdoor events. It would have been a full seventy-feet tall, had it ever worked. Actually it did work once in Florida, but that was the end of it. Later Dad sent me a postcard that simply stated the obvious.

'Penguins don't fly.'

Not everything was totally fabulous, as I recall. There were dark moments when the tremendous tensions and the inability to separate personal and business lives erupted into fierce battles, but the band never once let it affect the live shows. Perhaps as a result, our cocaine intake skyrocketed. The drug was rationed, according to our system, with people getting their supply at showtime in Heineken bottle caps. Lives were torn and frayed by the topsy-turvy of the road. The peak of our working day came after the shows, between midnight and one, when the rest of the world slumbered in their own beds. We were students of dislocation. All we wanted to know was, how's the coffee shop in the next hotel? And how late does room service serve?

There were also concerns for Stevie's instrument. Singing with her throat rather than her diaphragm, she began to have problems, and her voice changed into a lower register. Was this caused by overwork? I don't know, but we took her friend Robin Anderson, a voice therapist, on the road with us to try to train Stevie to use her voice differently. But it was like trying to tame a wild thing. Every night, at the climactic end of 'Rhiannon', Stevie would rip her voice to shreds. It was a sacrifice she chose to make.

We then rested for a few weeks. By the time we went back out, during the last week of August, *Rumours* had already sold four million copies. It was double platinum in Britain and selling well all over the world. Yet for me, with good times came bad as well. We were playing the Aladdin Theater in Las Vegas when I got a call from my mother on 25 August 1977. I'll never forget how it felt when she told me that my dad had been diagnosed as having cancer, and that the prognosis was not good. Mother told me that Dad was declining conventional chemotherapy treatment, preferring to use other, more holistic ways to fight the disease.

On this somewhat devastating note, we next went to Tuscon, where Fleetwood Mac played a heart benefit organized by Stevie's father, Jess Nicks, beginning a long professional association with Jess that the band has really enjoyed. Then we did three sold-out nights at the Forum, at home in Los Angeles. Fleetwood Mac always played a little tougher and sharper for the home-town audience – like all bands. I still think those Forum shows during the *Rumours* era were some of the best the band ever gave.

In September we went up to the Pacific Northwest, and from there to western Canada. It was there the old Veal Viper got me into trouble.

My basic premise has always been that I'm not a pig on the road. I've never chased girls in my life. Of course I've had one or two, but they were supplied or seduced by their own dreams rather than myself. My usual after-show posture was a position I call *Transcension*: prone on bed with bottle(s) of beer and good sounds on the box, friends in the room, TV on, sound off.

Every time I ever tried to pull some girl, I got caught. Some rock star! Every fucking time! The lads would poke me and say, 'Go on Mick, she fancies you.'

Every time. Caught red-handed.

I think we were playing the Calgary Stampede, and we got drunk and wanted some women. We were too tired to go to a club, so we thought, let's get some call girls! No sooner said than done. Blind drunk, back to the hotel – which is in the process of undergoing some kind of riot. The memory of it fades in and out . . . nice black girl . . . *real* nice . . . I'm unzipping the old fly buttons, preparing to launch the One-Eyed Trouser Snake . . . and the phone rings!!!!

The blood in my veins ceased flowing for a trice, and then froze. I *shot* to the phone, pants flapping around ankles, but couldn't quite . . . get there in time. The girl picks up the phone on some insane impulse. ''Allo?'

It was Jenny.

I'm dying. Oh my God!!

'Who's that?' Jenny asks.

'Oh, a few people in the room after the gig.' But Jenny knew, of course. I was caught fair and square. Jenny was disappointed and angry. So I've learned it's just not worth it. I always suffer for it.

We continued at an exhausting pace through the autumn of that year. After twenty-three shows with only a day off here and there, travelling the length and breadth of the land, we were almost spent. Lindsey was so exhausted from fronting the band that he passed out in the shower in his Philadelphia hotel suite and was later diagnosed as having a mild form of epilepsy.

We finished the American leg of the *Rumours* tour and took a few days off in October, during which time Jenny moved us from rustic-but-removed Topanga to a New England colonial white clapboard home on Bellagio Drive in Bel Air. It was a lovely place that Jenny had found, on a quintessentially suburban street with a pool for the girls and multiple garages for my growing collection of automobiles. Mike and Biddy came to stay with us, and Jenny tried to find a therapist who could help my father with his illness.

I was a complete wreck.

Later that month, we released 'You Make Loving Fun', which immediately sold another two million copies of *Rumours*. After only ten days at home with the family, Fleetwood Mac took wing for our late autumn turn around the Pacific – Australia, New Zealand, Japan and Hawaii. It was on this tour that some of the accumulated effects of the romance and passion that accrues to life on the road caught up with me. It was in Australia that I really fell for Stevie Nicks.

Our affair actually began in LA even before we left for the Pacific. I'd sneak away from home to spend most of my time with Stevie, picking her up in one of my cars and driving along Mulholland. She was seeing a record executive and I was married and my parents were living with me, so everything was very secret, imbuing subsequent events with a kind of supercharged aura of romance. In the Antipodes this blossomed into a full-on love affair.

It started up in New Zealand. Late one night, after the concert, a Samoan limo driver took me and Stevie for a long cruise along mountains and ridgebacks at dawn. At one point we got out and walked a bit in silence, waiting for the sun to rise. There was a mist that turned to a gentle rain, soaking us to our skin.

We were driven back to our hotel room in a ferocious downpour, clinging to each other in the back of the car.

I said, 'I think I'd like to stay here tonight.'

Fleetwood Mac had been received in Australia with great fanfare and tumult. Everywhere we went – Sydney, Perth, Melbourne, Brisbane – the shows were sold out, the press was agog, and the fans delirious. When Stevie performed the rites of the Welsh witch, the kids went bonkers. Something about Australia – the climate, the people, the beer, the unbelievable landscape – made me want to settle there and be part of this last great frontier.

On to Japan, where Fleetwood Mac had been popular since the late sixties. At the Tokyo Budokan, Richard Dashut started a riot among the normally staid Japanese fans when he cranked Lindsey's guitar solo on 'Go Your Own Way' up to 120 decibels. Richard had been moving audiences all year by 'riding up' the guitar solos, but at the Budokan, the audience snapped and rushed the stage as the guitar filled their eardrums.

We returned to California early in December, to find that *Rumours* had passed the eight million mark in sales and showed no sign of slowing. It was still the number one album in the country, and was selling an estimated 800,000 copies every week!

Understanding the past relationship between Lindsey and Stevie, as a point of honour I went to tell Lindsey that I was in love with Stevie. However, my relationship with Stevie continued, awkwardly. I ran the gauntlet, trying to be in two places at once, fairly torn by guilt and responsibilities. The whole thing was kind of on and off, and that suited both of us, Stevie and myself.

CHAPTER EIGHT

Not That Funny

Stevie Nicks gave a gala New Year's Eve party at her house to welcome in 1978 and celebrate Fleetwood Mac's stunning victories of the year just past. Jenny and I went, all our friends were there, and in many ways it was the prime of that era when we all still felt like innocents, and triumph filled the air.

We were all agog and somewhat dazed by this . . . success. We were also prepared for it, especially McVie and myself, who remembered that we'd been huge in Britain once upon a time, and lost it. But the whole band felt so wonderful about the end result – *Rumours* would soon sell its ninth million copy – because we'd worked so hard to get that result. All that time, we knew what we were doing. The best part for us was that we still felt good as a band. Through everything, Fleetwood Mac was still a road band, and the trappings and trimmings just didn't affect us that much because we didn't have much time to think about it. We just carried on and played.

The difference this time was that now we were millionaires. I made approximately three million dollars from *Rumours*. The three writers made much more. *Rumours* was for a time the best-selling album in the history of the recording industry. Its sales were eventually surpassed only by the two soundtracks from *Saturday Night Fever* and *Grease*, and later by Michael Jackson's *Thriller*. Today, with sales of twenty million plus, *Rumours* still remains one of the best-selling records in history.

Our sales figures were validated for us both by the press and our peers. We swept the American Music Awards in January 1978. At the Grammy Awards that February we sat nervously while the presenters fumbled with the Album of the Year envelope. We thought award shows were horrible, but it was a chance to march in front of your generation and be recognized. We heard *Rumours* named Album of the Year and were thrilled. *Rolling Stone* put us on the cover (me in lascivious cheerleader drag) to commemorate our receiving their reader awards for Artist of the Year, Band of the Year, Best Album and Best Single ('Dreams'). To my great satisfaction, the Eagles and *Hotel California* came in second in all categories. Many theories again appeared in the press to explain Fleetwood Mac's enormous new audience. One held that our three singer/songwriters and their different voices kept the public from getting bored with a monolithic Big Mac sound. Another postulated that the group represented various deeply-engrained Anglo-American archetypes, with myself as the Public School Aristocrat, McVie as the English cloth-cap Working Class type, Christine as an English Rose from the Midlands, Stevie as the California Girl and Lindsey as Byronic Rock Star. Along these lines, I remember Stevie remarking, as she looked at the motley Mac about to take the stage of some stadium in various costumes comprising bits of Dodger uniforms, chiffon outfits, waistcoats and breeches, silks and bell-bottoms: 'This is weird. We all look like we're going to a different place.'

Most critics seemed to agree that our writers were producing hit songs that fitted into the modern romantic tradition established by the Beatles. But my favourite theory was that we were one of the first white groups since the Mamas and the Papas to successfully bring female voices into the context of rock music. We didn't sound like anyone else.

My life at that time was appropriately chaotic for the proprietor of what one London paper called 'far and away the most commercially successful rock band since the Beatles'. Running a rock band, managing Bob Welch, husband and father in ever-decreasing frequency, secret lover, budding real estate mogul, the son of a dying father, sideman to many musician friends, interviewee and spokesman for the group – all of these roles began to jingle in my head. Add to this my contracting a thoroughly unamusing case of severe hypo glycaemia (not enough sugar in the old blood), and a neo-Falstaffian intake of alcohol and cocaine, and what do you have?

Someone often described in the press as 'gruff', 'soft-spoken', 'unapproachable', 'heavily-bearded'. Such was my image in this era. Looking back now, I think it was my reality as well.

All I can say is that I was trying to live many different lives, and sometimes it worked and sometimes it didn't. Even my memories of this time, post-*Rumours*, are hazy, as if the borders between what I experienced and what I dreamed are indistinct.

I remember going to Hawaii by myself in February. I told Jenny I wanted to inspect some property I had bought on Maui, but the real reason was to visit Stevie, who was renting a house with her friend Sara Recor and another lady. They were supposed to meet my plane, but they had taken a dot of acid and gone to the wrong airport. We rendez-voused later at a restaurant, and then went to Stevie's place.

There were a bunch of hammocks on the beach in front of Stevie's house, and that evening we lay in them, swinging gently in the mid-Pacific zephyr, watching the stupefying purple sunset and dreaming of nothing but peace and serenity.

But all that was Maya, the illusion. Reality awaited me at home, the house on Bellagio with the red Ferrari in the driveway. My parents were visiting from England, and the Wing Commander, my beloved dad, was clearly in a bad way. My parents felt that the British doctors had been unhelpful and cool towards alternative cancer therapies. They had come to California in part to try and find a holistic treatment so Mike might have as much time as possible. Although they were hopeful, I was in despair about my inability to really help my dad out of this one. Seeing my father in this predicament sent me off the deep end. Unable to deal with this, leaving it all to Jenny, I started going mad – out all night, lots of cocaine, immersing myself in the band and all its works, trying to deny the crushing portent of my father's illness. Jenny took up the slack and rallied the family around Mike. In the course of finding an acupuncturist for Mike and exploring other treatments, Jenny stopped drinking herself, and the gap between us began once again to broaden.

One night at the house on Bellagio, my father sat me down to talk to me as his heir and the man of the family. I was dead drunk and almost in tears. He spoke about death and how sad he felt at the finality of it all. He told me how he wanted my mother taken care of, and what he wanted done with the voluminous amounts of poetry he was writing. When he finished speaking, my father looked up at me, only to hear me say, 'We don't have to discuss this now, Dad. There's plenty of time.' I just couldn't accept his impending death.

The image of a wheelchair now swims into focus. It's early spring, 1978. Bob Welch's *French Kiss* album has come out and the single, 'Ebony Eyes', is a hit. While auditioning players for Bob's touring band, I liked to whizz around the huge soundstage at SIR Studios in this lovely wheelchair I had bought. It was collapsible, well-made, and you could move around whilst sitting down, which appealed to me. In fact, you could do almost anything in it. There was also a certain sick humour involved, which upset a lot of people including my father, who felt it was decadent. But I loved the wheelchair. My father and my daughter Amy decided eventually that having the wheelchair around the house was in poor taste, so they destroyed it by pushing it down a flight of stairs into the basement, much as Richard Widmark did in that pinnacle of *film noir*, *Kiss of Death* (except his wheelchair had a little old lady in it).

Jenny and I flew off for a vacation on the island of Bora Bora in the south Pacific around then. The atmosphere in our house had become oppressive to us both, and we left the children with their grandparents in an attempt to get away from our problems for a while in order to sort them out. Amid the lush, tropical, sleepy atmosphere of this faraway paradise, we tried to talk about our marriage. We felt worn out, and we wearily realized that all the long separations, affairs and alcohol had taken their toll. I wanted to tell Jenny about my feelings for Stevie. But I was too afraid of losing her and the children, and I couldn't get the words out of my mouth. The truth was, I wanted to have my cake and eat it too.

So I returned to Los Angeles as confused as when I had left, but as soon as I plunged back into the bustling world of the band, my spirits improved. 'It's really Fleetwood Mac you're married to anyway,' Jenny had said while we were away, and she was right, and there was nothing I really wanted to do to change that situation.

Meanwhile, we were in the midst of fevered negotiations to play a concert in Russia, with American network-TV support, to benefit Unesco. We flew to Washington to meet with a delegation of Soviet diplomats, and John Courage made a couple of trips to Moscow to seek approval. It would have been the first time one of the big western rock bands ever played in the Soviet Union, but a political crisis in Afghanistan wiped out months of planning and the concert never worked out, much to our disappointment.

The attentive reader will recall that for the past four years, Fleetwood Mac had been engaged in cripplingly expensive and painful litigation with Clifford Davies over the sordid events of 1974 – Fake Mac, and all that.

All that was resolved on a cold English morning that spring. John

McVie, Mickey Shapiro and I sat in our West End solicitor's office, and there appeared our former manager. It was time to settle up. Clifford and McVie looked at each other darkly. If looks could kill, our ex-manager would have been brown bread. It was so vitriolic – there was so much hatred in the room one could cut it with a switchblade. Despite the cold, the office felt like a sauna bath after five minutes.

We could have spent another half-million dollars to fight for our publishing, but in the long run it was just too draining. I was starting to talk like a lawyer myself. As unsavoury as it felt giving anything to this man, we finally said, look, this is hurting us needlessly, let's just give it to the guy. Let's give him his fucking money and be done with him. He's won. Parliament had passed a new copyright bill, which fell in his favour, and to this day he still gets Fleetwood Mac's royalties from 'Albatross' and the other old hits. We in turn had our arrangement with our label restructured so future payments from old albums wouldn't be channelled through him. Thus one of the saddest episodes in the history of the music industry was finally laid to rest. When we walked out of that lawyer's office and into the bracing air, we felt like free men again.

I was still trying to run my married life, but being close to Stevie was a preoccupation for me. Finally Jenny was wise enough to realize that our remarriage was over. She sent my parents back to England before leaving herself. Nothing much was said. It was just understood by us all that this was the best thing for Jenny to do.

Jenny recalls:

At the time, I was getting healthier, and Mick was getting sicker. He couldn't help himself, and wouldn't let me try either. He was angry with me, and I felt it wasn't good for the children to see him like that. His parents saw what a state he was in, but he was their only son, and they didn't feel they could support me against him, so to speak.

So I took the girls and went home to England. I knew he was devastated. He felt deeply, but couldn't express it, which was the pattern of our whole relationship. When I got back to London, I thought: how tragic! But I wanted to protect the image of their father for the girls, before Mick accidentally ruined it forever.

Jenny called a limousine. I watched her pack, and then she and our daughters literally walked down the garden path, stepped into the limo, and that was it.

I couldn't feel anything except numbness. If anyone had been there, I'd have turned around and said, 'I don't know what to say.' I felt like I had been anaesthetized. I continued living at the house by myself. I can't even remember being upset until I wrote to Jenny some weeks later in a moment of delirium. That's how long it took me to realize what had happened.

I didn't know what to do, so I just carried on.

During May 1978 we began to make the follow-up album to *Rumours*. Fleetwood Mac now found itself whipped by backlash of all stripes. First there was the general backlash that perennially affects rock music's biggest acts – ask Michael Jackson, Madonna, U2, Bruce Springsteen. How do you follow, let alone top, the best work you've ever done in your life, work that almost killed you to complete?

Then we had to contend with the cultural backlash within our industry. In Britain the punks (in America the New Wavers) were trying to build careers and gouge a niche for themselves by declaring all the old bands – the Stones, Led Zeppelin, Elton John, David Bowie, Fleetwood Mac – to be a bunch of decadent and boring old farts, completely out of touch with their audience and the real world. We of course knew that this was just a big wank, but it did make us think about what we were doing and how we were presenting ourselves.

And then there was the very real backlash *within the band*! Success put us into a state of shock for more than a year. Suddenly, in some circles, it was hip to like Fleetwood Mac and *Rumours*, and we weren't ready for it. Lindsey Buckingham was especially perturbed; he felt that with the success of *Rumours*, 'the work' was being ignored in favour of 'the phenomenon'. This was important because Lindsey was our chief architect and creator. He was totally dedicated to the art of it, and driven by pure intentions. He lived for his art the way Brian Wilson did, with few outside interests and a dislike of distractions. Lindsey wasn't even in it for the money any more. He just wanted it to be good.

Lindsey was always listening to the new stuff. On tour in England he went to see the Clash and some of the other new bands. It was like he couldn't stay still when there was this revolution going on. As such, Lindsey wanted to be part of the revolt; when it came time to start work on our next album, Lindsey made it clear that this record was *not* going to sound anything like *Rumours*.

Of course, he was right. The old 12-bar blues of Fleetwood Mac had now completely mutated into the *Rumours* groove, but that wasn't what we were about either. That was just one epoch in a long history, but suddenly we were being lumbered with the general impression that 'this' was Fleetwood Mac. We didn't feel this way, but people around us did. Thankfully, we were still on our own, and were spared having a business cadre whispering 'creative' ideas into our ears. We were still in control of our own destinies, with total creative control and almost no outside input. By now, we felt, it was part of our mystique within the industry.

These were the psychic conditions under which we proceeded to work for the following year on the massive double album that we eventually would call *Tusk*.

Recording *Rumours* had been a nightmare for us, studio-wise. Trotting around to countless different studios to get the right sounds was something we swore never to do again. This time we said OK, let's start at the bottom. I wanted us to buy a studio for the band and tailor it to our sonic team's specifications, but this notion was poo-pooed as too expensive. Instead we ended up spending an immense fortune building Studio D at the Village Recorder in Los Angeles. Everything about this custom-designed, state-of-the-art laboratory was built for the needs of Fleetwood Mac as ordered by Lindsey, Richard Dashut and Ken Caillat. The sound boards were the best in the world, the control room was nice and comfy, and the lounge had English beer on tap. We incorporated every studio innovation we could think of. A parabolic dish was even built over the drums; the engineer could hit a button on the board and move the dish and various louvres around, making for adjustable room acoustics.

We spent a lot on craft. When it was all over, we'd spent $1.4 million on the studio, and we didn't own it! And, of course, when the album eventually came out, the whole temper of the interviews changed. Before it was always, 'When are you breaking up?' But now it was 'How much did the album *really* cost?' We were accused of gross indulgence because we'd spent the most ever to make an album. It became a joke within the band. I'd just say that we ended up a huge success and made a lot of dollars and *spent it on craft*. People think that a record company pays you to record your music, but it's not like that. The musician pays out of his and her advances. We felt it was a privilege to put our money back into our craft, *not* an indulgence.

As I've said, Lindsey was fairly disgusted with people's expectations for our next album. He was acutely aware of the New Wave criticism of the so-called dinosaur bands, and wanted desperately to make a contemporary artistic statement in our new album. The musical appeal of *Rumours* had been no accident. Lindsey and Richard shared a house and spent their 'spare' time listening to records, trying to discover what worked and why. They'd pick a hit record – the Supremes, or the Beach Boys – and spend hours working them out for the mechanics of the sound. Lindsey was now bored with the normal pop framework. He wanted to experiment as much as possible within the context of the band, and this led to some serious discussion between the two of us. Right at the beginning of the album, Lindsey came over to my house and we sat on the lawn for three days trying to answer the question, What the fuck were we going to do now? I knew Lindsey was frustrated about his own music. 'Mick,' he told me, 'I feel like I'm sacrificing too much for the band. I'm giving it all away. If I have a great idea I'll put it on one of Stevie's songs, and I don't feel like I have anything left over for myself.'

'Lindsey,' I'd reply, 'this has been an issue for at least the past five years, man. It's the old dilemma – you're either in a band or you're not.' Lindsey wanted to stay on the fence. One day he'd be full of ideas for the band; the next he'd say he didn't really wanna be in the band any more.

'All right, Lindsey,' I finally had to say. 'Where is this gonna end? What do you want? What's the compromise going to be?'

The usually reticent Mr Buckingham had a ready answer. 'What I want to do is some serious recording at home. Sometimes I'm at the studio and I can't quite bridge the gap between the sounds I'm hearing in my head and the music I'm actually able to get on tape. Other times I'd like to play some of the other parts myself, like drums or the bass line, but I feel too intimidated to ask you and John to let me. It boils down to this – I want to do some of the work at home.'

I had to smile and say, in all honesty, 'Well, Lindsey, if it sounds good, we don't give a shit where it's recorded. It doesn't say much for the band's situation if, after fifteen years, we can't take care of everyone in it. Go ahead and do it.' The result was that some of Lindsey's things were recorded in his basement at home. Some of the rhythm tracks are Lindsey banging on shoeboxes. Some of the vocals were overdubbed on his hands and knees in his bathroom. I understood what Lindsey was going through, but neither John nor Chris really appreciated this method. It was felt that this kind of segregation away from the cauldron of traditional Fleetwood Mac group creativity in the studio was . . .

unhealthy. Lindsey himself later speculated that he might have been selfish. On the other hand, he continued to labour in the studio as part of our regular production team. He and Stevie worked closely on some of the sublime new music she had written – 'Angel', 'Beautiful Child', and the mysterious piano demo that would become the brilliant 'Sara'. In fact, rather quickly we fell into our usual lunatic studio habits, working for many days straight, and then sleeping for three.

That summer, we took a break from recording and embarked on the 'Penguin Country Summer Safari 1978', beginning at the Alpine Valley Music Theater in Wisconsin on 17 July and then moving to a monster show at the Cotton Bowl in Dallas on the 23rd, where we topped a sold-out show supported by the Little River Band, Bob Welch (whose *French Kiss* was now a nationwide hit!) and Steve Miller. At JFK Stadium in Philadelphia on the 30th we played with the same group, except that Sanford & Townshend opened. We played a dozen more stadia that July and August, flexing our collective muscle as the Biggest and the Best in the Land. Let the punkers rant about the dinosaurs, we laughed, as we watched our fans fill up arena, colisseum and bowl.

Did this spectacle give me joy? Did the old gigster enjoy being back on the road?

The answer is no. It was the summer my father died.

We were on the road. Sally phoned from England and said simply, Mick, you better get over here. In anguish I was bustled into a Lear jet to Washington DC, where I boarded the Concorde for London. Twelve miles over the north Atlantic, flying at twice the speed of sound, I could see the curve of the earth through Concorde's small windows. At the great height I saw the surreal blue of the upper stratosphere begin to turn dark. But my mind was focused instead on the life of my dad as it reached ebb tide. I was in shock.

Sally picked me up at Heathrow and drove to the hospital in Hampstead. There in bed lay the Wingco, quite heavily sedated. He smiled when I came into the room, and took my hand. 'Mick,' he said with his usual irony, 'they've got me high as a kite.' My father knew too well my naughty ways. I tried to smile. 'Careful, Dad,' I told him, 'you'll catch up with me.'

Mike went off to sleep then, and Sally and I went out for some bacon and eggs. When we walked back to the hospital he had slipped away. I said out loud, 'Dad you look so beautiful.' Mum and I went out to the garden and sat on the grass and looked at the trees for a long while. The next day I flew back to the tour and did the gig. I felt it was my duty, and Dad would have wanted it. His ashes were soon scattered to the breezes at Bucklers Hard on the Hampshire coast, where he used to moor his sailing boat.

I never got over his death. Does one ever?

At that point the tough carapace I had built around me, which I thought essential for survival in the professional world I inhabited, began to crack. Anyone who has lost a parent knows the difficult period of grief and deep reflection that follows.

In the early summer of 1978, when I had some time away from Seedy Management and the world of Fleetwood Mac, I met up with Jenny in southern Ireland. We left the kids with our friend Alice Ormsby-Gore, and rented a car to drive about the still-green winter landscape and be alone. I begged her to come back to California with the children. I'll get you a little house, I said. Jenny didn't want the girls to be living with me in the state I was usually in, and I told her she didn't have come to back to Bellagio, that I'd find her a separate house up by the ocean somewhere. We had a good time together, and she said she'd consider my request.

On this same trip, I visited my mother at a house my sister Sally had rented in the village of Barfleur, Normandy. It was a healing balm to be with the other Fleetwoods at that point, and I fell in love with the cozy charm of French provincial village life. There was something contagious in the *joie de vivre* of the villagers that I resolved to somehow recapture later, in the new music that Fleetwood Mac was trying to create, six thousand miles away in southern California.

When I got back there, I bought a house for Jenny and the girls in Little Ramirez Canyon, just off the Pacific Coast Highway in Malibu. It was a small English-style cottage, quite charming, and my family was persuaded to come back to California.

After they were settled in, one evening I waited until our daughters had gone to sleep, and tried to wipe the slate clean. 'Look, Jenny, there's something I want to tell you. For the past year I've been seeing Stevie, off and on. It was very intense at first, but now it's cooled down, and I think it's important you hear about it from me before anyone else tells you.'

Jenny didn't say anything, but she looked very unhappy. Finally she very softly replied, 'Thanks for telling me, Mick.' And that was the last time she mentioned it, but I knew her well and could tell this had come as a blow.

I was still living in Bel Air and despite what I said to Jenny, I spent as much time at Stevie's house as I could. I was also drinking quite a bit, which Jenny found distasteful, and eventually she decided the reconciliation wasn't going to happen. Once again she and the girls returned to England, and I finally realized that it was all over between us, and this time it was for good.

At this point, someone new entered my life.

I had known her as Sara Recor, the beautiful model and wife of Jim Recor, who had worked for Loggins and Messina and had managed the Sanford Townshend Band. Sara had become very friendly with Stevie Nicks from the days when we were all touring together. Sara was a good singer, and she knew all the old country songs that Stevie liked. They'd get together at Stevie's and sing and have fun all night, calling themselves the Twang Sisters. At the time, Sara was working as a model for the Elite and Johnny Casablanca agencies. She was gorgeous, charming, gregarious, funny and extremely warm. I'd first spent time with her when I was snuck off to Hawaii to visit Stevie, and Sara was staying in the house. Later, Sara and I made contact again at Stevie's 1978 New Years' Eve party, but I really got to know Sara much better at Stevie's old house in the Hollywood Hills when I was hanging out there. In October 1978 Lindsey gave a Halloween party at his house on June Street, before which I went over to Stevie's house to have my make-up done and put on my Halloween disguise. Sara was there. I was feeling extremely alone, and that's when it started with the old eyes, back and forth. What, I thought to myself, was going on? I remember saying to Judy Wong that I knew that Sara was married but I was feeling very attracted to her in every sense. Being a coward, I said to Judy: talk to Sara and find out what's going on here. One day late in 1978 I went over to see guitarist George Hawkins, who had played with Kenny Loggins' band and was now living at Sara and Jim's house in Sierra Madre. Sara was there; I took her for a ride in my Porsche and we talked. I was crying a bit over Jenny leaving me for the third time and Sara told me in her touching way that she wanted to try to help me through this. I was feeling, as I recall, quite bewildered and not a little moved by Sara's beauty and humour. I left my car at Sara's house, because she was trying to fix the phone in my car, and took a limo to a photo session for Fleetwood Mac. We arranged for Sara to pick me up later at the house on Bellagio; she knew where it was because she had often driven Stevie to meetings there. Well, she came and got me and took me back to her house. Nobody was there. We locked eyes, had a hug, and both said, 'This is insane!'

I said, let's go for a drink. We went up to visit Jenny's now empty house in Little Ramirez. Sara called Jim and told him what was going on. From then on, she stayed with me on Bellagio, calling home every day. Eventually she went home to pack, and I'll never forget going over to pick her up in my little MG. Jim Recor was a friend of mine, and it was very civilized. We shook hands and reaffirmed how much we liked each other. I looked over and Sara was sitting in a corner, holding a teddy bear, crying miserably. I felt bad, but look: this was *love*. It had already started, and we couldn't stop it. It wasn't the sweetest of things to happen in a very difficult time. It was a situation I somehow wandered into. I'm a person who counts his relationships on one hand. It wasn't a habit of mine to steal a wife. But it happened.

And Sara was as confused as me. She moved into Bel Air with me in November and promptly lost all her friends. Our extended family sharply disapproved of Sara leaving Jim, whom everyone liked, and of my making off with another man's wife. Stevie Nicks was upset enough to lock herself in her room for a couple of days. When I tried to explain, she cut me off with, 'Mick, I don't want to talk about it.'

So our lives changed quite a bit. I stopped seeing Stevie and settled into a restless domesticity with Sara. My mother and children were very annoyed. Sara became immersed in the isolated and claustrophobic life of the rock star. The phone was off the hook all the time, so no one could contact her. Her new friends became the other Fleetwood Mac road widows – Julie McVie, John's former secretary whom he had married earlier that year; Lindsey's girlfriend Carol Harris; and Christine McVie's new live-in boyfriend, Dennis Wilson of the Beach Boys. I had known Dennis from years of gigging with his band and had introduced him to Chris while we were making *Tusk*. Within a few days of their meeting, Chris and Dennis fell wildly for each other. Our lighting director Curry Grant moved out of Chris's hillside re-creation of an English country house, and Dennis moved in. It was December 1978, and for the next three years – as long as that tempestuous relationship lasted – there was never a dull moment, Dennis being the complete wildman so accurately depicted by his enduring legend.

Peter Green liked Sara too.

He was living in LA, having arrived in town late in 1977, looking for a new life. Since leaving Fleetwood Mac he'd worked as a gravedigger and hospital orderly, spent time in prison (which he said, as an old blueser, he actually quite liked – plain food and plain people) and in various mental hospitals and private clinics, where he'd been given many drug therapies. He seemed on a more even keel when he arrived on my doorstep one day. He'd been staying in some downtown hotel and had been befriended by a black woman cabbie who was driving him around. I was terribly anxious to help him in any way I could. He married his girlfriend at my house in Bel Air in January 1978. Later, when Sara moved in, he'd show up and gruffly ask her to cook him some breakfast. The best thing was that Pete had started playing the guitar again. We formulated many great plans together. Peter would become a client of Seedy Management. We'd get him a record deal. Pete was as enthusiastic as I'd ever seen him. It was like having old Greenie back in the fold again. He came to the studio and played on 'Brown Eyes', one of the songs Chris had written for the new album. Then we tried to get him a record deal as a solo artist. 'Wait a minute,' the executives said, 'didn't this cat go a little haywire on you once upon a time?' But I was adamant. 'Peter Green is one of the *greats*,' I insisted. 'Ask Eric Clapton! Ask B. B. King! This guy is a *legend* . . .' In the end, we arranged a sweetheart deal for Peter with Warner Brothers. I worked my tail off, and things seemed to be great until his marriage started to go downhill.

I'll never forget the meeting in our office to sign Pete's contract. I was elated that morning. Pete was doing well, I had sold him hard, and Mo Ostin had said yes. Bob Welch had a hit record and I knew we could do the same for Pete, who had once done so much for me. *This would show the world that Fleetwood Mac took care of its own, that we were a family as well as a business.*

As soon as Pete showed up at the office I looked at him and felt sick. Dishevelled, his deportment gone slack, Pete had that desperate look in his eye, a look that cried out that Pete was flashing back to the bad old days. I tried to cheer him up, showing him the contract, at which he looked with undisguised loathing.

'This is *evil*,' he said. 'I'm not doing it.'

The men from the record company nervously shifted their weight. No one said anything. Then I excused ourselves, and took Pete into another room. 'Please, Pete,' I pleaded, 'I'm *not* pressuring you, but I wanna remind you that this deal is worth nearly a million dollars. Many people worked very hard to make it happen, and the record company is very eager for it to happen.'

'No thanks,' Pete said. I wanted to cry.

'Look, Pete,' I started, 'could you just . . .'

'I hate signing things, Mick. You *know* that,' Pete said gently. He sighed. 'I feel very close to the Devil right now, Mick, and it scares me.'

Eventually it came out that Pete thought the contract was with the Devil, and he'd had enough of that Devil business. To him, it was Babylon. (In fact, Pete always did have a thing about signing stuff.) In any case, Pete freaked out, he wouldn't sign, I looked like a total idiot and that was the end of that. Eventually Peter Green went back to England, and the following year released a (quite good) album called *In The Skies*. It was a haunting and somewhat ghostly record; later we heard that most of the guitar had been played by somebody else, a guitar player called Snowy White.

By early 1979, many of the songs for the new album had been dreamed up and were in various stages of production. Our writers were prolific, and very early on we realized we had a lot more good songs that we could fit on a single album. I wanted to make a statement too, some special contribution that would reflect my vision of what Fleetwood Mac was all about, a sense of grandeur with intimacy, if you will. That was the vision that came together in the aural collage called 'Tusk'.

It started as a riff we used to play when we took the stage and the lights went off and we were being announced, right before our first number. It was our way of having a live sound check so Richard Dashut could set his levels. It was just a little riff that Lindsey started playing one night, and I'm tapping my drums. We used to play it in the dark for less than a minute every night. When we began the new album we tried doing something with it, but the idea was scrapped. Months and months went by, but that riff just would not leave my head. One night Richard Dashut assembled a 20-second tape loop of this 4-bar riff. A bunch of us physically held the tape loop aloft in the studio so it wouldn't sag as we dubbed it from one 24-track recorder to another. Then we sped it up, I did some overdubs, and we had a basic track.

The next day I was at home, thinking about 'the riff', and my memory returned to my visit to Barfleur in Normandy the previous summer.

One Sunday morning I had been awakened (with a *serious* hangover) to the raucous music of the village brass band, which was circling through the town blaring away in honour of the festival of the local saint. I tried to get back to sleep after the band had passed, to no avail. Just when I thought they had stopped for half an hour, back they came roaring through the village again. It became clear there was to be no relief, so I got up and opened the shutters onto a wonderful scene that could have been painted by Breughel: old peasants with bloodshot noses, young women garbed in colourful local costume, kids running around, drunks staggering after the band, the village all garlanded and festooned, everyone having a grand time *à la fête*.

Now, back in Los Angeles, I had a brainstorm. What was music all about anyway? Here was this brass band that was the catalyst for the village, bringing old and young together, playing and laughing. Why not try to re-create this ambience at Fleetwood Mac shows, with local brass bands, maybe from the high schools, playing 'the riff' at every stop on the tour? We could bring the intimacy of the village fête with us as we travelled around the world.

That, in any event, was the basic idea. One day in the studio I volunteered to pay for a marching band to record this riff. In a typical burst of grandiosity, I said I wanted to go for an immense wall of sound, that I wanted to record the band in Dodger Stadium. Silence. They looked at me as if I were mad. Someone murmured that this idea was a little off the wall. Dark mutterings that Fleetwood had gone round the bend on this one. Then Judy Wong, bless her, said she knew someone at Dodger Stadium.

Ha!

I forget exactly how the University of Southern California's Trojan Marching Band was chosen to play the part of the village band on the album. I went to one of the marching band's meetings, played them a tape of 'the riff' and asked if they could manage an arrangement. The kids liked the idea. The band director, Dr Bartz, came over to our studio a few days later, and gradually the village band came to life. By this time, I was frothing at the mouth. We could do this in Augusta, Germany, Rio, anywhere! The fans would love seeing the locals up on stage with us. It would be incredible. A few weeks later Fleetwood Mac, the 112-Member USC Trojans and a film crew met up on a beautiful southern California afternoon in an empty Dodger Stadium. (Richard Dashut fulfilled a boyhood fantasy by sitting down in the Dodger dugout and smoking a joint.) The band had the riff down pat by then, and the recording went smoothly. Stevie, in a summer dress and a broad-brimmed straw hat, brought the gathering to its feet with a solo baton twirling performance.

That's how 'Tusk' was recorded. The title refers to a jocular term of affection for the Male Member: old habits die hard in Fleetwood Mac. (When Stevie heard that we had decided to name the album *Tusk*, she

171

threatened to quit the band in revulsion. But I chose to ignore her and nothing ever came of it.)

Incidentally, the film that documents this Dodger Stadium event shows only the fully costumed marching band and four members of Fleetwood Mac. John McVie is represented by a life-sized photo of himself mounted on board, which I dutifully carried around under my arm as we changed location around the ball park. This was because the studio-loathing McVie had played his bass parts early in the process, and then set sail in the broad blue Pacific. He set out for Hawaii with three friends on his ketch; none of the four sailers could use a sextant. Following the jet contrails, they made a perfect landfall straight into the channel at Maui. While we were actually recording at the stadium, John and eight other lads headed for Tahiti, thirty-five days at sea. One clear night, with stars you could read by, shooting stars everywhere, total peace and quiet on the smooth down-wind run, dolphins cruising alongside . . . suddenly the whole boat tipped sickeningly. Twenty-eight tons and it almost keeled over. In the cabin people were on the floor, smashed crockery everywhere. They'd been rammed by a whale! At Tahiti the boat was hauled and they found a huge ding in the transom. Fleetwood Mac had almost lost Mr McVie.

The other track from *Tusk* that had the most meaning for me was 'Sara'. I remember the time when Stevie was writing the song, up at her old house on Doheny. Stevie and Sara would be working and they'd hear me coming up the drive in my throaty red Ferrari. That's me in the lyric, 'just like a great dark wing'. Stevie brought the song to the studio as a piano track, and I worked for days, sweating bullets to put the time to it. The softness required was a drummer's nightmare, but a great challenge. In the end it took three days to get the brush work to accompany that piano and vocal. The result was, in many ways, the ultimate Fleetwood Mac song of that era, the late 1970s: breathless, ethereal, almost ecclesiastical and somehow reverent, as Stevie pays tribute to her muse. (Much later, when an obscure songwriter filed a plagiarism suit against Stevie over the song, we all knew it was a farce because we'd seen how much work Stevie and Lindsey had poured into this masterpiece. There was a small out-of-court settlement so that litigation would not be prolonged, and Stevie was hurt by the allegation.)

By the early summer of 1979 we had finished recording, although 'finish' is a relative term. Like the proverbial poem that's never complete, but only abandoned in despair, the recording process was finally ended. We had twenty good songs, and we didn't feel there was any more we could do with them. Indeed, we had so much music that we liked, we couldn't bring ourselves to get rid of any of them. Many of the tracks, especially most of Lindsey's (but 'Tusk' as well), were rather eccentric in a new-wavey style; this was a direct reaction to the middle-of-the-road feelings of *Rumours*. But we all considered the *Tusk* songs to be the crowning jewel of Fleetwood Mac's recorded work. In the end, we decided we could get away with releasing *all* of the music on a left-field double album.

Warner Brothers had been wonderful in not pressuring us to duplicate the sound that had been a mega-hit on *Rumours*. But when we finally gave them the tapes of *Tusk*, they told us flatly we were crazy to release a double album. Mo Ostin explained that the record industry in that time, 1979–80, was in the midst of a severe slump (few if any of the much-vaunted New Wave bands sold many records), and that a big double album might not be a very commercial proposition. The Warner Brothers executives, meanwhile, listened to *Tusk* and saw their much-anticipated Christmas bonuses fly out the window. No way, they said, was this package going to sell tonnage. But we didn't waver. We were too far into what we were doing, and at that point there was no question of hacking the album down to one record. The whole thing had become just too massive. Word on the street was that we were going to go into the record books as having spent the most money in history recording an album, but we didn't care. (We knew, incidentally, that the Eagles had spent more.) We understood the company's point of view. They wanted us to continue in our usual groove and make a lot of money for everyone. That was their measure of success. But Fleetwood Mac's measure was the art. It would be dishonest to say that we were oblivious to the money, but the music came first. *Then* maybe you make some money with it. We didn't want to approach our lives with the understanding that 'Soft Rock' is the sort of music we have to do to make money. I shit on that whole concept, because the point of the music is lost. It becomes nothing more than another business. The company ordered up a huge, expensive advertising campaign to hype the record, which we had to veto as vulgar and very un-Mac. They began to panic. You've *got* to sell so many units, they warned us. And we said that we had to please ourselves first, that was the point of what being an artist was all about. If you didn't keep your integrity in the face of hard commercial decisions, you were lost. Your soul was dead.

Such was the high creed of Seedy Management.

But there was also some nervousness within the band, and some of this anxiety did emanate from me. I was very aware that Lindsey had set certain creative processes in motion. The definite New Wave spin on *Tusk* was a signpost of what was going to happen to Fleetwood Mac; that after *Tusk* everyone would go off on their own and do separate things, which usually meant the end of a band. There was quite a debate within the band on the disparate nature of the record, each writer doing his or her own thing instead of the unified sound of *Fleetwood Mac* and *Rumours*. I argued this issue with Lindsey, sometimes bitterly. I kept saying that I didn't want the album to be so segregated that people couldn't hear the band. When we were mixing I'd beg Lindsey to make his songs more recognizable as Fleetwood Mac. His songs were fantastic, but my reservations were that they might be too alien for our fans. Do what you're doing, I'd say, but don't forget the ingredients we worked on for years as part of the band. Don't go *too* far.

To this day, Lindsey feels I wasn't enthusiastic enough about the album. I know he feels I got it all wrong, but in fact I loved *Tusk*. I think it's a great album, and probably the only artistic reason Fleetwood Mac is still together today. As a double album, it released a lot of creative frustrations. The extra space let us delve and experiment and hone art. And in the end, I think I was right. *Tusk* did well when it came out, with its Peter Beard collage and postmodern graphics, but it was mostly Stevie and Chris's music you heard on the radio.

Tusk, incidentally, was dedicated to my father and Lindsey's dad, Morris Buckingham, who had also recently died.

We released *Tusk* in late September 1979. Its list price of $16 was considered uncomfortably high at the time, and it was calculated we had to sell about half a million records and tapes to break even. In the end, *Tusk* sold about four million copies and was considered by some a failure, considering *Rumours'* astronomical numbers. Ironically, one of the big promotions Warner Brothers arranged backfired on us badly. With as much hype as possible, *Tusk* was broadcast in its entirety on the Westwood One rock radio network, which comprised most of America's FM radio stations in major markets. This was an unmitigated disaster, as millions stayed home that night and *taped* the whole album, avoiding record stores completely. Then the other networks got mad and blacklisted us.

But other publicity stunts were more fun. One crisp October afternoon, Fleetwood Mac congregated inside Frederick's of Hollywood, the famous nasty lingerie emporium. Outside, several hundred fans were seated on bleachers lining Hollywood Boulevard. It was Fleetwood Mac Day, time to have the 156th star on Hollywood's Walk of Fame dedicated to the band.

Inside the store, we were presented with special commemorative underwear. Much hilarity, whirring of cameras, popping of flashbulbs. Outside, loudspeakers played *Rumours* to the crowd. Suddenly a hundred USC Trojans filed into Frederick's playing 'Tusk'. Consider the bedlam! We had been told that having a star on Hollywood Boulevard brought good luck. We walked out into the street and the girls in the crowd screamed like banshees when they saw Stevie and Chris. Mo Ostin was up on the podium making a speech: '. . . don't think we can measure how important Fleetwood Mac has been to Warner Brothers and the record industry in general.' Polite applause. Then we filed up to say thank you into the mike. McVie deadpanned, 'Thank you all for being . . . er . . . Americans.' He was followed by Stevie, in billowing white satin. 'Thank you for believing in the crystal vision,' she said sweetly. 'Crystal visions really do come true.'

The plan now was to spend almost a year on the road in support of *Tusk*. Fleetwood Mac would play all over North America, Europe and the Pacific, carrying our music to all parts of the globe. We scrapped my idea of having local brass bands play with us every night because the logistics were impossible to work out.

Although we'd done some big shows the previous summer, it had been a year since Fleetwood Mac had been a working road band. So I ordered up six weeks of rehearsal that autumn of 1979. We met almost every evening at the Sunset Gower Studio complex, in an immense and damp old soundstage where Busby Berkeley and Fred Astaire once staged lavish film production numbers.

I usually arrived around seven. Our Japanese masseur had been on duty since 4:30, and an immense buffet which no one ever ate waited at one side of the room. I can see Christine circling the big room on a bicycle, trailed by a small dog. People came in and out. Lindsey is noodling on his guitar; a transmitter sends every random note blasting out of a tower of loudspeakers. Outside are four gull-winged Benz sports coupés, which Richard Dashut and I are inspecting for a possible purchase. While we look at them, Dennis Dunstan comes over and introduces himself. He's from the Bob Jones Karate School in Australia, which did our security when we were Down Under on the *Rumours* tour. We liked them so much we've hired them to do the *Tusk* tour, and Dennis will be working with me.

After a band meeting, in which we sat cross-legged on the floor and tried to firm up our set list, we finally begin to play. Lindsey has a new look, very modern: hair cropped short, narrow lapel, grey suit, quite ascetic. Stevie is in her customary high heels, a long skirt and dancer's woollen leg warmers. She runs offstage in the middle of songs when she isn't needed and huddles with her girlfriends. Christine is in black, and looks over to where Dennis Wilson sits. 'Do I have any free time this week?' she asks plaintively. McVie chain-smokes behind the amplifiers. He's restless tonight, playing bass lines by himself, concentrating, getting his all-important chops back. I'm at the drums, heavily bearded, raring to go. The scent of someone's extra-potent Afghani pot tickles the hairs in my nose.

We take a break, and the five members of Fleetwood Mac scatter to different corners of the room. Stevie later tells me that there are nights she doesn't want to come and rehearse. I know how she feels. We all know that Fleetwood Mac is a job, a lovely sort of job, but hard work all the same. There's a frayed edge to tonight's rehearsal. We all sound a bit tired, and the tour hasn't even begun. Yet other nights we sound sharp and stirring, even to ourselves. We know that somehow this long year on the road will be one of the linchpins of our career together.

We didn't know at the time that it would almost kill the band.

The 'Tusk' single went right to number one in Britain and Australia, but in America the record started off slow. Radio was tentative; they told us it didn't sound like Fleetwood Mac. The press was decidedly so-so; reviews were positive, and congratulated us on our experiments, but the critics said it didn't sound like us. There was much ado about the expense and length of the recording process, and the by-now-expected accusations of saurian obsolescence.

The whole point of this long tour was that John Courage and I had finally said, does the band just sit back and take all this flak, or do we go out and try to put this album over the hump? Looking back now, I can see that the tour was hugely successful from an artistic standpoint, but something of a financial debacle. The big money we earned was offset against the luxurious way we liked to tour. The Tusk Tour turned out to be the zenith of Fleetwood Mac living up to its reputation for spending lots of money and going first class all the way. If we were going to be on the road for a year, we damn well wanted to be comfortable. To this end we hired an airliner so we wouldn't have to fly commercially. We ordered some of the priciest hotel suites in the world, repainted in pastel shades for Stevie and Chris at fabulous expense. The refreshment rider written into our contracts with the local promoters provided an immense backstage buffet for an army of Californian gourmands, although many of us were too coked-up and glazed-over to actually eat anything. A king's ransom was spent on keeping the tour's cocaine supply adequate. Every time our BAC 1-11 jet roared into a new airport, six black limousines pulled up to the tarmac and whisked us hither and yon. It was all wonderful, occasionally depraved, and ruinously expensive; but it also helped to keep us going during the most challenging and exhausting year of our lives, from October 1979 to September 1980.

We started at the Pocatello Mini Dome in Idaho on 26 October. Two nights later at the Salt Palace in Salt Lake City, Fleetwood Mac began to turn into a hot band again, but the press was asking why the hall wasn't quite sold out tonight and whether I was disappointed by the sales of *Tusk* – 2.5 million after about a month. Backstage a playful Miss Nicks danced into the lounge, her hair an unruly mass of golden ringlets, a plastic hairbrush poking out of her coiffure. 'Well, how does everyone like this?' Dressed in a leotard top and her stacked heel boots, she got a big laugh from everyone except John Courage. Two roadies mirthfully pushed Stevie back into her dressing room to complete her toilette.

Three shows down the road, in Albuquerque, Sara stole the house cat from the venue and had a confrontation with Courage, who didn't want a cat on the plane. Suddenly our tour party was split down gender lines. The women wanted the cat. The men didn't. Guess who won? Sara was congratulated by our female cadre as she and cat defiantly took their seats in the back of the plane for the hop to St Louis . . . where as usual film crews from the local news stations were positioned at the bottom of the steps as Fleetwood Mac disembarked and stepped into the limos. By this time, I had my Spokesman Routine down pat, pulling myself together from in-flight stupor as soon as the plane touched down. As we pulled up to unload, I was filling my eyes with Visine, inhaling mouth spray, checking my hat, adjusting my shades and wrapping the right scarf around my neck. 'No, we're *not* breaking up,' I hear myself insisting. 'No, we *love* the album, it's doing great. We're playing the Checkerdome on the 5th and 6th and want to see everybody there.'

Warner Brothers filmed the St Louis shows. Stevie went through six costume changes and poured herself into 'Sara' wrapped in a long red shawl that made her look like a High Priestess. For the first encore, 'Sisters of the Moon', she sang the verses while tapping on a cowbell, telling the story of the song, communicating with the enraptured audience. I looked out and saw they were hers. Her intimate gestures, soothsayer's words, and majestic raised palms were magic. The girls in the crowd strained to hear the unheard lines Stevie liked to chant out of range of the microphone. She shouted and wailed the climax, and the audience screamed and whooped in return as she thanked them profusely from the lip of the stage.

A week later and we were in Manhattan, playing two nights at Madison Square Garden. Lindsey was cruising away, picking out spare riffs on his custom guitar. A guy in the front row said to him, in the quiet moment between songs, 'You sold out.' We guessed he meant that Lindsey had sold out the old Mac style in favour of the new wave thing. It made Lindsey think about what he was doing. He confided to *Melody Maker*: 'It's been a strain personally for me in that I can't believe in myself as much as when I put the album out. I was busting out to do something that had depth to it, but then I realized people aren't getting the message. You wonder whether you've been deluding yourself, especially when the rest of the band starts telling you it's time to get back to the standard format.'

We spent the rest of November playing the cities of the northeast and upper Midwest. In early December we played five sold-out nights at the Los Angeles Forum, then three nights at the cavernous Cow Palace in San Francisco. There we sat down to a press conference, to which I arrived late in a semi-comatose state due to warring bouts of hypoglycaemia and a mild touch of diabetes. For the next hour we fielded questions:

Stevie, who is Sara?

Stevie, when are you leaving the band?

Stevie, when are you making a solo album?

Stevie, what about the 'Rhiannon' movie?

Stevie, are you busy for dinner tonight?

Midway through this ordeal my entire body began to shake. I was wracked with severe muscular spasms, and when I realized the cameras were still rolling and clicking away, I had an anxiety attack as well. Mercifully, Christine reached over and began to massage my shoulders and the pain subsided. Thank God the healing touch seems to run in the Perfect family.

A few nights later, backstage at the Cow Palace, our dear friend Bill

Graham paced the dressing room as John McVie and Dennis Wilson tried to drink each other under the table. I told an English reporter that, no, Fleetwood Mac is not breaking up, but, yes, we'll all probably do some solo recording after this long tour is finished. I also spoke for the first time about a plan I had to return to Africa to record with local musicians in an attempt to fuse the standard rock beat with more complex rhythms. He took copious notes but looked somewhat dubious, as this synthesis had been tried before without much success. Later that evening, Fleetwood Mac took the stage and burned with a specially bright flame since we've always had an ardent love affair with our San Francisco fans. Halfway through, Stevie stepped to the mike and dedicated the show to Lindsey's late father, Buck.

These shows were Fleetwood Mac's last of the decade; after San Francisco, we planned to break for the holidays and take some time off. My own plans were to go to England and spend Christmas with Jenny and the children. Sara was upset about this and we had several terrible rows. This was fairly typical of the hell I put poor Sara through over the next eight years, but I had told her when we started out that living with me would never be easy.

Before the band left San Francisco, we decided to play a prank on John Courage, who had been ushering us around America like a herd of dazed cattle for the past three months. The prank came on Colonel Courage's birthday and was entirely John McVie's idea. We bribed a bellboy at the St James Hotel to look the other way while a barnyard scene was lovingly recreated in Courage's room. When he returned to the hotel that night, he opened his door to find fifty hens and roosters had turned his room into an immense chicken coop. The whole suite had been filled with fresh hay, and the chickens were everywhere – all over the bed, stuffed in drawers, and one hen had even layed an egg in the smashed TV set. There was chicken shit all over his clothes. All the hay made it a fire-hazard, and when I walked in, there was Dennis Wilson lying drunk in the bathtub, smoking two cigarettes at the same time. It was actually quite scary, but the Colonel took it in good humour. In the end we rounded up the chickens, shoved them in the elevator, and pushed 'Lobby'.

In January 1980, Stevie Nicks wrote me one of her rare notes, this one full of portents, news, and admonitions. After pointing out that Ted Kennedy had beaten President Jimmy Carter in the Iowa Democratic caucuses, that the Russians were moving slowly into Afghanistan, and that American hostages had been held in Teheran for seventy-eight days, she said: 'It is a fearful time. Things are becoming less exciting and more real.'

She also wrote that she had started work on her first solo album. 'Recording has begun, and Rhiannon is afoot.' Then she told me she had moved to a small house by the beach and that I was a cheap bastard, so she was sending the girls in our office an extra $250. Stevie signed the note 'Katherine DeLongpre', one of her many pseudonyms of the period.

In February 1980 Fleetwood Mac landed in Tokyo to play three nights at the Budokan. But first we held a hilarious press conference at the Roppongi Samba Club, where Japanese reporters grilled us about our attitude towards drugs in the wake of Paul McCartney's recent stay of two weeks in a Japanese prison after some grass was found in his luggage at the airport. We swore up and down that we never touched the stuff. The next day's paper headlined WE DON'T SMOKE MARIJUANA SWEARS FLEETWOOD MAC. After the Tokyo shows, we boarded the Bullet Train for concerts in Kyoto, Sapporo, Osaka and Yokohama, laden with samuri swords, new cameras, and lots of then-new Walkman portable cassette players. I was very pleased that our Japanese fans seemed to love the song 'Tusk'. I had been disappointed that my idea of having a local brass band play the number with us at every gig had been too complex to implement, but instead Christine played 'the riff' on her accordian; the effect was understated and endearing as opposed to brassy and pompous, and I learned to love it the way she played it.

Sara had stayed in California while Fleetwood Mac toured the Pacific, but that didn't stop our bitter fights. Confronted with my general craziness, we fought pitched battles over the phone. One night in Japan, Dennis Dunstan came into my suite to find me naked in bed except for a bowler hat and a bottle of brandy. I was alternately shouting terms of endearment and death threats to Sara back in Los Angeles. Then she would harangue me, and I would record this on a cassette player and play the tapes back to Sara to show her what she sounded like. This went on for hour after cognac-soaked hour in what we estimated was the most expensive phone call in history. When we checked out of the hotel, the bill for this single call came to more than $2000.

After three weeks in Japan, we were due to fly to Perth, Australia, on 20 February. At this point Richard Dashut and I developed a horrendous fear of flying. We discovered that the plane scheduled to take us Down Under was a DC-10, and DC-10s had been crashing all over the world that winter with great loss of life. So Richard and I mutinied. We flatly refused to get on the plane with the rest of the band, convinced as we were that we'd never make it alive. 'Where's Fleetwood?' John Courage asked Dennis Dunstan when I wouldn't board the plane. Dennis explained the situation, and Courage told him to get us on the fucking plane or Dennis would be fired. So Dennis got me very drunk, swore to me that the aircraft had been changed to a 747 at my request, and poured me into my first class seat. Somehow my bleary eyes managed to focus on the emergency procedures card in the pocket of the seat in front of me. Somehow I managed to read the card, which stated unequivocally that I had just boarded a DC-10. 'YOU LIED TO ME!' I screamed at Dennis, and rose out of my seat to de-plane. The big jet had already sealed its doors and left the gate to begin to taxi down the runway, but I didn't care. 'GET ME OUT OF HERE,' I howled, and actually managed to have the plane return to the gate before threats of air piracy charges convinced me that it would be better to take my chances in the air than land in a Japanese jail myself. I fumed all the way to Australia, and an equally furious Dashut vowed to leave the tour for good.

I had been enchanted with the idea of living in Australia ever since going there on the early Fleetwood Mac tours. There're only fourteen million people on the continent. I'd look around and get a lost frontier sort of feeling, like California must have felt sixty years ago. There are great modern cities where for three weeks we played to immense crowds – 48,000 in Sydney, 60,000 at a Melbourne racetrack with Santana opening – but you go five miles out in the sticks and *there's no one there*. To me, it was paradise.

Which is not to say that we didn't have problems. The Australian police were convinced that Fleetwood Mac was a bunch of international dope smugglers and they were determined to give us a hard time. John Courage had flown in our gear on sixteen palettes on a chartered DC-8. (Our crew sat on the seventeenth palette.) Somewhere in all those tons of equipment, the customs came upon a couple of crates of Gatorade, which I liked to mix with vodka to achieve a state of Transcension. Convinced the bottles of Gatorade were spiked with LSD, the customs officials impounded them. To get around this, Courage had a crate of canned Gatorade flown in from LA the next day.

There was also a moment of panic at the Melbourne Hilton. Some of our smokers were getting desperate from abstinence, and one of the roadies' girlfriends had sent him a joint from California, which had been intercepted. Next morning at seven, after an all-night fight with Sara, seven cops burst into my suite and rousted me, looking for heroin! 'All right, Fleetwood,' they shouted, 'we know you're an addict!' They turned the suite upside down. They even looked between my toes! To their dismay, they found nothing!

Yet I didn't care. The more time I spent touring the outback, the more I loved Australia. Between gigs I began to look at property. On 16 March 1980, I signed an agreement to buy a huge stud farm near Sydney for three million dollars.

The property was called Wensley Dale. It was a colonial homestead with a mansion house and ranch of 620 acres at a place called Colo Vale. It was gorgeous, and protected as a historic landmark. There was a good-sized herd of cattle and the whole place functioned nicely as an ongoing bull-breeding concern. I was in heaven, but I knew I was stretching myself thin financially. All my money was now tied up in real estate in Hawaii, California and Australia, and I had bought these properties at the absolute top of the market at astronomical interest rates. In the back of my mind I began to worry about making the mortgage payments, because I could see that our touring expenses were so high we weren't going to earn much from this tour. We expected to sell a lot of records to compensate. I had a business manager, an old school chum of Richard Dashut's, but he told me not to worry about it, so I didn't. Anyway, at that point I was quite anxious to get out of LA because I'd been having apocalyptic dreams about 'The Big One', the giant earthquake that's supposed to dump southern California into the Pacific some day.

In mid-March we flew off to New Zealand to play in front of 60,000 thousand fans in Auckland. The show also went out live over the radio to the rest of the country. By then, the exhaustion of constant travel began to set in, and we were all pretty brain-fried. Lindsey hit the old scotch bottle a little too hard before the concert, and halfway through the performance he snapped like a guitar string tuned ten octaves too high. First I noticed that he was playing out of tune. Then he started to clown around and mimic Stevie while she was dancing around the stage. Then, while she was hunched over, upstage of Lindsey, during her 'Rhiannon' performance, he stopped playing and pulled his jacket over his head in a grotesque imitation of her pose. At that point he lost all control, playing anything except 'Rhiannon', and laughing like a madman. Then he started to kick Stevie while she was trying to salvage the number. Sixty thousand people were watching! Lindsey would flick his foot at her and Stevie would shy away, trying to cover up his stoned-out behaviour to save us all from dying of embarrassment. The rest of the band could only look at each other in disbelief!

The show finally over, we stumbled into the stadium's rugby changing rooms, where we were dressing. There would be no encore that night: we were all freaked out. I could hear the crowd screaming for more as Christine McVie stormed into the room, utterly hell-bent, and made straight for Mr Buckingham, who was slumped miserably on a bench. Lindsey stood up, and Chris smacked him – *crack!* – right in the face. Then she threw her drink at him for good measure. 'Don't you *ever* do this to this band again,' she shouted. 'Ever! Is that clear?' Then she stormed out again.

Silence. Then someone pulled on my sleeve to tell me I had to go on live radio to say a few words – and I'm completely traumatized! They moved me into a trailer and started to ask questions. I dreaded talking about the incident with Lindsey, but it turned out they either didn't notice it, or thought his behaviour was part of the act, or just a joke. All credit went to Stevie, who had kept her dignity and salvaged the show, and Christine and Lindsey didn't speak to each other for a week afterwards.

At the end of March we flew to Hawaii to play three nights in Honolulu. At that point we were really dragging. The whole band was wrung-out, burned-up, dead tired, jet-lagged, sick of Fleetwood Mac and about to go our own ways into solo albums. Yet we were also determined to keep this thing we'd built from crumbling like so many other successful groups. In a crucial business meeting, we managed to form a consensus to renegotiate with our record company and plan for the future. We decided that, no matter what anyone said or did to pull us apart, Fleetwood Mac would not dissolve. We'll stick together, we resolved, and *damn* the rumours!

In Hawaii we also said goodbye, with much regret, to Richard Dashut, who was sick of travelling and was leaving the tour. We hated to see him go; for the past five years he had been like the sixth member of band. We gave Richard a huge farewell party that turned into a bacchanal. John Courage went out and bought a Rolex watch, and had it buried in an immense cake. In order to get his watch, we made Dashut crawl through a gauntlet of crew members who drubbed him and taunted him with cruel ditties whose lyrics suggested that he had lost his 'ears' and that he would never work in this town again. Then he had to grovel before Fleetwood Mac. When his degradation was complete, we made him swear eternal fealty to the band and gave him his watch after an appalling cake fight that sent us all – even my mother who had flown in from England to join me as a witness to this sorry spectacle – to the showers.

We all collapsed for a month. I felt like a wounded animal, but also felt an exhilaration because most nights the band was cooking and our front-line – Stevie, Chris and Lindsey – was such a treat to play behind. Yes, we fought with each other, but so did members of my family, and that's still what Fleetwood Mac felt like to me.

So in May 1980 we pulled ourselves together to tour the US. We hired a Las Vegas casino's private 707 ('Caesar's Chariot') to whisk band and crew about the northwest, western Canada and the Midwest. Opening was the former roadie Christopher Cross, who one night told us he had chauffered a previous incarnation of Fleetwood Mac around Austin, Texas, ten years earlier.

This leg of the tour saw some of the best and worst of the Tusk tour. On good nights it was like magic, on others the show was phoned in. Some nights were dominated by Chris and Stevie as star vocalists, others turned into a guitar clinic by Lindsey. We learned to compensate for each other's moods and bio-rhythms. 'FANS FORGIVE FLUBS AS FLEETWOOD MAC POURS ON THE ROMANCE' read one typical review headline. Others were less kind, and Stevie, who among us took the greatest artistic risk by opening herself up the most in performance, also took the most heat. 'Each of [Stevie's] songs seemed like a celebration of some dated hippie ritual,' observed one typically acerbic critic. But we knew differently. We on stage could look back out at Stevie's ecstatic, entranced fans who by the thousands turned out at our shows to worship her like the Queen of Rock she had become. *Sod the critics*, we thought, as Stevie and her legions of faithful fans created their own almost private communion at Fleetwood Mac performances in those days.

On 16 May we played a second political benefit for Senator Birch Bayh in Indianapolis. Our friend the senator was in a tough re-election campaign, which he would lose later that year to a young Indiana congressman named J. Danforth Quayle, now the vice-president of the United States.

We were glad to help Senator Bayh.

At the end of May, after sixteen shows that month, we flew to Europe, where we had experienced trouble with the police on the *Rumours* tour three years earlier. Then we had used a plane to fly around, and the Dutch airport customs had become convinced Fleetwood Mac was a cover for big time international drug smuggling. In Holland there'd been a nasty incident when customs officers body-searched Stevie Nicks, Christine McVie and our wardrobe and make-up girls. An enraged John Courage swore this would never happen again, so this time we hired a private train to take us from city to city by rail, which was much more convenient since inter-European train passengers are rarely harassed by officialdom. John McVie, who maintains a collection of Third Reich memorabilia, almost went out of his mind when we were told that the opulent, overstuffed lounge car had belonged to Adolph Hitler. The train even came with a little old German in a starched white jacket who had waited on the Führer. (The band was actually afraid to ride in Hitler's creepy coach, and preferred to hang out in the dining car.)

On 1 June, Fleetwood Mac headlined an immense outdoor show, one of the biggest we ever played, at Munich's Olympic riding stadium. Bob Marley and the Wailers warmed up the hundred thousand kids to a fevered degree, despite storms, wind, rain and cold. When we finally got on stage and hit them with 'Say You Love Me', I knew it was going to be one of those shows that transcends space and time. Later, from my seat behind the drums, I could see that even the riot cops were dancing in Munich that night.

From Germany the Tusk tour proceeded to Switzerland where, in Zurich, I introduced my young nephew Kells Jesse to some of the fruits of life. The son of my sister Sally, Kells had been invited on this leg of the tour so he could see what the life of his rock star uncle was like. Join the army, I told him when he signed on, and see the world! When I learned that young Kells was still an innocent virgin I felt I had to do something; so after the Zurich show Dennis Dunstan and I plied him with strong drink and embarked on a tour of the red light district. At the same time there were some serious housing riots going on in the city as the local youth battled police over the eviction of some squatters from abandoned buildings. This added a surreal touch to the scene as we crept from one shady club to another, trying to find the right girl for Kells. Making our way through intense clouds of tear gas, we finally located the right club, chose a woman for my dear nephew, haggled over the price, and got Kells deflowered on his twenty-first birthday. I felt like a truly wicked uncle, and I loved it!

Then we played Belgium, Holland, Paris, two nights in the midlands, and on to London where Fleetwood Mac played six sold-out nights at Wembley. By this time I was so sick from the hypoglycaemia that I'd require nursing from Dennis all night. It was a total nightmare. Before the gigs I would vomit and break out in terrible sweats and shivers, although paradoxically I'd sometimes find myself playing better under the threat of this blood-sugar terror. At Wembley I went into a sort of coma while the band was onstage, and my drum roadie, Tony Todaro, would have to come up behind me and burp me like a baby so I could play for another ten minutes. At the end of the final Wembley show I was so ill I couldn't play the encore, and I almost cried backstage as I heard the crowd hollering for more Mac. But I just couldn't give it to them, so Chris went out alone and sang 'Songbird' by herself.

It was lovely to be home again. We had many reunions, both wonderful and strained. One night I took over the bar of the Carlton Tower Hotel for a big family get-together. My mother, my sisters (Susan was now an actress with the Royal Shakespeare Company; Sally was recently remarried and was now Mrs Hartnell), my daughters, Jenny, her sister Patti, who brought along her then husband Eric Clapton, all crowded in. Christine McVie and her dad Reg played piano and we sang until late – 'I Left My Heart In San Francisco', 'A Foggy Day In London Town'.

And then we found Danny Kirwan.

I was determined, in a low-key way, to try to help everyone who'd been connected with Fleetwood Mac. We'd tried and succeeded with Bob Welch. We tried with Peter Green, to no avail. Jeremy had written to me from Sri Lanka. That left Danny. While we were in London, I got his number, and in due course he showed up at the hotel. I was having breakfast in the suite with Jenny and the kids when he appeared, looking grubby and very unwashed. It was heartbreaking. He'd lived with us at Benifols, the kids loved him, and he'd been a good-looking chap. Now he looked derelict. He told us he had worms, and that he'd slept on a park bench the night before. He looked lousy. Mind if I use the toilet? he asked. When he was out of the room, Jenny and I looked at each other in embarrassment.

Then we had to go downstairs to catch the transportation to Wembley. Danny refused to go, and got quite paranoid. I still hadn't been able to elicit what he'd been up to, or how we could help. The buses pulled up to the kerb, and I tried to give him a hug. 'No,' he said. 'Don't do that. I don't want to be touched.' I got on the bus, and never saw him again.

Back at home, we took two weeks off before going back in the studio for three weeks to record, overdub and remix tracks for a live album. It was controversial within the band, this record, because I was the only one who wanted to do it. It was *not* a popular decision. Both John McVie and Lindsey Buckingham thought it was a negative move, but I always bought greatest hits albums myself, and I strongly felt there had to be a live document of the band at this point. Besides, we had great material to work with, recorded all over the world: 'Monday Morning' from Tokyo, 'Say You Love Me' from Wichita, 'Dreams' from the Paris sound check, a psychedelic 'Oh Well' from St Louis, 'Rhiannon' from London, and so on. We also set up our gear and played three new songs 'live' for an audience of crew and friends at the Santa Monica Civic Center – Stevie's 'Fireflies', Chris's 'One More Night' and a Fleetwood Mac harmony orgy in homage of Brian Wilson's 'The Farmer's Daughter'.

Later in the year, we released *Fleetwood Mac Live* as a double album, and it wasn't a big success. There were many accusations of 'We Told You So', but I have no regrets.

And so we went out for a final month in August, beginning at the Lakeland Civic Center, Florida. There Stevie's fans threw her dozens of scarves and flowers. One girl threw her crutches on stage; it was a bit like being at Lourdes. When Stevie's voice cracked dangerously during 'Rhiannon', she turned to Lindsey and hid her face behind the microphone. Eight months of touring had taken its toll on all of us.

Lindsey himself collapsed about a week later in Washington DC and was hospitalized. We cancelled the gig. The doctors couldn't agree on a diagnosis and ordered a spinal tap, but they didn't put the cork back right when they had finished, and a day or two later Lindsey was in such pain that he was crawling around Caesar's Chariot on all fours. That night we were scheduled to play before 80,000 in Cleveland, with Bob Welch opening. Lindsey couldn't go on; we sent John Courage out front to say *please* don't riot, we'll come back later in the month. (This worked out OK, as we later sold out three nights instead of just one.)

In Atlanta, Stevie stole the show. In San Antonio she gave such a beautiful performance of 'Landslide' that the audience stood as one and gave her an ovation as moving as the song itself. In Mobile, Alabama, a teenage boy was stabbed to death in the hall while we played. In Dallas, Rocky Burnette, who was opening this leg of the tour, joined us on stage. (John, meanwhile, left the stage half an hour into the show, having come down with food poisoning in New Orleans the day before.) Also in Dallas, Stevie took 'Rhiannon' to its outermost limits, chanting 'Is this what you want from me?' during the crashing finale of the song.

We had worked ourselves down to the bone.

Late in August, rumours started to fly. *The Los Angeles Times*, *The Herald Examiner* and *The Hollywood Reporter* claimed that Fleetwood Mac's upcoming pair of concerts at the Hollywood Bowl would be our last, that we were breaking up. These reports cited the reasons for the putative split as solo albums, creative differences, and drugs. It was all rubbish. In Tucson, right after 'Say You Love Me', Lindsey told the crowd that we'd been touring for a year, and that it would be a long time before we'd be back again. Hopefully he added, 'and we're going to take some time off soon!'

Three days later, in front of a sold-out audience at the Hollywood Bowl, Lindsey leaned into the mike and announced 'This is our last concert . . . for a long time.' I'll never forget Stevie's 'Landslide' that night, the way she sang about growing older in her scratchy, uncertain voice. It was an ineffable moment. After the show, we had a classic locker room victory celebration – kisses, hugs, champagne, intense feelings of relief mingled with fatigue. To me it felt like the end of an era. And it indeed turned out to be exactly that.

CHAPTER NINE

Transcension

The story I am about to relate, which I somewhat ruefully call The Blob, is perhaps representative of my general state of mind in this post-*Tusk* era.

It started in New Orleans while we were still on the road. One afternoon the phone rang in my suite, and was answered by my right-hand man, Dennis Dunstan. No idea how they got my number, but Dennis, back then a bit of a lad, handed me the phone. It was a young girl trying to get tickets to the show. I ended up on the phone with her for about an hour. She had a wonderful voice, sounded very interesting and completely drew me into her world. The girl said her name was Whitney. Sure, I said, we'll leave tickets and backstage passes for you and your friends. After the gig, a guy and a girl came back and said thanks, but Whitney had to get home.

That was the start of the Blob.

I wanted to meet this girl with the wonderful voice. I had her number, called her up and invited her to the record company party in the French Quarter that night. She said she'd love to come, but she didn't show.

I talked to this girl on the phone for almost the next year. In the back of my mind I knew this was pretty odd, but it got even odder, and I found myself doing it – falling in love with this woman on the phone. I swear to God. I was still with Sara, but I was talking to Whitney on the phone day and night. Any subject, from Aston Martins to Tibetan monasteries – this girl had it covered. She sent me pictures of herself after she had told me she did some modelling in her spare time. My hands shook as I removed the photos from the envelope. She was a blonde goddess! When I'd call her, a black maid answered the phone. Whitney explained that she was just a rich brat who liked

189

to stay home, but I had to meet her. She was too good to be true!

I called Sara from the road. She and I had been fighting a lot. I said, 'Look, I know it sounds crazy but I've fallen in love with someone on the phone. I can tell you more when I get home. I don't know what's going on, but I'm obsessed, it's in process. I can't stop it.'

Sara said forget it, and moved out.

We had a few days off that August, and I begged Whitney to join me, but she had some excuse. Meanwhile, everyone on our plane was convinced that old Mick's mind was finally fucking *gone*. John McVie told me I must be nuts. Richard Dashut had somehow gotten sucked in by a friend of Whitney's, and now *he* was on the phone too. Whitney wrote me beautiful letters. I'd call and beg her to come. She said she was only eighteen and her parents were in Gstaad. I mean, she had it *nailed*. 'Please,' I'd beg, 'this is crazy, I wanna come see you.' But there was always some fabulous excuse.

Back in LA at the end of the tour Fleetwood Mac was playing the Hollywood Bowl, based at the hotel L'Ermitage. Whitney's friends would show up in limos, pick up tickets, and vouch for her! 'Oh yes, she's very beautiful', a model, and so on.

I couldn't figure it out. I wasn't giving her any money, so fraud was out. But why? Why can't I see her? She must exist. Meanwhile, I'd broken up with Sara, was living alone at Bellagio, getting more and more twisted. I kept calling Whitney and threatening to get on a plane. I finally called our New Orleans promoter, told him the story, and asked him to have this girl followed or something.

Finally, after eight months of talking to this person every day, a private detective sent me the real photos – of an overweight young woman in a VW who worked for the post office. I don't mean to be cruel, because she was a genius, brilliant at doing voices (she was the black maid too) and stringing me along. I phoned her up immediately. 'Whitney, the game's over, and what you've done isn't right. You need help, and you've got to stop.' I tried to arrange counselling for her because I still cared for that voice, but I never found out if it worked. I was prepared for this ending right from the beginning, I told myself, but I thought it might be worth the risk. A long time later, I dialled her number again. The answering machine played me 'Still Crazy After All These Years'.

Less than a month after the end of the *Tusk* tour, I realized I was in trouble with the rest of the band.

By this time, other managers began to enter the picture. John, Chris and I were still with Mickey Shapiro, but Stevie had signed with the tough industry mogul Irving Azoff, who managed the Eagles at the time, to represent her with regard to her looming solo career. Lindsey was with somebody else.

The shit hit the fan at a business meeting held to overview the *Tusk* tour with reference to the European leg. This turned into a vitriolic review of my behaviour and management skills. The basic complaint, of course, was that we'd been on the road for eight months and hadn't made much money.

I explained that we'd undertaken this tour in order to sell a difficult record, which by that time was up to five million in sales. Yes, we grossed some big numbers, but our overhead was murderous. We spent a fortune on the road, running a fat ship. We decided to be comfortable, and we lost control. If Stevie wanted a hotel suite painted pink with a white piano in it, what are you gonna do? Say no? You can't do that in a Holiday Inn! Pink rooms and pianos cost real money. These were my decisions, because they had to be. There was no management company as a buffer between me and the band. To complain about anything, as musicians love to do, they had to address a band member – me. People were honest with their feelings under this system, but they didn't like complaining about money. Even so, early in the tour I tried to change to cheaper hotels. All the others complained and I said the hell with it. From then on we went first notch. We had everything.

Irving Azoff: 'You should've made more money. Why isn't there more money after a year on the road?'

The accountant, meanwhile, was looking over the books and frowning. Impressive amounts of cash were missing, having been spent on various extravagances. The accountants and lawyers were not used to this. They didn't understand how to run a rock band. They said to me, 'How can you consider yourself a manager when you let this kind of thing happen?' But had they ever tried to say no to friends who also happened to be members of the world's biggest band? But that didn't matter.

John Courage was fired by the band's lawyers right after this meeting.

My turn came a bit later. It was a very shifty scenario. The lawyers didn't say we had done anything wrong, but it was bordering on that. There was an unspoken implication that money was missing. We felt unjustly accused by ignorant laymen. It was most unpleasant. John Courage had been working for Fleetwood Mac for almost ten years, and is one of the most honest people I've ever known. And my end had consisted of taking ten percent of the band's net, not the gross like most managers. I got paid after expenses and had no publishing, and got to work my brains out.

Granted, some kind of split was inevitable, but it was really ugly, the way it was done. It was a big meeting. Everybody was there, and all the recriminations about the past eighteen months were played out. We had been pilloried for making the most expensive record in history. *Tusk* had only gone to number three, whereas *Rumours* had been number one. We made no money on tour. Some money was unaccounted for. It was like an Indian council, everyone seated in a circle, five musicians and the lawyers with their wretched files in their laps.

I didn't say anything.

Irving Azoff made it plain that he was there to clean up the mess and take care of business. 'I represent Stevie, and she ain't doing nothing unless . . .'

His basic message was this: 'Hey, Mick, *it's over*. From this point forward, we ain't paying no management commission, no office overhead, legal fees, accounting fees, nothing. We're out for now, goodbye.'

Stevie had given Azoff the power to lever a position in the band, and Azoff had just taken us over. Running through my mind was our ongoing friendly rivalry with the Eagles, the other California glamour band of the 1970s. Fleetwood Mac and the Eagles were like Coke and Pepsi, Hertz and Avis: same age, same look, same demographic. Who is this guy? The Eagles' manager! Does he want to kill Fleetwood Mac?

But he wasn't trying to wreck anything. He was one smart fucking guy, that's all. None of the other members of the band said anything.

The end result was that I was off the throne. It was the democratization of Fleetwood Mac. Ever since, we've had review by committee – managers, lawyers, business managers. The Gang of Four.

I was very hurt by all this. I walked outside into my garden and just sat for a long time. Chris, John, Stevie and Lindsey tried to make it clear that they weren't mad at me, that they considered me to have acted like an over-indulgent father. But I felt humiliated and flogged in front of my community. It was horrible. If that's what they want to do, I thought, *fuck it*. At that point there wasn't going to be much to manage anyway, since we were all about to devolve into solo projects for a few years. John Courage went off to Hawaii to live, and I headed back to Africa, feeling a bit like King Lear.

Fortunately for me, before I left I managed to get Sara back.

When the true nature of the Blob came to light, I felt very needy and full of remorse for the pain I had put Sara through. I felt like a cad and a dupe, and I just wanted to prostrate myself before Sara, with whom I had been through so much, and say – don't abandon me now. Give me just one more chance. I was prepared to beg for it. My friends in the band were all annoyed with me, and for a while I couldn't even find her. At the same time I was feeling very lonely and dislocated. I had put the lovely house in Bel Air up for sale as part of a tax fiddle my business manager had cooked up. I had purchased a cubbyhole apartment in Monte Carlo and technically become a legal resident of Monaco, thus hoping to avoid American taxes. I figured to commute between Australia and LA, and my mum could use the Monaco place for holidays.

When Sara left, she had moved into her own place in Marina Del Rey, but she wasn't there. Then I heard on the Fleetwood Mac grapevine that Sara was in Hawaii with a boyfriend. This concept made me so queasy that I flew to Maui, arriving in time to practise in the afternoon with the Fleetwood Mac softball team, which was seeing action that night. John McVie and I were in the outfield. 'Looking for Sara?' he asked contemptuously. I gulped. 'You'll find her over at my house with . . .' And McVie named one of the dashing technicians on our crew. My heart did a backwards flip! I dropped my glove and drove over to McVie's. I knocked on the door, but there was no answer. So I went in and knocked at the bedroom door. 'Wait a minute,' Sara said.

She came out in a robe; she and this guy had been asleep. She was very angry with me. I got down on my knees, told her I was sorry and asked her to marry me.

'Mick,' she said. 'You must be really out of your mind. I'm not marrying you.'

I told her the whole story of the Blob, and Sara laughed in my face. 'You jerk,' she said.

She was right, so I grovelled. I swore I'd be good. I swore I'd reform and not be crazy. I swore I'd take care of her. She said she'd think about it, and eventually I left.

In the end, she came home.

At the big meeting at which I had been deposed, it was decided that Fleetwood Mac would take a nine-month break so members could pursue other projects. They said, we're not touring, we're not going into the studio, go find something else to do.

Ever since my trip to Zambia, I'd had odd ideas about going to Africa to record. Beyond it all, I suppose, was the idea of some Big Statement; but I really just wanted to go there and play with some of the greatest drummers and singers in the world, to have fun.

So I started to research the idea after sitting around for five weeks talking about it. Early on I picked Ghana, where I knew we'd find some of the nicest people on the continent. (The original idea had been Nigeria, but other musicians told me the vibes there were too heavy to do what I had in mind.) Then we found that a Ghanaian master drummer, Kwabene Nketia, was lecturing at UCLA. I went over and told him what I wanted to do, and he put us in touch with some people in Ghana. In mid-December 1980, right after John Lennon was murdered, Mickey Shapiro and I flew to Accra, Ghana's capital, to see what was available.

As it turned out, what was available in Accra was chaos.

Ghana, the former Gold Coast, had once been the showplace of modern West Africa. The first African nation to receive independence from colonial Europe, Ghana prospered until oil prices rose while the price of cocoa, the main export, dropped. Corruption ensued, and Ghana went broke in the seventies. The place was going down the drain when a young flight-lieutenant in the Ghanaian air force took charge in a coup in 1979. Jerry Rawlings restored order, stabilized the currency, and then went back to his barracks. By the time we stepped into Accra's blistering equatorial heat, civilian government was back, and things were beginning to slide again. An old Africa hand, descending the aeroplane ramp ahead of me, turned and said, 'Beyond the airport, everything is bedlam.' Checking into the Star Hotel, we quickly discovered that the telephones didn't work, there was no telex or telegrams, the currency was useless, there were no taxis or rental cars, and the elevators were broken. It had been some years since Ghana had had any hard currency with which to buy spare parts. There was no way to communicate with someone across town, and forget about the outside world. Things at the American embassy were chaotic, and it turned out that the Ghanaian diplomats in the US, whose names we dropped, were particularly loathed at home, probably out of sheer jealousy. We had come from the capital of the planet's music biz into a sleepy backwater of the Third World, and it took some getting used to.

We did have a contact, a young American drum scholar named Craig Woodson, who was studying local rhythms, programming them into computers and the like. When we arrived, we found that Craig was away in the up-country town of Kumasi, attending a big regional convention of drummers. 'Let's go,' I said. We found some cool guy to drive us, a gold smuggler with a new Peugeot, a car stereo blasting out old Bee Gees, and a shotgun on the front seat. As soon as we got out of Accra, we found that the roads hadn't been resurfaced in decades. The potholes were like lakes. This immediately dashed one of my fantasies; I had wanted to bus a portable studio and generator around the country, going to villages, finding the best musicians and recording with them on the spot. Now I could see the roads were so bad it would never work. Meanwhile our driver was chugging beer, slamming into potholes, and I was getting nervous. We'd hit a giant crevasse in the road and lurch. You shouldn't do this, I said, please slow down.

Hey man, he said. It's OK. Everything cool. Finally – SLAM: two flat tyres in the middle of the bush. It's at least a hundred and ten in the shade. We're fucked. Our driver takes the shotgun out of the car and begins shooting birds! I can't believe it. Suddenly another car appears out of nowhere. Mickey Shapiro flags it down, and the guy happens to have a couple of spares, which Mickey buys on the spot. Eventually we got to Kamasi, in the midst of this tribal drum festival. We found Craig, and he took us around. I was jet-lagged and dazed, but with all this Big Beat around me, I felt like I was in Paradise.

I explained to Craig my idea to come back with a few musicians and some material, find some local players and record, amalgamating the two types of music. Nothing too fancy or ambitious, just a hodge-podge of music. He quickly disabused us of the notion of going on a sonic safari with generators and tents. We realized we'd need a base in Accra, a studio where the best musicians would be channelled to us. Craig told us, as others already had, that we'd best see Faisal Helwani.

Faisal was, and is, legendary in West Africa and Europe as one of the most important producers in Africa. At the time he *was* the music industry in Ghana. His 8-track studio was the only one in town and was currently occupied by Brian Eno, who was producing an album for the hot local band Edikanfo. Faisal also owned a nightclub, and casino complex that was the only action in town at night. He was wired into the government and could get things done. As far as the Ghanaian music scene went, he was like a king, a wild man, an absolute character dripping with gold chains and dark glasses. He was Extra Classic, this guy. Yet, through all his jive, he really cared about the country and its music. Meanwhile, he thought he had seen us coming. And I'll admit we probably reeked of money. Faisal knew exactly who Fleetwood Mac were. He began to smile as I told him I wanted to meet as many musicians as possible when we came back. I want a studio, I told him, and I'll bring all the equipment and engineers from LA.

'You can't use any musicians here unless you make a deal with me,' he answered. He told us he knew we were going to sell millions of records, and that he wanted a hundred thousand dollars cash to serve as co-producer. The whole thing almost collapsed right there, but I was determined. I didn't even care about the money. I was prepared to sacrifice to bring it off. So, after some haggling, we made our deal. Faisal would get his end. We'd make a $10,000 cash payment to the musicians' union, which would arrange the musicians and oversee royalties. We would use the technically obsolete 1950s soundstage at the Film Institute of Ghana for our studio, both to record and make a film of the expedition. In return we would give the Institute $20,000 worth of film stock (Kodak hadn't sold them any film in eighteen years because of unpaid bills), and we'd let some of their people work on cutting the film.

Eventually we got the whole thing organized with much craziness. *Nothing* worked. We'd have meetings on the seventh floor of buildings without lifts or air conditioning. There were no phones to confirm meetings, so you didn't even know if your ministerial assistant would be 'on seat'. It was so hot we were even afraid our sensitive 24-track machines wouldn't work in the humidity.

Just before we went home, we had to find a good location to hold an outdoor concert which would unite the African and Anglo-American musicians, and which we'd film to use as the centrepiece of the video we wanted to make. Mickey and I went out to dinner with Craig Woodson, and after midnight he drove us to see Black Star Square in the middle of town as a possible concert site. We get out of the truck and started to wander around. Mickey took along his briefcase, as he always did, and Craig says, 'You can leave it, there's no one around.' We got thirty feet from the truck, heard something, turned around, and there's a shadowy figure darting into the night with Mickey's briefcase, which of course contained our whole paper lives and identities – passports, money, credit cards, kids' pictures, plane tickets back to the US. The poor man came apart right there. The briefcase was Mickey's security blanket and office. He looked at me in desperation and I could only laugh. 'C'mon, Mickey, it'll be good for you. You can't use the fucking credit cards here anyway. Forget it.'

We went to the police station to file a report. There were three chickens scratching around the floor. The constable told us he couldn't take our report because he didn't have any paper. At that moment, I whipped out my trusty Polaroid SX-70 and snapped a shot of Mickey, which was later published by *American Photographer* magazine in a celebrity snapshot section depicting the most dejected man in the world. The next morning, Mickey stormed into the offices of British Caledonian Airlines, explained the situation, and said, 'I want you to give me two first class tickets from Accra to London, then London to LA.' And the guy gave them to him.

I spent Christmas with Jenny, Lucy and Amy, and then flew back to LA to try to make a deal to get our African odyssey financed. We had to explain ourselves to some American recording executive well enough to get him to sign a cheque for half a million dollars so we could fly a recording studio halfway around the planet. Mo Ostin looked at it, blinked at all the zeros, and Warner Brothers passed the next day. Then we heard that RCA was developing their laser videodisk technology and were desperate for programming. Bill Summer, the president of the company and a sophisticated guy, flew out, had lunch with us, and eventually gave it the green light. They loved the idea, God bless 'em, and they paid for *The Visitor*.

I asked Bob Welch to come back to Ghana with me, but he passed. So I took my friend George Hawkins to play bass and sing, and guitarist Todd Sharp, who had just left Bob Welch's band. This would be our core trio that would interface, we hoped, with the cream of Ghana's pop and folkloric musicians. Richard Dashut, who would produce the sessions, bought two 16-track machines, because we figured one would break in Ghana (where we couldn't even replace a battery), as well as mounds of tape, cable, microphones, everything we would need, serviced by a five-man crew of good mates and buddies. All of this, plus the film gear, was loaded into a chartered jet and flown from LA to Gatwick, and then down to the west coast of Africa in January 1981.

Richard Dashut flew with me and Sara to Australia first, so we could spend a few weeks at Wensley Dale to which I was still planning to move. It was the first time I had actually lived in the old mansion, and we soon discovered the place was really haunted. Richard watched doors open by themselves and saw strange, faint apparitions. You could hear the sounds of children running on the floor above, which we knew was quite empty. Bureau doors slammed shut by themselves. There were bizarre cold spots everywhere in the place. But it was also extremely beautiful, a frontier paradise with gum trees and kangaroos.

One day, just before we left, we were off away from the house, taking a walk. We turned around and saw that huge dark clouds had formed over Wensley Dale. The dry wind came up with a rush, and the moment felt dramatic. Richard and I looked at each other and had the same thought – that once we left, we'd never see this place again.

Then we flew west, towards Africa. We stopped in Singapore to change planes and went on a shopping spree. On a whim I bought an $8000 Rolex President watch with a credit card. (Later, after weeks stumbling around impoverished Ghana, I was in a bar in Accra late at night with Richard and some people. I was *very* drunk, and I looked around and thought, what am I doing wearing this big gold watch amidst such poverty and privation? I took one of the big club beer bottles they had, laid the Rolex on the bar, and bashed it to death with the butt of the bottle. It was a stupid gesture in a drunken rampage, but to me it had some small meaning.)

We were in Ghana for seven weeks in early 1981, making music, throwing feasts and having incredible fun. We got a Mercedes bus and drove to musicians' homes, auditioning and taping songs to use on the album. Everyone was broke and wanted money, especially the giant unhinged bureaucracy we had to deal with. But in the end, people were simply too nice to put the heavy screws on us, and we got along very well. Eventually we learned that you don't need phones and freeways to be happy. In fact, I gained a tremendous sense of how *little* I actually needed to consider myself doing OK. It was a very African lesson for The Visitor to learn that winter, as the arid *harmattan* winds blowing south from the Sahara pushed the wet monsoon out into the sea.

We all lived dorm-style at the Star Hotel and commuted to the studio every day. As a drummer trained to play steady purist rock style – sixteen beats, classic 4/4 rock time – it took me a while to get used to the Africans' 12-beat drum music. I wasn't used to the constant embellishment at the heart of the Ghanaian hand-drumming. In a typical five-man drum group, only *atumpan*, or talking drums, are allowed to improvise. The others are secondary drums and bells. In a group like that, I was really just a support player with my big, Western drum kit. But we also learned that the place where sixteen rock-beats met twelve Afro-beats was the Land of Funk, where your bum begins to twitch involuntarily. Guided by this knowledge, we cut a new version of 'Rattlesnake Shake' with a children's drum ensemble, Ebaali Gbiko. We did a song, 'You Weren't In Love', with drummer Lord Tiki and added backing vocals by the Accra Roman Catholic Choir that were otherwordly. A group called Adzo came in and we cut several things: 'O'Niamali', 'Amelle', Buddy Holly's 'Not Fade Away', and

Lindsey Buckingham's 'Walk A Thin Line' from *Tusk*. We recorded 'The Visitor' with the Ghana Folkloric Group, some of the best harmony singers I ever heard, and a track called 'Super Brains' with the impossibly hot band of the same name. Todd Sharp strung together some of the hortatory slogans on the back of local buses (DEATH MAY BE WORSE; WHY WORRY; NO MONEY, NO FRIEND) into a song called 'Don't Be Sorry, Just Be Happy'. As we had feared, sometimes it was so hot that our machines stopped.

All this time, we were living about four doors down from the military strongman, Jerry Rawlings. They kept asking us if we wanted to meet him, and we remembered that when he seized power he had executed three former heads of state and five of their aides, all for gross corruption. With that in mind, we passed on an introduction. There was one high official who helped us, de Graft Johnson, then serving as Ghana's vice-president. (When Jerry Rawlings got fed up with economic anarchy a year or so later, de Graft Johnson was the first guy he threw into jail.) But before we left, the vice-president and a host of other local lights crowded into the open pavilion of the Star Hotel to hear the concert we played, supported by the best musicians in Ghana – Edikanfo, Super Brains, Adzo Cultural, a group called Ebaahi and the guitarist Koo Nimo, head of the Musicans' Union of Ghana. At first, when we started to play our Afro-rock 'Rattlensake Shake', there was only silence from the 2000-strong audience. Then a rock-starved marine from the US Embassy got up with his date and began to boogie. Soon the cheap seats emptied. Then, up on the balcony where the VP and other VIPs were sitting, some wiggling started, then dancing. Then everyone was up and the place went mad. We played for *hours* that night. My arms felt like they were falling off, but I kept riffing, unable to stop. 'Thank you,' George Hawkins said to the spent dancers at three in the morning. 'We love you very much.'

After a couple of months, we realized it was time to leave. We took the film crew up the river by boat and into the markets for some local colour, and then ran into some horrible problems when the Ghanaian film people insisted on doing post-production work themselves, and it didn't get done. (Eventually we had to hire a BBC director to finish *The Visitor*.)

During these weeks in Africa, I had begun to forget about Fleetwood Mac, its trials and tribulations. But the reality to which I would soon return was brought home to me in an interview I did with the Ghana Broadcasting Corporation (whose bunker-like studio was guarded by two purple tanks) to plug our concert. After a fairly pat welcome, the interviewer began to pepper me with questions. Why had *Tusk* been so raw and experimental, coming in for criticism from both the left and the right? That one floored me. Why do John McVie and Lindsey Buckingham have their ex-wives in the band? I tried to stammer an answer to this most African of questions, but it was really too much.

My job now was to get our African tapes mixed.

Richard and I left Ghana and flew to England where we met Sara and settled into the oldest inn in Britain, Ye Old Bell, near my ex-brother-in-law George Harrison's place in Henley-upon-Thames. I had asked George if I could use his studio to mix my tapes, but it wasn't possible. Instead, he contacted Jimmy Page and arranged for us to use Jimmy's studio nearby, in an old mill. There we decompressed from Africa, overdubbing and mixing *The Visitor*, eating like pigs in the inn and resting in between. We had recorded 'Rattlesnake Shake' with the idea that Peter Green would sing over it. If he didn't, it wasn't going to be on the album. I called Pete, and he was kind enough to come out to sing and play on the track, as well as the one we did with Super Brains. I found him quite together and objective about himself. His deportment was better, and being with him wasn't as upsetting as it had been.

But that was the last time I saw the old Green God.

We finished *The Visitor* towards the end of April. George Harrison came over and put some slide guitar on 'Walk A Thin Line' for me. Other English musicians added a lead guitar part here, a synthesizer there. When the whole project was done, we'd spent about half a million dollars. The album was released soon after and didn't make one fucking dime, but I had learned and experienced more than money can buy.

Meanwhile, there were rumblings back home.

'LOOKS LIKE END OF THE LINE FOR FLEETWOOD MAC' screamed the headline in the *New York Post* in March 1981. 'There's big trouble among members of rock's hottest group,' the story continued, 'and some highly placed music industry sources are saying the band is swiftly headed for the rocks.' Citing creative differences and a loss of income on our last tour, the paper concluded: 'The untimely breakup of Fleetwood Mac could send shock waves throughout the music world unlike any since the Beatles split eleven years ago.'

Well, that was nice, but as usual it wasn't true. In fact, when Richard and I finished mastering *The Visitor* in London in early May 1981, we got into my old Bristol car, headed south for the Channel, and boarded the night ferry to France, where the rest of Fleetwood Mac was waiting at a rented sixteenth-century château in Herouville, about sixty miles from Paris, to begin work on our next album.

We arrived as the sun was rising on the day we were to actually begin recording. As we drove down the château's long tree-lined lane, Richard and I marvelled that no sooner had we laid the whole African chapter to rest than it was time to begin yet another era, with scarcely pause for breath. We pulled up into the drive, looked up and saw Stevie Nicks peering out of the ancient leaded glass window of the château, looking like Queen Guinevere in the misty early light. It was as if she were waiting for us, being the dawn-type lady that she is.

I had asked the band to record outside the United States, so that as a citizen of Monte Carlo I wouldn't be liable for American taxes. I was beginning to get into dire straits with money, having taken bank loans out at some of the highest interest rates in living memory to pay for real estate. I had to prove this new album was recorded out of the country. I was still thinking of emigrating to Australia and giving up my American green card to live as Lord of the Manor at Wensley Dale, but at the same time, Lord of the Manor was getting more nervous every day. In the back of my mind, I knew I couldn't operate out of the US. If I stayed away too long, Fleetwood Mac might drift apart, and I was obsessed with keeping this band together and working – no matter what.

It turned out that the writers had some splendid new music together, and recording was fun. Le Château, the 'Honky Chateau' of Elton John fame, was a much-favoured studio of the Euro-rock aristocracy – private, very romantic, with great food and stupendous ambience. (We had it redecorated for the girls, spending the usual pile.) Plus it wasn't too far from Paris. So into Paris I'd go, with our crew member Dennis Kean. One morning on the way back from one of these forays, we passed a stable and I decided I had to ride back to the château through the ancient fog-shrouded countryside. So I got this big grey mare, took a long pull from my ever-present silver flask of good cognac, and rode home, and then right up the stone steps of the house's main entrance. *Quelle scandale!* Amidst a grand to-do, Stevie swept down the big staircase, leapt on the back of my horse, and cantered off through the greening orchards, her long cape billowing behind her.

Mirage, the album we recorded in France, was an attempt to get into the *Rumours* groove again, but in an updated style. Chris's songs,

especially 'Hold Me', reflected her bittersweet reflections on her relationship with Dennis Wilson, which had almost resulted in marriage
but had ended instead the previous December when Dennis had moved
out of Chris's house and her life. Christine had loved Dennis with all
her heart (we all did), and it was a fascinating if exhausting episode in
her life. I felt some responsibility, because I had introduced them.
Dennis was an utter loon, and Chris was like my sister. I watched in
trepidation as Chris almost went mad trying to keep up with Dennis,
who was already like a man with twenty thyroid glands, not counting
the gargantuan amounts of coke and booze and pills he was always
shoving into himself. I was very torn, because Dennis was a
friend, and I'd see him fucking up and chasing skirts and didn't know
whether it was my role to say anything to Chris. In the end I didn't
have to. She got tired of spending a fortune and her health on
maintaining Dennis on the road to his eventual destiny. In any
case, 'Hold Me' was a great song, and became the first hit single of
the new album.

Stevie's songs – including the utterly majestic 'Gypsy' – were what
she had saved for us after recording her first album, *Bella Donna*,
which was about to sell ten million copies and make Miss Nicks the
Queen of Rock. Some leftover! 'Gypsy' is one of Fleetwood Mac's
greatest works of art; for me that whole period of the early 1980s is
crystallized in it.

Lindsey Buckingham had also been recording a solo project, which
became the *Law and Order* album. He arrived in France with two good
songs, 'Can't Go Back' and 'Eyes of the World'. Three others – 'Book
of Love', 'Empire State', and 'Oh Diane' – were written with Richard
Dashut at the château and in the three other studios in LA where
Mirage was wrapped up over the next seven months. Tired of being
typecast as the archetypal northern California hippy, Lindsey had now
veered from his new wave sound into a 1955 Eddie Cochrane rock &
roll feel. (I remember some semi-tense conversations on musical
direction in this era, as Lindsey still felt that I blamed him for the
relatively weak sales of *Tusk*. I thought we should do what we do best,
and insisted on doing this album as a band. This time, the whole band
played on almost every track; then Chris, Lindsey, and I spent months
in the studio, overdubbing in typical Fleetwood Mac fashion.)

I returned to southern California during the summer of 1981, after the
French recording sessions, having been away most of the year. The
house in Bel Air had been sold, and all my things moved to the new

house I had bought in Ramirez Canyon, which I called the Blue Whale. So begins one of my most notorious epochs.

The Blue Whale was a huge house surrounding a pool. I had watched it being built while staying in Jenny's little house nearby, and fantasized about living there. The property had an ample guest house, and I thought it would be a perfect place where lots of people could hang out and play music. Barbra Streisand and Don Henley were neighbours. I was dubious about whether I could afford the place, but my business manager said no problem, and I paid $2.4 million for the property. Sara and I moved in, and over the next couple of years, it turned into a real zoo.

Mirage was released in mid-1982, an artistic and financial success. Both 'Hold Me' and 'Gypsy' were hit singles in the US, and 'Oh Diane' was a British chart hit as well. I think we sold about five million albums. It didn't hurt that *Rolling Stone* had crowned Stevie 'The Reigning Queen of Rock & Roll', and that a new cable television channel called MTV was broadcasting our new videos – 'Hold Me' set in desert dunes, 'Gypsy' in a Stevie fantasy world – to the American suburbs twenty-four hours a day. *Mirage* went to number one, and it felt great to be back on top for a while.

Mirage also marked the first time that Fleetwood Mac didn't automatically tour to support a new album. Stevie's solo career was now in full swing, and she obviously didn't want to do a long Fleetwood Mac road-binge in the midst of becoming one of the biggest stars in the business. We did do an eighteen-show stint during the summer of 1982 that was booked around two big outdoor festivals in Florida and the immense US Festival in California (for which Fleetwood Mac received $800,000 for one show).

I felt sick when we stopped touring. *Mirage* was number one and sales were strong in cities where we'd played. I wanted to be on the move, touring until the cows came home, but the others were less enthusiastic. Christine had sessions for her own solo album scheduled, and we'd been lucky to get Stevie at all. As soon as we left the road, *Mirage* died after five weeks at number one. The Australian band Men At Work, who had opened for us on the road, saw their album go to number one shortly thereafter.

The US Festival was also the last time I saw Robin Anderson.

Robin had been Stevie Nicks' best friend for years and years, and I had known and loved her ever since the wild days in Sausalito recording

Rumours. Robin was a voice therapist, and had often accompanied Fleetwood Mac on the road to work on preserving Stevie's voice. One of the most beautiful and beloved members of our extended family, she was married to Kim Anderson, a Warner Brothers promotion guy. She had also been ill with leukaemia for the past two years, beginning around the time of the *Tusk* tour. Although she had been in and out of hospital, and against the advice of her doctors, she became pregnant and was determined to bear her child before she left this earth. The baby boy she bore definitely shortened her young life, but that was part of the heroic nature of Robin's determination.

When we came off the stage at the US Festival, a giant outdoor event in the desert organized by a computer mogul, I asked where Robin was, because I'd had this gold and ruby crucifix made in Malibu, which I wanted Robin to have. Someone yelled that she had already gone to the helicopter that was shuttling musicians and friends to and from the site. I ran up to the chopper as it was about to take off, and there was Robin looking gorgeous, but as frail as a petal. I took the cross from around my neck and put it in her hands. I removed my heavy black cape and wrapped it around her, and hugged her as lovingly as I could. She smiled at me, and began to brush back tears. The helicopter took off with her into the western sky, and the dust made my own eyes teary.

A bit later, I was fishing up in Lake Shasta when I was called into the lodge. Stevie was on the phone, very upset. Robin had died, Stevie sobbed, clutching my crucifix.

We all went into something of a spin over these sad events. Robin's death was a terrible loss. And there were more repercussions to come.

In late January 1983, I was home at the Blue Whale, working on the second of three solo albums due under my deal with RCA. The phone rang, and someone told me that Stevie was on the line. I knew something had to be up, because Stevie only called me when the news was important. I usually called her. She said, 'Mick, you better sit down.' I remember it like it was this morning. I was all sweaty from recording, sitting on the interior balcony that looked out over the big living room of the Blue Whale. She said, 'Are you sitting down?'

Thank God I was.

She told me she was going to marry Kim Anderson, Robin's widower. Stevie was emotionally involved with Robin's new baby, and felt an overpowering responsibility to care for this child, even to the point of wedding Robin's husband. My mouth opened, but nothing came out.

I realized my old feelings for Stevie had never been resolved. I was dumbfounded. I just didn't know what to say. I went downstairs to the bedroom and burst into tears. I came back up to the room we were using as a studio and said to Richard, 'You won't believe this. Stevie's getting married to Kim.'

We all knew it was too soon, only weeks after Robin had gone. It was a dramatic gesture by two people bonded together only in misery. Christine and I went to the ceremony, at some born-again type of church. Stevie's bridal veil was one of sorrow. I could see on her face that she knew it was a mistake.

This marriage was very short-lived. To this day, Stevie won't talk about it.

The Blue Whale was also known in our social circle as both the Ice Palace, and Hotel Hell. It was sort of like a rock & roll boarding house, or a boys' clubhouse for about ten people – almost like an updated version of Benifols. It grew into a hang-out, a meeting place for lots of people; there were tons of the old blowski on the premises, and many days and nights of lost memories. Dave Mason lived in my guest cottage, and there was much great fun and comradeship. We also recorded an album there called *I'm Not Me*, which was the first manifestation of the continuing enterprise known as Mick Fleetwood's Zoo.

The Zoo had its roots in the loose musical scene around the Blue Whale. The original idea had been to follow up *The Visitor* with a Brazilian project. George Hawkins would go to Rio with me, and we'd record with the cream of Brazilian musicians. To this end we bought a portable studio, which we instead set up at the Blue Whale when the South American project was scrapped. Then I got a little band together, with George on bass, Steve Ross (a friend of Richard's) on guitar, and Billy Burnette doing the vocals.

I had met Billy in early 1983, when we had both been celebrity guests at a Dick Clark TV taping. Billy was just getting a solo career together, but I knew that he was of Memphian royal blood. Billy's father and uncle, Dorsey and Johnny Burnette, were friends of Elvis Presley who had formed the Rock & Roll Trio in 1956 with guitarist Paul Burlison (who in turn had been a heavy influence on all the English guitarists, including Peter Green). Trio hits like 'Trains Kept 'A Rolling' and 'Tear It Up' are keystones of the music we all play. Billy was born in Memphis in 1953, but raised in Woodland Hills in the San Fernando Valley. He'd also been in the music business most

205

of his life, opening for Brenda Lee when he was thirteen years old. I'd heard the music he made, and after this TV show I simply went up to him and said, 'We're going to do something together someday.' It was just a feeling I had.

I called Billy and invited him over to the Blue Whale, where we played some, and it felt good. We've been like family ever since. Then Lindsey Buckingham asked us to back him on *Saturday Night Live*, the first time we appeared in public. Then we did a paying gig at the 'Rock & Run' event in LA and a couple of charity gigs, one for the Pepperdine University Medical Center. It felt like a working band, so we decided to make it one. We cut *I'm Not Me* almost entirely at home, with Richard producing. The material was a mixture of oldies ('Tear It Up' and Lloyd Price's 'Just Because'), a couple of covers (like the Beach Boys' 'Angel Come Home') and new songs by the band and various other writers. Both Lindsey and Christine McVie played on the album; it was my intention that other Fleetwood Mac members could drift in and out at their whim. Richard Dashut came up with the name Mick Fleetwood's Zoo, a tribute to the bestial nature of life at the Blue Whale. It was an appropriate name. But this would be the sort of zoo where the animals come and go from the cages all the time, at will.

I really liked *I'm Not Me*, but it stiffed. When I listen to it now, I'm amazed to hear how much we were influenced by the Beach Boys' sound. (It also reminds me of how much we all loved Dennis Wilson, who got drunk and drowned in the Marina late in 1983, much to our general misery.)

Lord knows, we tried to make the Zoo album a hit, touring throughout America. We bought ourselves tuxedos and played bars, travelling by bus – the old-fashioned way. It was like a scene from *Spinal Tap*: we'd arrive at these clubs and there'd be nobody there. The lads in the band were embarrassed for me when we'd go out and play for fifty people. But I loved it. It was a total failure, and a lot of fun. Some of those moments were classics, like the time in Maui when Stevie joined the Zoo to sing 'Rhiannon' at a restaurant gig and three thousand people heard about it and showed up. The place opened its windows and the mob was dancing in the street.

That was pretty much the end of my deal with RCA. I bailed out of the third album I was supposed to do for them. *The Visitor* hadn't done well either, and with two stiffs they didn't need a third. They treated me with respect, and gave me some money to live on.

I went home to England that year, 1983, in part to work on Christine's solo album at Steve Winwood's studio in Gloucester. One night I had a yen to visit my old school in nearby Sherbourne. At three in the morning, we drove down to what had been King's School. The place was ghostly and bare, and was obviously no longer used as a school. Yet I could almost hear the laughter of excited boys, could almost feel the twinge of loss for my relatively cozy and secure childhood. How different the man from the boy, I thought, and yet how much the same as well.

Adding to the Felliniesque atmosphere of the old Whale were the genuinely surreal episodes when deranged fans would stumble into the place. I remember one episode vividly. It started on the *Tusk* tour. I'd met this girl somewhere in the Midwest, and she pulled me. We went back to the hotel; she ended up staying the night. She read the Bible, and I read some of my Dad's poetry. We slept together, nothing else happened. She was young, unhappy, divorced, very good looking, with two kids. I thought that was it.

Somehow she got the tour itinerary. Soon the phone calls started and didn't stop. Then, off the road, she got my address, and letters started coming. Sara went through my drawers and found them. Great! So I said, 'Yeah, OK, one night!' It took me a full year to live this down! Then the telegrams started, saying she's having my child, accompanied by thick religious letters running to hundreds of pages. 'I see the Lord in your eyes', in all its obsessive variants. The letters got more heated. She got the phone number, somehow, but I wouldn't talk to her.

Two years went by. I started to get letters postmarked Phoenix, and Sara said, 'She's getting closer.' Not long after, Sara and I were in bed at the Blue Whale, comatose after a two-day Transcension. Suddenly, the huge French windows of our bedroom rattled us awake, and we heard breaking glass. It was *her*! She'd tracked me down! Three years later, paying for the Veal Viper!! She had metamorphosed into a crazy hag – fat, pink polyester coat, no shoes, brown paper bag in hand. She wanted in!

'Go away!' I shouted. 'I'm calling the police.' Which I did. So she left, walked up the canyon towards the Pacific Coast Highway, where she was picked up hitching by a friend of mine. He left her off at the highway, where the police found her in the foetal position, screaming. I felt terrible, and talked to her doctor at the asylum where she'd been taken. 'Try not to feel responsible,' he said. 'If it hadn't been you, it would have been someone else.'

Eventually, of course, the bottom dropped out. In the spring of 1984, I was forced to file a bankruptcy petition.

I also had a young manager who became out of control, got me into some dumb investments and the worst real estate market in this century. On some of my mortgages I was paying well over twenty-two per cent. To keep up the monthly payments for Wensley Dale and the Blue Whale, I had to cough up $40,000 a month. I had to make a million dollars a year to cover that, which was fine when I was making a million dollars a year. We had planned for Fleetwood Mac to go back to work much sooner than it did, and when the band stayed off the road, my income couldn't keep up with the expenditure. I had said to this manager, when I was allowed to buy these properties, 'You know what's gonna happen, don't you? In eighteen months it's all gonna be over.' But the manager didn't want to say no to me. We fell right into it, and I was too preoccupied and blind to rein it all in. Eventually, I woke up and tried to save myself. Dear Christine McVie lent me $50,000 at one point to cover myself, but it was a drop in the bucket. I sold my gold records for $1500 and put the Blue Whale, my car collection and about $50,000 worth of recording equipment on the market. It was a humiliating ordeal, attended by abominable publicity. 'MICK'S INCREDIBLE MISSING MILLIONS', ran headlines in the London papers when word got out. People were saying that I'd put $8 million up my nose, but if I'd done all the things they said, I'd have been dead long ago.

I also didn't care *that* much, and tried to maintain my sense of humour and a stiff upper lip. I remember sitting there, watching the movers taking our things out of the Blue Whale after it had been sold off and thinking, Oh my God! I've managed to lose eight million dollars. But I've never been terribly attached to material things, and have often thought the whole 'Ruptcy', as Sarah and I called it, was probably a blessing in disguise. We split up, and she went to work, and re-entered the so-called Real World.

Fifteen years earlier, back in 1969, Jenny and I had gone to see a famous American astrologer in London named Liz Green. I was never a rabid astrology buff, but Jenny and Judy Wong were really into it, and the whole family had charts done. Mine sounded very interesting. She told me that I was going to make a lot of money and be a very wealthy man. She also told me that I'd go through a fallow period and lose it all. But don't worry, she said, because after this you're going to start acting.

I only remembered this after the bankruptcy, and it gave me hope.

When I closed down the Blue Whale, I moved into the back room of Richard's house, nearby in the canyon. As I lay down to sleep there that first night, I told myself that everything would be fine, that I'd make it back for the sake of the kids and my mother.

And I was relieved that my father hadn't lived to see this day.

CHAPTER TEN

Comeback

It's like a living thing, this Fleetwood Mac.
It's a source stronger than its various members.

Christine McVie

Time passed. It took another three years to get the next Fleetwood Mac album made, and the band back on the road.

Most of 1985 was spent trying to re-group and re-order my life after the bankruptcy. There were many changes to cope with. Gone were my various properties and my fleet of cars, sold off at fire sale prices. Richard and I decamped from Little Ramirez, which had begun to give us the creeps. Instead we rented a big house overlooking Point Dume in Malibu. Dispersed was the wild and crazy entourage that had eventually turned the Blue Whale into a pool of leeches. In its place was the core of hearty lads who played in the Zoo, which continued to function as a glorified bar band in the saloons of Hawaii, Trancas Canyon and points eastward. But as much as I love the Zoo, my main concern was the revivification of Fleetwood Mac. The problem was how to make it happen? Stevie had a booming career of her own now. Her second solo album, *The Wild Heart*, had sold in the millions, and now she was working on her third, *Rock A Little*. It would be hard to persuade her management that she should come back to us for a while. Lindsey was also working on his third solo project, and Christine was enjoying a huge solo hit with 'Got A Hold On Me'. John McVie seemed quite happy in semi-retirement, sailing his boat and playing occasional gigs with John Mayall and Mick Taylor in a reformed Bluesbreakers.

I was the only member of the band desperate to see it back together.

The reformation process started somewhat inauspiciously, when the rest of the band visited Stevie Nicks backstage at a benefit she was playing with her own band at the Universal Amphitheater for a local environmental group called Mulholland Tomorrow. It was the first time Fleetwood Mac had all been together since the end of the *Mirage* tour, three years earlier, and the tension was so thick you could choke on it.

As it happened, it was really Christine McVie who reunited Fleetwood Mac.

It started when she called John Courage out of his Hawaiian exile to help her make an album in Switzerland, and eventually to manage her career. Christine had been asked to record Elvis's 'Can't Help Falling In Love' for the sound-track of the film *A Fine Mess*. She called in Richard Dashut to produce, who in turn said that Lindsey was a real Elvis fan and might like to get involved. Then John Courage called me and John McVie, and in August 1985 four-fifths of Fleetwood Mac found themselves in the studio, cutting this record. This was fun, and the seed that eventually grew into *Tango in the Night*.

But it was far from easy. Our natural group chemistry was still pretty weak at that point, and it was really the lawyers and managers – what we call the Gang of Four – who tried to work out a structure in which we could create together. I have to say that from the outset, Stevie's people were great. Mick's in a jam, they said. How can we help him? John McVie said he would be there. Christine said she was in. Lindsey Buckingham alone was fairly reticent about Fleetwood Mac. He was enjoying his hard-won independence and deep into his own album with Richard Dashut. Eventually we worked to build enough momentum that we were able to convince Lindsey that it might go off without him. When Lindsey said he was in, things went forward. Since Mr Buckingham was immersed in his own record, we felt it necessary to bring in an outside producer for the first time in years. First we met with Nile Rogers, but it didn't work out. Then Mo Ostin at Warners gave us some money to hire producer Jason Casaro from New York, who had coaxed such an astounding sound from the pickup band Power Station earlier that year. We booked into Studio One and held a week of glorified rehearsals without Stevie, who at the time was touring Australia with fellow Frontline client Tom Petty and Bob Dylan. (She appeared onstage with them a couple of times to sing 'Knocking On Heaven's Door' until the authorities discovered she didn't have the right visa and prohibited her from performing.) Nothing came of these sessions; in fact it took us about a week to realize that any outside producer who tried to harness the old Mac at that point was going to be in way over his head. So Mr Casaro went home, and for a while in early 1986 it looked as if this record wasn't going to get made. In the end, to salvage the project, Lindsey and Richard decided to continue the now hallowed tradition of producing Fleetwood Mac themselves.

It took us eighteen months, working under completely different conditions than what we were used to. We had started out at Rumbo Sound in the Valley, where the basic tracks were cut. We then moved production to the studio Lindsey had built in the garage of his house, called The Slope, where we would mix and do the overdubs. It wasn't really a proper studio *per se*; everything is recorded right in the control room. The acoustics were the wooden floor, the bathroom, the carpet, the hallway. To minimize wear and tear to the property, John Courage brought in a trailer with phones and a TV and a place to hang out.

This arrangement changed everything. We began to work regular hours. We were all sick of cocaine and had given it up, so it was all very organized, and we got into a nice routine with few delirious moments as of yore, and almost no all-night Transcending – wot I was used to. (Actually there was a *little* splurge of villainy early on; 'Tango In The Night' was the result of a two-piece drunken Transcension between Lindsey and me. We used the drum track as the basis for the song.)

Recording proceeded slowly at first. It had been a long layoff for Fleetwood Mac and some of us were a little rusty. John McVie had spent the last couple of years drinking at a sailing hideaway he maintained on the Caribbean island of St Thomas. John's a great musician, but he had hardly played in two years and his chops were way down. At first he'd come to the studio and hold court with his bass in his lap. Then he'd go home, having forgotten to lay down his bass parts. Then he started to get worried that he had lost his touch completely. I'd have to say, 'C'mon, John, you *know* what you're doing; you've been at this for twenty-five years!' He stopped drinking for a while and tried to play it stone-cold sober, and this didn't quite work either. I began to get really concerned. The others asked me, 'What's going on with McVie? Why is this taking so long?' But I could tell John was suffering a serious artistic block, a blind panic of the kind I used to feel when they asked me questions in school. I was so worried that I took him out to dinner and said, 'John, you've got to tell me what's happening. What's the problem playing these parts?'

He looked miserable. 'I don't know what it is, Mick,' he said. 'I don't feel part of the creative side of this record. You know I've never had much input into writing. I just like to go out and play the music.'

'Look, John,' I ventured, 'this is our first record in years and years, and maybe you shouldn't take it all *that* seriously. We know you've long suffered little traumas in the studio. Do you remember *Kiln House*? When you said you were sick of playing and just wanted to be a roadie for a while? Well, you got over that, and you'll get over this too.'

McVie smiled ruefully, and said he'd go back to the studio and try again. From then on things went more smoothly for him. A few months later he was stricken by an alcoholic seizure on St Thomas that scared the life out of him and his wife, and John stopped drinking completely with the help of a therapist. As always, John McVie came through for Fleetwood Mac.

Christine McVie came through too, with some of her most wonderful songs – 'Everywhere', which glistened like gemstone even in Chris's original demo; 'Little Lies', destined to be a hit single on both sides of the Atlantic; and 'Isn't It Midnight', which she co-wrote with Lindsey and her new husband, Eddie Quintela (who Chris married in October 1986).

Lindsey Buckingham dipped into his postponed solo album for four new songs for Fleetwood Mac: 'Big Love', 'Caroline', 'Tango In the Night' (which originated in the live versions of 'So Afraid') and 'Family Man'. Lindsey and Christine also co-wrote two more album tracks: 'Mystified' and 'You and I', which came in two parts. We used Part II to close the album, and Part I appeared on the reverse of the first single, 'Big Love'.

Through all this, Stevie Nicks had been working and touring to promote her third solo album, *Rock A Little*. She had spent a million to make it, and Frontline kept her away from us while they were selling it. I went on part of her long 1986 tour, playing percussion in a hot band that included Waddy Wachtel on guitars, and I could see that Stevie was running herself right into the ground. She was drinking and doing a lot of cocaine. Every night I'd watch her launch into one of her dancing spins on stage, and each night the spins got more and more dizzy until I was afraid she was going to fall off the stage during a show. 'Stevie,' I said, 'you're going to hurt yourself. You've got to work on getting away from being so high while you're on stage.'

She would cry to me, 'Oh Mick, I know it! I don't wanna be like this. I don't wanna need this stuff so much. I'm gonna do something

– after the tour's over.' I knew what Stevie meant. You can't go cold turkey on a major tour after years of partying and having a good time. But now the party was over. It had become an addiction, a way of life. Later, while Fleetwood Mac was labouring in the studio, Stevie and her band went to Australia, where her drinking worsened and she fell off the stage twice. I was afraid she would injure herself, or worse.

Stevie finally showed up in January 1987; we'd been working six months, and it was the only time the whole band was in the studio together. We had been sending copies of our working tapes to Stevie's home in Arizona. For her part, she was dreading that Lindsey, in his producing capacity, would be sarcastic towards her, but he made an effort not to be as much of a martinet as he was with the rest of us. He was under some strain with this project, and lost his patience occasionally, but with Stevie we wanted him to be more objective and professional. He tried to make her feel great in the studio, and they got on well. (The love-hate saga between those two will never end.)

Complicating matters slightly in the spring of 1987 was Stevie's admission to the Betty Ford Center in Palm Springs to get her life under control. This was done through an 'intervention' by friends, members of her family, and her management company. Stevie spent twenty-eight days in a successful treatment for alcohol problems, but she didn't like being coerced into entering this facility, and Frontline was fired shortly thereafter. (Later she told me that the treatment made her change her way of thinking, and was worth it.)

So the little time we had with Stevie was somewhat disoriented, but she did come through with good songs. 'Seven Wonders' was written by songwriter Sandy Stewart and augmented with new words by Stevie in the studio. 'Welcome to the Room, Sara' was a graphic depiction of her experience at the Betty Ford Center, where she had checked in under the pseudonym Sara Anderson. (This song is extremely moving when understood in that context.) 'When I See You Again' continued Stevie's string of touching songs of farewell, and was used on *Tango* in favour of a fourth uptempo number that Stevie brought in called 'What Has Rock & Roll Ever Done for You'.

We did have one blow-out with Stevie when she came to the studio to listen to the mixes before *Tango In The Night* was released. After the playback was finished, she began to storm around the studio like a tornado. 'It's like I'm not even *on* this record,' she complained. 'I can't hear myself at all.' I knew Stevie pretty well, and could tell she was angry. Then she threatened us. 'All right, maybe I wasn't able to get to the studio that much, but how is it going to look when the record comes out and I might have to tell *Rolling Stone* that I didn't work on it?'

Christine McVie's eyes narrowed. She'd had a couple of glasses of wine, and wasn't about to be trifled with. 'OK, Stevie,' she said, 'what are you so upset about?'

'I should be singing on "Everywhere",' Stevie said. 'You should hear me singing harmony on that song.'

'I *wanted* you to sing on it too,' Chris said in measured tones that signalled she was furious, 'but you weren't here. In fact, we've been working for a year and you were only with us for a couple of days. Now why don't you just say you're sorry and we'll work it out?'

Quite gracefully, Stevie capitulated in front of the whole band, and we gleefully layered her vocals into the mix of the album, which now sounded indeed more like Fleetwood Mac. Stevie had been right after all, and so had Christine.

Tango In The Night was released in the spring of 1987 amid much hoopla. We spent a quarter million dollars on the totally surreal video for 'Big Love', the single of which quickly jumped into the top ten. Who, the media wanted to know, was responsible for the song's carnal love grunts? Stevie Nicks? Lindsey's girlfriend Shari? (Actually it was Lindsey's voice sampled through a variable speed oscillator. 'FLEET-WOOD MAC SHIMMERS BACK' said *Rolling Stone*. The *New York Times* described the album as having 'a mood of edgy, sophisticated wistful-ness'. Calling the record 'exquisitely produced', the paper went on to say that 'Mr Buckingham's arrangement . . . evoke the members of the group calling to one another from mist-shrouded turrets, across vast distances'. *Tango* quickly became a top ten album in America and reached number one twice in Britain, selling more than eight million records, tapes and compact discs to date. Fleetwood Mac was back!

When you have an album in the top ten, things sometimes begin to revolve in a widening gyre over which no one has any real control. So now events began to accelerate for Fleetwood Mac. The issue was ostensibly whether to tour in support of *Tango*. The rest of the band was ready to go, but Lindsey was saying he wanted to stay home and work on his own record now, effectively hanging up Fleetwood Mac. We all knew how he felt, and we were upset. Lindsey had made his feelings clear to other musicians around town, and was quoted in *Creem* magazine to the effect that he could no longer do what he really wanted to do in the context of Fleetwood Mac. To the rest of us, it was like he was giving his notice in the press.

We had a big confrontation over this at a much-dreaded band meeting on the white leather sofas in Stevie Nick's living room that July. 'Lindsey,' I said, 'we want to go back to work, as you know, and I think it's about time you gave us an answer.'

'I'm feeling a lot of pressure,' he said quietly. 'I know the band should go out, but check it out from my point of view. I just finished *Tango* and I'm fried. I've got my own album to do. Why should I go out and kill myself on the road?'

'Because Fleetwood Mac has to play this new music live if we are going to survive,' I said. 'It's simple, Lindsey. I want to know what this band is doing, and whether we go on the road or not, we all would like to hear what you want in connection to this band. You've aired your feelings to friends and to the public. Why don't you give us a clue?'

There was a pause, and Lindsey looked at the floor. 'Mick,' he said. 'You're not letting go of this, are you?'

'No, Lindsey, I'm not. It's not fair to the rest of us. The days of five years between albums is over. We're musicians and we just wanna go back to work.' Stevie, Chris and John nodded in assent. We were all focusing on Lindsey, and he was writhing.

'What should I do?' Lindsey groaned. 'I don't want to tour – I don't *need* to tour – but I feel funny leaving the band. I might regret it later.'

'You probably would,' Stevie said. Lindsey looked at her darkly.

I intervened. 'C'mon, Lindsey. People are upset.'

'Are you gonna go on the road without me?' he asked.

'Yes, Lindsey, we are. We wanna go back to work. Now it's cards on the table. We know you're the one on the spit here, but we just want to do our jobs. Are you on the pot or not?'

'Yeah, yeah,' he said, stalling. 'How long do you want to go out for?'

We looked at John Courage. 'Eight months, give or take,' the Colonel said.

'*C'mon, Lindsey*,' I said. 'If you wanna leave the band, go on the road with us and *then* go your own way.' Lindsey shook his head. 'I don't need this,' he said.

Then Stevie decided to swallow her pride and have a go.

'Hey, Lindsey,' she joshed. 'It won't be so bad. We can have a great time out there. Let's do it for old times' sake, just once more.' Stevie stopped and blushed, and we all laughed. For the first time that evening, Lindsey smiled. Somehow, Stevie almost broke through. 'Lindsey,' she said. 'I can *promise* you this tour won't be a nightmare.'

'OK,' he said, 'let me think about it.' And then he left, saying he would meet us later for dinner with his answer.

'The old boy's got his screws turned pretty tight,' John McVie observed a bit later.

'Too bad,' I said. 'If it's considered pressure, then pressure it has to be.' But when we met later that evening at the restaurant, Lindsey didn't show. Actually he drove up to the place, and then turned around and roared off again.

'Well, lads and lasses,' I said, 'looks like he's packed it in.' But the others didn't want to give Lindsey up so easily, and we were determined to try to convince our singer and guitarist to stay with us.

Finally, Mo Ostin persuaded Lindsey to tour with us for ten weeks. The news was flashed over the telephone. Hey! It's on! Fucking hell! Great! There was a big meeting at Christine's, and Lindsey was enthusiastic. I was thrilled! It's on!!

A week later, we were doing a Zoo gig in Salt Lake City. All that spring, Stevie had been coming along and singing with the Zoo, and she was there that day. Back in LA Fleetwood Mac had started rehearsing, signing on roadies, confirming dates with booking agents. We were *rolling*. Then Dennis Dunstan called me at Stevie's house in Phoenix. 'Are you sitting down?' he asked. Oh no, I thought, what now?

'The tour's off,' Dennis said. Lindsey had called John Courage and said he had changed his mind, that he couldn't go through with the tour. Courage told Lindsey that the rest of Fleetwood Mac deserved an explanation, and a meeting was set up for the whole band to have it out.

It was a real showdown.

7 August 1987.

We gathered at Christine's house, where from the start feelings ran high. No one wanted to face the humiliation of a cancelled tour – it was like a hideous spectre from our distant past – except for Lindsey, who just wanted out. The meeting was civil for about five minutes. Stevie felt devastated. She took Lindsey's rejection of us personally. 'You can't do this,' she said. 'Why are you doing this?'

Lindsey apologized. 'Look, I'm sorry. I just can't do any more. I've given twelve years of my life to this band? I've done it all – arranged, produced, played guitar, sang. I just can't . . . hack it . . . and do it all any more.'

Christine spoke now. 'What do you mean, Lindsey, do it all?' Her tone was withering. It was her singles, after all, that got played on the radio, not Lindsey's. This was a sore spot, because in interviews Lindsey had been describing his role in the band as the grand interpreter of Chris's and Stevie's music to the world – as if he felt he had carried the rest of the band. Nobody liked this, especially now. Lindsey was silent. No one knew what to say. Lindsey had given his answer.

I looked over at Stevie, who was brushing back tears. 'Lindsey,' she said, 'you've broken my fucking heart on this.'

'Hey,' he said, turning on Stevie and becoming agitated, 'don't do this again. Don't start attacking me.'

'Watch out, Lindsey,' Stevie said. 'There's other people in the room beside yourself.'

'Oh shit!' Lindsey shouted. 'Get this bitch out of my way. And fuck the lot of you!' A great hue and cry now ensued. Lindsey headed out to his car, and Stevie followed him outside to the courtyard, trying to change his mind. It was a terribly sad moment, because I could tell that even in her anger, a part of Stevie still loved Lindsey Buckingham and didn't want him to leave Fleetwood Mac. She didn't want him to go. They exchanged words in Chris's courtyard for a few moments. I didn't hear what he said, but Stevie cried out, 'Hey, man, you'll never be in love with anyone but yourself!'

Then it got physical. Lindsey grabbed Stevie and slapped her and bent her backwards over the hood of his car. Was he going to hit her again? He'd done it before. Suddenly Dennis Dunstan and Stevie's manager, Tony Dimitriades, pulled Lindsey off her and told him that was enough. Lindsey then came back into the house, very distraught. He shouted, 'Get that woman out of my life – that schizophrenic bitch!'

Christine sounded furious. 'Lindsey, look at yourself, screaming like a madman.'

There was a silence. And John McVie quietly said to Lindsey Buckingham, 'I think you'd better leave now.'

'You're a bunch of selfish bastards,' Lindsey said, and walked out. He sat in his car in the driveway for fifteen minutes, obviously distraught, but nobody wanted to go to him. Eventually, we heard him start his motor and leave.

I've put down as complete an account of this incident as memory allows, because I want it clear that Lindsey Buckingham was not fired from Fleetwood Mac. He left the group on his own.

We sat around for a bit after Lindsey had left. 'It didn't take a rocket scientist to figure out this was gonna happen,' John McVie said.

'We've got a great record,' I reminded them, 'and we're gonna look like a lot of bloody idiots if we don't go on the road. Let's keep our momentum and use it to find new people.'

A few days later, over lunch with John and Chris, I suggested replacing Lindsey with Billy Burnette and his guitarist friend, Rick Vito. A look of relief came over their faces. We arranged to meet them over dinner the next evening. When Stevie heard where I was going, she asked if she could come along. (She and Billy had recorded an unreleased version of Red Sovine's 'Are You Mine' together during the *Rock A Little* sessions.)

During that dinner, Fleetwood Mac was reborn.

I had actually thought of asking Billy Burnette to join Fleetwood Mac the instant Lindsey left the room that afternoon. Billy was a skilled writer who had done seven solo albums and had written both R&B and country material for Loretta Lynn, Irma Thomas, Levon Helm, Conway Twitty and others. Billy was a good singer with real presence, but we also needed a world class lead guitar, which is where Rick Vito came in.

As a teenager in Philadelphia in 1968, Rick had seen Fleetwood Mac play the blues (and display dear Harold the dildo) at one of our Electric Factory gigs. Peter Green had been one of the reasons Rick had learned to play his instrument. Rick now earned his bread by handling lead guitar on tours by Bob Seger and Jackson Browne, among others. But Rick was really an old blueser at heart, just like the core of Fleetwood Mac. (He had even played with John Mayall!) He had his own little band on the side, Rick Vito and Blues Moderne, that played in bars around Los Angeles.

As usual there were no auditions. As always, Fleetwood Mac hired musicians on intuition and instinct. That night I asked Billy and Rick if they wanted to join the band. They both said they'd think about it, but the answer was yes.

A few days later that August, we all met at Stevie's house during the observance of the Harmonic Convergance, on the theory that some good harmony might converge on Fleetwood Mac. By early September 1987, we were holding secret rehearsals in Venice, for a long journey we undertook that autumn, which we called the Shake the Cage tour.

And so, almost exactly twenty years after Fleetwood Mac's debut at Windsor, the band's eleventh line-up hit the road in late September,

1987. We had earlier introduced Billy and Rick at a press conference, and worked for a month to craft our new show. Gone were most of Lindsey's signature tunes. Now the focus was on our girls, Chris and Stevie. Now we spent more time exploring the band's history. Billy Burnette handled 'Oh Well' with all the bitter sneer Peter Green had intended when he wrote the song. Rick Vito chimed the blues with touching fidelity on Peter's beautiful 'I Loved Another Woman' and we revived 'Rattlesnake Shake' to powerful effect. (We had discussed adding 'Black Magic Woman', but John McVie vetoed this because he felt the song was too identified with Carlos Santana.) We also brought along Stevie's fine backup singers, Sharon and Lori, and added a blistering version of 'Stand Back' to the set.

I augmented our rhythm section with the brilliant Ghanaian percussionist Isaac Asante, with whom I'd played in Accra years before, and who had just come off Paul Simon's *Graceland* tour. (*Graceland*, which fused Paul's music with South African township jive, had been a big hit. I was proud that *The Visitor* had obviously been five years ahead of its time.) I also had a new waistcoat made, with concealed touch-sensitive drum pads. Now, during my spotlight bit on 'World Turning', I came upstage and started doing hambone stuff on my body. We had sampled various sounds, and when I hit my chest the vest would scream 'HELP ME' or 'OH GOD'. We also had sounds of heavy breathing, tablas, and car crashes, plus a wild blood-curdling scream when I played my balls. It was a touch of High Tech that I tried to accompany with a tribal dance of my own inspiration.

Well, we charted our own 727, and off we went. At first Stevie had some rather strong doubts about the tour. She was used to Lindsey being there, and it was difficult to convince her that this was still Fleetwood Mac. But she looked beautiful and sang great, which was rather heroic since she'd been diagnosed as having debilitating glandular fever less than a year previously. By mid-October, Stevie had earned some rave reviews in the press and was starting to ask for road rehearsals so we could re-weave the harmonies to our current hit, 'Little Lies'. By then, *Tango In The Night* was the number one album in Britain (ahead of both Michael Jackson and Bruce Springsteen) and was number eleven in America and climbing. In the end, the tour was a big success. Most of the shows sold out, we made *Tango* a hit, we taped the San Francisco show for video release and, most of all, had a lot of fun and grew to love our new line-up. There was even a return to the somewhat loony antics of yesteryear. In Boston on Halloween, I was carried onstage in a coffin, emerging as a dancing vampire after

Chris had pried the lid off. And, to be honest, there were moments of trial for both Billy and Rick, who knew they were stepping into some pretty heavy boots. Yet never once did anyone ask, Where's Lindsey?

Oh yes, the fellow from the BBC did. They did a special on us, and the interviewer broached the subject with Stevie. 'I gave Lindsey up,' she told him. 'He's a thing of my past. I hope he finds what he's searching for, and I hope he's happy, and I wish him well. And there's nothing left to say.'

We were off the road by Christmas. On the eve of the New Year, 1988, Stevie Nicks accompanied the Zoo to a club in Aspen, where we were joined (on a stage the size of a large bed) by Eddie Van Halen. So the Zoo expands and contracts to meet the needs of the inmates. So it ever shall be.

We were scheduled to tour Australia in March of that year, but Stevie's ill-health intervened, and we were forced to cancel.

But in May 1988 we went off to Europe. A ferry strike forced us to cancel Dublin, and we played a couple of shows at Manchester and Birmingham before coming down to London for ten sold-out shows at the Wembley Arena. This was a big deal for the English members of the band, as we had not played at home since the halcyon days of the *Tusk* tour, eight years earlier. What's more, a royal prince had requested tickets for opening night and had been invited backstage afterwards. We were all a little nervous, I recall, as Ziggy Marley's tape faded off the PA, the crew climbed their rope ladders like spider monkeys, the lights went out and we heard our capacity crowd, some of whom had been paying to see Fleetwood Mac for two decades, began to roar like the sea.

A month earlier, the BBC had shown its documentary on the band, which they called 'the epitome of adult rock music'. Somehow they had tracked down Peter Green and obtained some film of him, against his will. Peter Greenbaum was now unrecognizable as Peter Green. His hair was long and matted, and his fingernails were drawn into four-inch wizard's daggers. He shuffled about the streets of suburban Richmond, whose children referred to the Green God as 'The Wolfman'. He didn't even own a guitar any more, he told them. 'I'm recuperating from treatment for taking drugs,' he said. 'At least I hope that's what it is. I only took it [LSD] eight or nine times, but it lasted so long. That was my failing, I guess.' Questioned about whether he would rejoin the band under any circumstances, Pete answered: 'If

221

Mick called and said they needed me, I'd be tempted to cut them [referring to his nails] . . . but I'd probably let it pass.'

Have you ever regretted leaving Fleetwood Mac? they asked.

'Yeah, I've regretted it,' Pete replied. 'But then I also regret joining them as well.'

Anyway, opening night at Wembley went swimmingly. Stevie dazzled everyone and Chris's songs had young Prince Edward, his leather-jacketed girlfriend, and his minders up and dancing in their seats. Afterwards there was hot food and cold lager in the dressing room. The prince was led in and proved gracious and complimentary, and the whole company was flattered that he came to see us.

Later on, as usual, I was the last musician to leave the hall for our hotel in St James's. On the way, I asked the driver to take the big Daimler limo through the deserted wet midnight streets of Notting Hill Gate, where I had come to live with my sister Sally as a Beatles-smitten fifteen-year-old, twenty-five years earlier. We pulled up to darkened Hawbury Mews and I got out. There was the garage where I set up my drums. Here was Peter Bardens' house. The night was very quiet, and I could almost hear myself banging away behind the big carriage doors, a young kid dying to be a West End drummer. It was almost like astral travel, that night.

The faithful reader will by now have realized there's quite a bit of pain in this story. But playing music for a living has its many joys as well, among them long friendships. I try to keep in contact with as many old friends as possible. The question I'm most often asked by strangers is, whatever happened to . . . ? So let me try to account for some of the major players in this drama.

My mother Biddy is wonderfully healthy and lives down in Salisbury in Wiltshire. My sister Sally lives nearby. My sister Susan Fleetwood is a pre-eminent British actress, to be seen both on screen and onstage in London's West End. Peter Bardens, who discovered me, recently released two fine albums for CBS; in fact I did a little tour of northeast clubs with him in early 1989, since we're now both managed by Dennis Dunstan.

Jenny Boyd Fleetwood eventually brought Amy and Lucy back to southern California when she married drummer Ian Wallace in 1984. Jenny has been studying to be a psychotherapist, and has written her own book on creativity and the musical arts. My oldest daughter Amy is living in Hollywood, pursuing her own fledgling career as a model, following in the footsteps of her mother and her Aunt Patti. Lucy just got her driving permit!

Peter Green, now Greenbaum, still lives in west London. His fate haunts a generation of successful English musicians, all now entering middle age, who saw one of the authentic geniuses among them withdraw from the lists, refusing to sell out or play the fool. He not only started Fleetwood Mac and gave the rest of us a career; he also taught me something about my playing that's very important to me. He gave me the feeling he understood who I was as a person. He understood that I played like that person, without a lot of flash, but steady-on, like a rock soldier. Most of all, he gave us that magical, ongoing gift of a name – Fleetwood Mac. This book is for him.

Jeremy Spencer is said to remain with the Children of God. He and his family were last seen at the Children's HQ in Sri Lanka, but the violent Tamil insurrection there reportedly forced the cult to flee for their lives. At last word, Jeremy was hiding out on an atoll somewhere in the Indian Ocean. Not long ago, a strange young girl approached me on the beach in Malibu and handed me a cassette. It turned out to be Jeremy, singing and playing his guitar, but when and where it was recorded, I have no idea.

Danny Kirwan lives in a south London mental hospital.

Bob Welch, still a buddy, lives in Phoenix and is doing movie soundtracks.

Harold the dildo? I still have him. He sleeps in an old drum case in my basement.

Christine McVie is as great as ever. Right now she's working on her songs for our next record, thinking up blissful new ways to say she loves us. The healer's daughter will always be my sister and inspiration.

Stevie Nicks? Better than ever, in my opinion. (Although she doesn't let us play 'Rhiannon' in concert any more.) Not long ago, she told me: 'Sometimes I think I should go back to being a waitress; maybe I would enjoy life more.' She's still writing great songs, one of the major stars of our era. Along with John McVie, she remains a sometime member of the Zoo (we call Stevie 'the Zooette') and someone on whom I will forever rely. (Recently, we did sessions together for an album by one of Fleetwood Mac's earliest heroes – B. B. King.)

And I'm most happy to say we're friends with Lindsey again. He came to the wedding when Sara and I married under a marquee outside our house in Malibu in the spring of 1988. Later that year we dedicated *Fleetwood Mac: Greatest Hits* to him, with much love.

John McVie is still my closest friend. He and Julie had a daughter, Molly McVie, in March 1989, which served to mellow the once-wicked McVie, who is now sober, funny, and still a hell of a bass player. His spare time is devoted to the majestic *Challenger*, his 63-foot Sparkman and Stevens sloop.

Richard Dashut is currently producing Lindsey Buckingham's next album.

Judy Wong remains one of Fleetwood Mac's dearest friends. She lives and works in LA.

As does Mickey Shapiro, now in the film business.

Flight Lieutenant Jerry Rawlings took over Ghana again in 1983 and has held power ever since, steering his country into an unexpectedly strong economic recovery during the latter 1980s. Record producer Faisal Helwani is reported to be currently operating in Liberia.

John Courage and Dennis Dunstan are still my dearest friends and associates. They continue to shepherd Fleetwood Mac in the studio and around the world. We would be lost without them. As for me . . . I've taken up acting, just like Liz Green the astrologer predicted, back in 1969.

For years, people had been telling me I had to get into film work. They'd see the death-mask faces I'd make while playing the drums, and I've always put on costumes and skits for friends at home. I've been a fan of travesty ever since I played Ophelia in that boarding school production of *Hamlet*. I enjoyed it and felt connected to the craft through my sister. Then I'd see scripts, and the old anxiety attacks would return. I didn't think I could memorize my lines – the old blockage from school days. But gradually I forced myself. Through my old friend Tom Ross, I got an agent and did the round of casting offices, eventually landing my first movie role opposite Arnold Schwarzenegger in *Running Man*. I played myself as an eighty-five-year-old rock star, despite a last minute panic attack as we were about to shoot. I was so scared I thought of breaking a toe to get out of it, but in the end I learned my lines and did it. I thought, I've got to make this happen.

Since then, I've done dramatic roles on television and seem to be in some danger of inventing another career for myself.

Yet I also want Fleetwood Mac to go on until eternity. If anyone else quits, John McVie and I would just go out and find another front line. As McVie says, it's too late to send away for a computer training course.

I'll keep playing forever. That's how I really feel. I'm going to be an eighty-year-old rocker, and they'll have to take me out and shoot me to get me to stop.

Which reminds me of a weird thing that happened just the other day.

I went to see this drummer friend of mine, Jethro, who lives in a trailer up in the hills behind Zuma beach. We happened to be talking about catching AIDS, and I said, 'You know that song that Peter Green wrote, "Rattlesnake Shake"? The lyric goes: *"I know this guy, his name is Mick. Now he don't care if he don't got no chick. He does the shake, the rattlesnake shake."'* Jethro said he always wondered what that was all about, and I told him it was about jerking off. We were talking while standing in the hard-packed dirt about two feet from the side of Jethro's caravan. Then I said goodbye, turned around, and started down the steps leading to where I was parked. Just as my foot hit the top step, I heard it: RTRTRTRTTTTT!! A huge diamond-backed rattlesnake blocked the path, coiled and poised to strike, rattling at me like mad.

Right on cue. I had to jump to get out of his way.

THIS BOOK

was recorded, transcribed and edited in Malibu, New York and London between 1985 and 1990. The authors wish to give thanks and praise to all present and former members of Fleetwood Mac who helped out with memories of their own, as well as Biddy Fleetwood, Sally Hartnell, Jenny Boyd Wallace, Dennis Dunstan, Richard Dashut, Judy Wong, John Courage, Paul Ahearn, and Sara. Ron Bernstein and Mickey Shapiro were instrumental in getting this mad endeavour underway, and Jim Landis, Jane Meara, Susan Hill and Roz Targ helped to see it into print. Special thanks to photographers Herbie Worthington, Sam Emerson, Richard E. Aaron and Neal Preston. *Ave atque vale.*

M.F. & S.D.
Malibu, California
1990

Index

Adler, Lou 117
Ahearn, Paul 125
'Albatross' 45, 48–9, 89
Ambrose, Dave 22, 24, 30
Anderson, Kim 204–5
Anderson, Robin 153, 203–4
Asante, Isaac 220
Asher, Jane 50
Australia: property 182; tours 156, 181–2
Azoff, Irving 191, 192

Baker, Ginger 25
Barden, Cliff 17–18
Bardens, Peter 14–15, 18, 23, 222
Bare Trees 82–3
Bartz, Dr 171
Bayh, Senator Birch 147–8, 184
BBC 221
Beatles 5, 9, 10, 12, 21, 25, 29, 50–1, 57, 75
Beck, Jeff 22
Belgium: tour 186
Benifols 68–9, 88, 101
Bennett, Duster 41
Birch, Martin 90
Blue Horizon Records 30, 54, 57
Blue Jam at Chess 57
Blue Whale 3, 203, 205, 207, 208
Bluesbreakers 16, 18, 23, 24, 25–6, 27–9, 210
Bo Street Runners 19, 22
Boilerhouse 43–4
Boyd, Jenny (Helen Mary) (later Fleetwood): affair with Bob 92–3, 97–8; astrology 208; birth of daughters 69–70, 90, 97; breakdown 133; catching Mick with girl 154–5; courtship 19–22, 49; giving up drinking 159; living with Mick 51–2; marriage breakups 132–4, 161–2, 166–7; marriages to Mick 65–6, 147; modelling 21; moves to California 101, 166; not part of FM's life 68, 69; relationship with Andy 138; remarriage 222; reunions with Mick 142, 160, 186, 197; songs 66; travelling with FM 91; views on marriage 97–8; visiting Mick's parents 95
Boyd, Patti 20, 21, 49–51, 98, 186
Brereton, Bridgid, *see* Fleetwood, Bridgid
Brown, J. T. 32, 48
Brown, Tara 25
Bruce, Jack 25
Brunning, Bob 30–1, 33, 34
Buckingham, Greg 112
Buckingham, Lindsey 110, 111–14, 114–17, 223; best man to Mick 147; collapse 155, 187; drunken behaviour on stage 182–3; experiments with musical sounds 164–5; joins FM 117–20; at loggerheads with John 121; made partner in FM 130; producing FM 212, 214; relationship with Stevie 113, 126, 132, 135, 137, 143; songs 113–14, 119–20, 140, 149, 162, 173, 178, 202, 213; stage image 158; unwilling to tour 215–18; work outside FM 152, 153, 202, 206, 210; with Zoo 206
Buckingham, Morris 'Buck' 112
Buckingham Nicks 110–12, 113–14, 114, 115, 120

Burlison, Paul 205
Burnette, Billy 205–6, 219–20

Caillat, Ken 137
Casaro, Jason 211, 212
CBS Records 36
Chess Records 47–8
The Cheynes 15–16
Chicken Shack 34, 40, 43, 64–5
Clapton, Eric 22–4, 25, 51, 186
Cornick, Glenn 77
Courage, John 87–9, 91, 93–4, 98–9, 110,
    124, 127, 144, 147, 160, 179, 181, 183,
    191–2, 211, 212
Cross, Christopher 184

Dashut, Richard 114–15, 116, 127–8,
    136–7, 164–5, 170, 171, 180–1, 183–4,
    197–8, 200, 210, 211, 212
DaSilva, Dave 26
Davies, Clifford 29–30, 54, 70, 87;
    arrangement with record companies
    99–100; difficulties of working with
    88–9; with Fake Mac 98–100; fight
    with 98, 99–100, 102, 104; with FM 37,
    76, 94–5; gun threat by Pete 150–1;
    litigation 130, 160–1; search for Jeremy
    72, 73
Davis, Spencer 63
Dawson, Dinky 47, 64
Decca 36
Dimitriades, Tony 218
Disc 61
Dixon, Willie 48
Dominic, John 19
Donovan 50
drugs 40, 45–6, 65, 70, 121, 137, 138, 153,
    177, 181–2; affecting concerts 53; giving
    up 212
Dunbar, Aynsley 26, 27–8
Dunstan, Dennis 175–6, 217, 218

Eagles 141, 142, 152, 158, 173
Egan, Walter 152
Egypt: childhood in 5
Ellsdon, Sandra 32, 55, 137
England: tours 150, 186, 221, 222;
    treatment of FM 86
English Rose 52
Epic Records 52
Epstein, Brian 21, 50

Europe: success in 147; tours 39, 44–5,
    59, 68, 185–6

Faithfull, Marianne 50
Farrow, Mia 50
Fleetwood, Amy (daughter) 69–70, 147,
    160, 166, 186, 197, 222–3
Fleetwood, Bridgid (Biddy) (mother) 5,
    142, 153, 155, 159, 186, 222
Fleetwood, Jenny, *see* Boyd, Jenny
Fleetwood, John (grandfather) 4
Fleetwood, Lucy (daughter) 90, 97, 147,
    166, 186, 197, 223
Fleetwood, Mick: acting 9, 224;
    bankruptcy 3, 208; birth 5; business
    ventures 158; childhood 5–6; confusion
    with beat 53; courtship of Jenny
    19–22; desolation 95; determination to
    revive band 4, 210–11; drinking 28;
    early groups 14–28; fans 207; fear of
    flying 180–1; fencing 8; financial
    problems 201; first drums 8–9; first job
    13; first sexual experience 20–1; in
    Ghana 194–7; girls in life 154–5;
    illness 186; immigration problems 147;
    leadership of FM 62; living with Jenny
    51–2; living with sister 10, 13, 29; low
    point in life 3–4; managing FM 102,
    191–2; marriage breakups 132–4,
    161–2; marriage to Sara 223; marriages
    to Jenny 65–6, 147; obsession with
    Fleetwood Mac 3; obsession with
    Whitney 189–90; relationship with
    Sara 179, 180, 187–8, 190, 193, 200;
    relationship with Stevie 127, 155–6,
    159, 167; removed from management
    of FM 192; reunions with Jenny 142,
    160; Rolex watch 198; schooling 6–10;
    stage image 158; visiting parents 95;
    wheelchair 159–60; wooden balls as
    totem 38; work outside FM 152; in
    Zambia 95–7
Fleetwood, Mike (father): career 4–6;
    death 165–6; illness 154, 155, 159;
    poetry 4, 10–12; retirement from air
    force 8; saving son's life 5; sense of
    rhythm 8; visits from 142, 153, 155,
    159; wartime service 4–5; work with
    farmers 9
Fleetwood, Sally (sister) 5, 10, 18, 22, 26,
    80, 165, 186, 222

Fleetwood, Susan (sister) 5, 10, 186, 222
Fleetwood Mac: albums, *see* titles;
auditions 78; awards 145–6, 157–8;
backlash to contend with 162; bad times
86–105; banned from clubs 42;
becomes 6-piece 87, 89; comeback
210–22; communal living 65–6; early
recording session 36; first gig 33;
formation 28–35; identity crisis 89;
launched as pop group 45; litigation
99–100, 160–1; management 102;
money 68–9; moving to LA 100–1;
name 30; name stolen 95, 98–100;
organization 79; PA system 47, 88;
penguin iconography 80–1; playing
festivals 33, 42; on radio 125–6;
recording for Chess Records 47–8;
rumours of breakup 89, 188, 200;
singles 37, 41, 45, 53–4, 56, 60, 61, 141,
149, 150, 152, 176; spending 176–7,
191; stage costume 144, 158; stage show
41, 144; on television 145–6;
temporary break 94–5, 193; threat of
breaking up 66; as touring band 123–4;
vulgarity of show 37, 38–9, 41–2,
46–7
Fleetwood Mac (1968) 37
Fleetwood Mac (1975) 121–3, 125, 136,
145; tour 141–2
Fleetwood Mac: Greatest Hits 223
Fleetwood Mac in Chicago 57
Fleetwood Mac Live 187
France: tour 186
Fritz 111, 112, 113
Future Games 80–1

Gentoo Music 145
Germany: tour 185
Ghana 194–7, 198–200
Ginny (girlfriend) 136
Gorham Hotel, New York 46
Graham, Bill 40, 101, 178–9
Grant, Curry 134, 151, 168
Grateful Dead 39, 40, 60
Graves, Doug 104
Grech, Rick 30
Green (Greenbaum), Peter: appearances
with FM 89; attracting girls 49;
background 22, 23–4, 25–6, 28–9;
dedication to 223; disillusionment 54,
55–7; fancies Christine 41; film 221–2;

forming FM 29–35; leaves FM 58–61;
life after FM 68, 74, 150–1, 168–70,
186; marriage 169; money to charities
57–8; rejoins FM 74–5; religion
57–60; responsibilities for FM 43;
royalties 150; scruffiness 146; songs
55–6, 60; support for Mick 53;
threatened by psychopath 46;
threatening Clifford 150–1
Green, Liz 208
Gunnell Agency 15, 16

Harris, Carol 168
Harrison, George 20, 49, 50–1, 98, 200
Hawaii: tour 183
Hawkins, George 197, 199, 205
Helwani, Faisal 195–6
Hendrix, Jimi 29, 46
Henley, Don 143
Heroes Are Hard To Find 104; tour 104
Holland: tour 185, 186
Hollis, Peter 15

I'm Not Me 205, 206
Ivory Hudson and the Harlequins 76

Jagger, Mick 50
James, Elmore 31–2
Japan: tours 156, 180
Jesse, John 10, 13
Jesse, Kells 13, 80, 185–6
Jesse, Tiffany 80
Johnson, de Graft 199
Johnson, Robert 31–2
Jones, Brian 21, 29
Joplin, Janis 47, 112–13

Kean, Dennis 59, 64, 66, 72, 201
Kells, Alice 4
Kiln House 62, 64–6, 68
Kiln House 66–7, 70, 74; tour 67
Kirwan, Danny 43–4, 52, 64, 66–7, 80,
83–5, 89, 95, 186–7, 223

Lennon, Cynthia 50
Lennon, John 50–1, 54
Levi Set 31
Limited Management 145, 153
Lord, Jon 84
Los Angeles: earthquake 70–1
Lynch, Eddie 15

McCartney, Paul 31, 50–1, 180
McDonnell, Phil 72, 73
McVie, Christine Perfect 34, 223;
  accepting women in band 118;
  background 62–5; body-searched 185;
  debut with FM 40–1; at family
  reunion 186; fights with John 81–2;
  fights with Lindsey 183, 218; healing
  touch 178; home-making 88;
  immigration problems 147; joins FM
  67, 68; living with FM 65, 69; marriage
  breakup 124–5, 132, 134, 137;
  marriage to John 43, 64; moves to LA
  100–1; reaction to stardom 146;
  relationship with Curry 134, 151;
  relationship with John 41, 42–3;
  return to England 119; reuniting FM
  211; reviews 129; solo work 210;
  songs 66, 80, 89, 90, 104, 120, 131, 140,
  149, 152, 169, 201–2, 213; stage image
  158; talents 69; with Zoo 206
McVie, John 223; background 17–18, 25,
  26; in Bluesbreakers 22–3; communal
  living 69; drinking 26, 28, 81–2, 179;
  fight with Lindsey 121; fights with
  Chris 81–2; immigration problems
  147; joins FM 334; living on boat 134;
  living with FM 65; love of penguins 80;
  marriage breakup 124–5, 132, 134,
  137; marriage to Chris 43, 64; meeting
  Mick 18; moving to LA 100–1; re-
  starting to play 212–13; in recording
  studio 139–40; relationship with
  Christine 41, 42–3; reluctance to join
  FM 30, 33; sailing 172; semi-retirement
  210; stage image 158; 3rd Reich
  memorabilia 185; work outside FM 152
McVie, Julie 168
Madge (fan) 56
Maharisihi Mahesh Yogi 49–51
Marsden, Beryl 25
Mason, Dave 205
Mayall, John 16–18, 22–3, 25–6, 28, 34,
  210
Melody Maker 37, 57, 65, 178
Mirage 201–2, 203
Morrison, Van 18–19
Mr Wonderful 40–1, 42
Munich Jet Set 59
Mystery To Me 90–1, 92, 101, 148; tour
  91–5

New Musical Express 60, 65
New York Times 215
New Zealand: tours 155–6, 182–3
Nicks, Aaron Jess 111
Nicks, Jess 110–11, 117, 154
Nicks, Stevie 105, 223; albums 202;
  background 110–12, 114–17; baton
  twirling 171; body-searched 185;
  courted by Don Henley 143; drink
  problem 214; fans 144, 187; illness 220,
  221; joins FM 117–20, 119–21;
  litigation for plagiarism against 172;
  marriage to Kim 204–5; mystical quality
  119; notes from 179–80; partner in FM
  130; reaction to Mick and Sara 168;
  reaction to stardom 146; rejoins FM
  214; relationship with Lindsey 113,
  126, 132, 135, 137, 143; relationship
  with Mick 127, 155–6, 159, 167;
  reviews 129, 142, 184; row with
  Lindsey 218; row over album 214–15;
  songs 111, 113, 119–20, 140, 149, 172,
  202, 214; stage costume 141–2; stage
  image 158; stealing show 187–8;
  strength 139; suffering on tour
  129–30; throat problems 150, 153;
  work outside FM 152, 210, 211,
  213–14; with Zoo 217
Nketia, Kwabene 194
Norway: childhood in 5–6

Oldham, Andrew Loog 54
Olsen, Keith 105, 110, 114, 121
Ormsby-Gore, Alice 51
Ostin, Mo 103, 122, 130, 173, 197, 211
Owsley, Augustus Stanley 40, 45, 46, 53

Page, Jimmy 22, 30, 200
Parker, Mick 22
Peacock, Roger 16, 20, 21
Penguin 89, 90
Penguin Promotions 145
Perfect, Beatrice (Tee) 62–3
Perfect, Christine, *see* McVie, Christine
  Perfect
Perfect, Cyril 62
Perfect, Reg 186
Peter B's Looners 22, 23, 24–5
Price, Hugh 38, 46–7
publicity stunts 174

Quintela, Eddie 213

Rawlings, Jerry 194, 199
RCA 197, 206
Recor, Jim 129, 167, 168
Recor, Sara 159, 167–8, 177, 179, 180,
    190, 193, 197–8, 200, 223
Record Plant 136–40
Regehr, Bob 123
'Rhiannon' 141–2, 144, 153
Richards, Deke 125
Rockhopper Music 145
Rogers, Nile 211
Rolling Stone 40, 104, 129, 149, 158, 203,
    215
Rolling Stones 10, 12–13, 16, 17
Ross, Steve 205
Ross, Tom 119
Rumours 148–50, 152, 153–4, 155, 156,
    157–8, 163, 192; tour 149–50, 151–2,
    153–4, 155–6
Russia: plans to play in 160

Santana, Carlos 40, 70
Scarrot, Mrs 80
Scotland: tour 69, 70
Seedy Management 102, 145, 173
Senders 15
Shankar, Ravi 50, 51
Shapiro, Mickey 102–3, 122, 130, 147,
    191, 194, 196
Sharpe, Todd 197, 199
Shelly's Mann Hole 76
Shotgun Express 25, 26, 130
Smith, Joe 122–3
Sound City 105, 114
Spencer, Dicken 64, 74
Spencer, Fiona 64, 68, 74
Spencer, Jeremy: disappearance 71–4;
    early band 31; Elvis impersonations
    67–8; with FM 32–3; leaving FM 70;
    living with FM 65; mimicry 37–8, 42;
    missing from album 54–5; personality
    37–9; problems 43, 70–4; quiet
    behaviour offstage 49; with religious
    sect 72–4, 75, 89, 186, 223; songs 47,
    66; onstage 41–2; vulgarity onstage
    38–9, 39–40, 47
Starr, Ringo 50
Stewart, Rod 24, 25, 26, 130
Strawberry Alarm Clock 102

Summer, Bill 197
Switzerland: tour 185–6
Sylvester, Andy 40, 63, 138

Tango in the Night 211, 214–15, 220
Taylor, Mick 29, 33, 210
Then Play On 54–7, 114
Todaro, Tony 186
Tusk 163–5, 170–5, 192; tour 175–9, 184,
    190–1, 207
Twang Sisters 167

USA: FM moves to 100–1; tours 39,
    45–8, 52–3, 67, 70–5, 81, 91–5, 141–4,
    166, 184; treatment of FM 86

Vernon, Mike 26, 29–30, 31, 36, 40, 47–8,
    54, 64, 89
The Visitor 197, 198–9, 200, 206, 220
Vito, Rick 219–20

Wachtel, Waddy 115, 213
Walker, Dave 87, 89, 90
Warner Brothers Records 54, 102, 103,
    122, 149, 173, 197
Webb, Stan 40, 63, 64
Welch, Bob 101, 129, 186, 223; album
    159; in charge of FM's money 118; clash
    with Danny 83–4; fighting Fake Mac
    98–9; help with career 152–3; joins
    FM 76–9; leaves FM 109–10;
    persuading FM to move to LA 100–1;
    songs 80, 89, 90–1, 104; work for FM
    102–5
Welch, Nancy 80
Wensley Dale, Australia 182, 197–8
Weston, Bob 87, 89, 92–3, 93–4, 97–8
Whitney 189–90
Wilson, Dennis 168, 179, 202, 206
Winwood, Stevie 63
Wong, Judy 21, 23, 39–40, 69, 76, 77,
    102, 145, 208
Wood, Chris 63
Woodson, Craig 194–5, 196

Yesterday's Gone 145

Zambia 95–7
Zevon, Warren 115, 116, 152
Zoo 205–6, 210, 217, 221, 223
Zoot Money 24